Operation
Peace for Galilee

OTHER BOOKS BY RICHARD A. GABRIEL

*The Antagonists: A Comparative Combat Assessment
of the Soviet and American Soldier*

The Mind of the Soviet Fighting Man

To Serve with Honor: A Treatise on Military Ethics

Fighting Armies: NATO and the Warsaw Pact

Fighting Armies: Antagonists of the Middle East

Fighting Armies: Third World Armies

*The New Red Legions: An Attitudinal Portrait of
the Soviet Soldier*

The New Red Legions: A Survey Data Sourcebook

Crisis in Command: Mismanagement in the Army
(with Paul Savage)

Managers and Gladiators: Directions of Change in the U.S. Army

Ethnic Groups in America

Program Evaluation: A Social Science Approach

The Ethnic Factor in the Urban Polity

The Environment: Critical Factors in Strategy Development

Operation Peace for Galilee

The Israeli–PLO War in Lebanon

Richard A. Gabriel

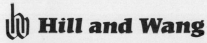 **Hill and Wang**

A division of Farrar, Straus and Giroux
New York

Copyright © 1984 by Richard A. Gabriel
All rights reserved
First printing, 1984
Printed in the United States of America
Published simultaneously in Canada
by Collins Publishers, Toronto
Designed by Charlotte Staub

Library of Congress Cataloging in Publication Data
Gabriel, Richard A.
  Operation peace for Galilee.
  Includes bibliographical references and index.
  1. Lebanon—History—Israeli intervention, 1982-
2. Israel—Armed Forces. I. Title.
DS87.53.G32   1984   956.92′044   83-26439

To my wife, Katherine,
and my two daughters,
Christine and Leah,
who have given me
years of happiness
and joy

Preface

This book had its beginning in March 1982—three months before the Israeli Defense Forces unleashed a lightning strike into Lebanon in the largest search-and-destroy mission conducted against the PLO since Operation Litani. I had been invited in March 1982 by the Israeli military establishment to visit Israel and to present a series of lectures on various military subjects to a number of commands and instructional institutions. During this visit I lectured at the Israeli Defense College, the IDF Psychological Research Center, the IDF Training Command, and the Brigade Commanders School. In addition, I had the opportunity to make presentations to members of the Israeli intelligence community gathered at the IDF Military Intelligence School outside Tel Aviv.

Although I had long been a student of Israel's military history, this ten-day visit provided me with an excellent opportunity to examine the IDF at close range. I was involved in a series of meetings and background briefings provided by a number of high-ranking officers and political officials. In addition, I was able to establish a number of contacts with field officers of all ranks, which, as the year passed, grew into genuine friendships. Some of these officers—many had attended military schools in the United States—visited my home in New Hampshire, where we had long talks that often lasted late into the night. We also conducted a voluminous correspondence. Sadly, some of the men

I met in Israel would soon be killed in the war in Lebanon. As a consequence of my visit to Israel and the experience gained there, I decided on my return to write a book on the IDF and to analyze the remarkable changes which had occurred in it since the near-disaster of the Yom Kippur War.

My work was interrupted by the events of June 6, 1982, when, with remarkable precision and speed, the IDF launched a large ground-force operation into Lebanon to destroy the PLO and root out its infrastructure, which supported terrorist attacks on the settlements and civilian inhabitants of northern Israel. Suddenly a study of the structure and doctrine of the IDF seemed somewhat misplaced. I decided to change the thrust of the book, to examine instead the military campaigns of the Lebanese war and assess how that war affected Israel's military forces.

For almost six months after the war began, I gathered information, drawing on press reports, scarce in-depth analyses of various aspects of the war which appeared in military journals, long letters sent by Israeli friends who held commands during the fighting, phone conversations with other friends, and long visits with officers and friends who visited the United States. And chance served me well. In 1967, while I was at the University of Massachusetts studying for my doctorate, one of my closest classmates had been a young member of the PLO, which was then in its formative stages. By the time the conflict in Lebanon broke out, my classmate—who had returned to his home in Jordan after the Six-Day War—had risen to fairly high rank in the PLO's political hierarchy. He was very helpful in providing me with his views on the situation in Lebanon, and he arranged for me to talk at length with other PLO members about their conflict with the IDF. Although I gathered quite a large amount of information, and often in great detail, I was still going to write about the war without having visited the battle front and interviewed those who had been directly engaged in it.

In November 1982, I received a call from a friend who worked with the *Time* bureau in Jerusalem, who asked if I would be interested in traveling to Israel and Lebanon for the express purpose of continuing my research on the war and the IDF. A number of my books and articles were standard reading in IDF military schools, and my reputation as a scholar of military affairs in Israel, he thought, might be put to good use in gathering more information to finish my book.

Within a week, I received a formal invitation to visit Israel for a period of three weeks. The independent group sponsoring my trip was the Inter-University Study Group for Middle East Affairs, associated with Hebrew University in Jerusalem. Although I was prepared to go, my previous experience doing research on the IDF in Israel—and later publishing that research —made me feel that it was imperative to establish certain ground rules for my visit. Two basic problems concerned me.

The first was the traditionally strict IDF censorship of all reporters and scholars in Israel writing on military matters. Generally, any information gathered on an officially sponsored visit must be submitted to IDF censors. Moreover, completed papers and articles must be submitted for a final review prior to publication. Having written an earlier work on the military psychology of the IDF, I was thoroughly familiar with the process. Having also witnessed nightly news reports dealing with the Lebanon war bearing the notice "Cleared by Israeli censors," I knew that the IDF was likely to be more sensitive than it normally was. I decided that if I was to make the trip and study the war, then as a precondition the IDF would have to waive its censorship requirements. I would not submit my notes or my final work for review. The IDF would see the results when everyone else did, when the book was published. If this condition could not be met, I wouldn't accept the invitation.

The second problem involved choosing a publisher. The Inter-University Study Group had indicated, albeit indirectly, that they might be helpful in finding one. I knew, however, that the book might then be unfairly viewed as being biased in favor of Israel or as being sponsored by the Israeli military. One of the conditions for accepting the invitation to Israel was that I find my own publisher, and certainly not one in either Israel or an Arab country. After a short delay, the conditions were agreed to, and I could begin my work in Israel and Lebanon with the clear understanding that I would be free of any censorship and publish what I wished where I wished.

In conducting field research for this book, I spent approximately twenty-one days in Israel and Lebanon. During that time I was able to meet and talk to a number of officers who had participated in the war. There were also officers and soldiers whom I had known from the year before, with whom I discussed various aspects of the war. Although the IDF arranged a number of formal briefings—many of which were valuable—much of my knowledge was gathered in private conversations with friends who had commanded major military units during combat. In this regard, my earlier lectures at the Brigade Commanders School were particularly valuable, since it was these men who led the brigades in the actual fighting. Important, too, were the friends I had made at the Defense College, some of whom commanded the divisions that struck into Lebanon. Using the official contacts provided by the IDF and my own "unofficial" connections, I had the opportunity to speak to almost every major military ground commander who was in the Lebanon operation.

Equally valuable were the discussions I had with lower-ranking officers—battalion commanders, company commanders, platoon leaders—and also with the common soldiers, who, as in all wars, bear the brunt of combat. Their stories and experiences formed a rich mosaic of information with which to check the perceptions of their superiors. Particularly helpful in this regard were the doctors, mostly reservists, who provided a highly accurate assessment of the treatment of civilians and the medical care afforded them and Israeli soldiers during the war. Of great interest were the in-depth conversations I had with a number of battle psychologists who performed under fire. Their experiences provided a close look at the horrors of war.

In addition, I conducted a number of lengthy and extensive interviews with key operations officers in the navy and air force, thus rounding out my picture of IDF field operations. I was briefed on the performance of equipment on the battlefield—sometimes by the very people who had designed the machines. In almost every case, that information proved accurate when checked against the battle experiences of the soldiers.

Although my research did not focus on the political aspects of the Lebanese incursion and especially not on the Israeli domestic political scene, it was difficult to ignore them entirely. I conducted extensive interviews with top political leaders, including cabinet members, and powerful leaders of the Opposition. These interviews proved valuable in assessing events in Lebanon, since a number of commissions had been established by the Knesset to conduct detailed investigations of various aspects of the war. My meetings with the individuals who sat on these commissions provided invaluable information.

Particularly informative were the seven days I spent in Lebanon. Equipped with a car, a driver, a friend, and flak jackets and rifles, I was able to travel all through the Lebanese battle zone. (The flak jackets and battle gear were very welcome when, as we were leaving the Palestinian camp at Rachidiya one evening, our car and others were fired upon.) I retraced, by car or on foot, the major routes of advance taken by major Israeli units: in the east, in the Bekaa Valley, to the outskirts of Yanta, overlooking Damascus; in the center, to the foothills of the Shouf Mountains, near Jezzine, across country, following the road taken by Avigdor Kahalani's forces from Nabitiya to the Zaharani Junction, south of Sidon; and north, to Damour and to the outskirts of Beirut itself. Armed with a map and a terrain analysis I had made before entering Lebanon, I was able to assess the terrain of the battle sites. As a former army officer and a reserve intelligence officer for eighteen years, I am familiar with the impact terrain can have on military operations.

In Lebanon, I held long interviews with Israeli ground commanders and talked to the men still dug in in their positions more than six months after the end of the war. I visited the major refugee camps in southern Lebanon, saw for myself the degree of damage, and spoke—unescorted by any Israelis—with civilians who had suffered through the war. I spent time with "PLO suspects" who had been detained both in Israel and at the Ansar camp, gathering their impressions of their internment. Doctors and nurses, all Palestinians, who had lived in the camps for years and attended the wounded during the fighting, provided me with insights which I don't believe I could have gained otherwise. To the credit of the IDF, I was allowed to move freely and talk to whomever I pleased, with no restrictions and no Israeli soldiers present. I am convinced I received accurate accounts of the events in the camps as they happened during the war.

Travel inside Beirut was necessarily restricted by the persistent daily threat of ambush and hostile fire, as PLO remnants attacked IDF soldiers, and members of confessional militias, rival ethnic and religious groups, engaged in their favorite pastime of ambushing one another. Yet my official—and unofficial—travels within the city produced an accurate picture of the death and damage that attended the siege. I interviewed a number of high officials in the Lebanese government, the Christian militia, members of the Druse militia, and the second in command of the Amal Moslem militia, all of which proved enlightening on the nature of ethnic and religious hatreds within Beirut and Lebanon.

Finally, my conversations with journalists—Lebanese, West European, Israeli, British, and American—who covered the war from the battlefront produced a kaleidoscope of information and impressions. I am now convinced that historians are at least partially correct when they assert that, to describe an event accurately, distance from the event and the passage of time are far more of an asset than actually having been present.

As I assess my studies of the war and the field research I carried out on the battlefields, I realize that, as in any given situation, there are probably many people who know more about the detail surrounding it. But only a few have been privileged to examine the totality of the Lebanese war as closely as I did. It is upon this assurance that I have ventured to write this book.

Manchester, New Hampshire
September 1983

Contents

Maps

Operation
Peace for Galilee

1
The Israeli Defense Force

HISTORY

For the past thirty-five years the Israeli Defense Force has been the shield protecting the country. Since its beginning in 1948, the Israeli army has fought no fewer than five major wars against Arab attacks, any one of which was capable of destroying Israel. To the average Israeli, it is impossible to separate the Israeli Defense Force from the history of modern Israel. It takes no stretch of the imagination to suggest that, given the continued imbalance of forces between Israel and its enemies, had the Israeli Defense Force not been as effective as it has been, the State of Israel would no longer exist.

Because war has been a constant threat, the role of the military in the formation and preservation of that state is of major importance. It is fair to suggest that the shape of modern Israel in its political, economic, and even in its social structure would have been far different had it not been for the central role played by the IDF. The IDF is one of the major social institutions of the state.

The Israeli Defense Force came into existence formally on May 28, 1948. It is most commonly known to Israelis as Zahal, a term derived from Zeva Haganah le-Israel, which means Israeli Defense Force. It constituted the first official army of an independent Jewish state in over two thousand years. The IDF had its origins in three illegal guerrilla organizations with a common purpose to drive the British out of Palestine: the Haganah, the

Irgun, and the Palmach. The most important of these was the Haganah.

The Haganah was formed in 1920 during the British mandate. Its purpose was to protect Jewish settlers in Palestine from constant Arab attacks. The larger goal was to prepare the nucleus of an army that could help Israel achieve independence from the British, and then to establish an army within the new state. Its initial activities involved organizing fighting groups and smuggling arms, to be funneled to Jewish settlements for self-defense.

In 1936, after a year of large-scale rioting, even the British came to see that the forces they had in the area were insufficient to defend all Jewish settlements against Arab attack. Inadvertently, they encouraged the Haganah openly to take on the role of self-defense. In 1938, under the command of Captain Orde Wingate, the British formed three legal counterguerrilla units whose job was to collect intelligence and to sustain the security of Jewish settlements. The establishment of legal military units was a boon to the Haganah. Many members of its secret army joined these legal units, where they gained considerable military experience. Moreover, since the Jewish soldiers in these units acquitted themselves well, they not only acquired leadership and combat experience but gained legitimacy, among the population at large, as a credible military force.

The major criticism leveled against the Haganah was that it adopted a strictly defensive posture: to protect the settlements against Arab attacks, but not to retaliate against Arab villages or Arab forces. A number of influential political leaders in the underground came to regard the Haganah's policy of "defense only" as not aggressive enough. Moreover, they saw it as a policy that was doomed in the long run because it would not bring to bear the strong pressures necessary to drive the British out of Palestine. As a consequence, another underground group, more radical and more aggressive, was formed—the Irgun.

Irgun, which means National Military Organization, was formed in 1937 under the leadership of Vladimir Jabotinsky, a radical socialist and terrorist. In 1937 the Irgun began its campaign of terror and retaliation against Arabs in Palestine. Its fundamental difference with the Haganah, from the military perspective, was its willingness to engage in offensive operations and retaliatory raids. In 1939, the British formally extended their mandate for ten additional years, a move which forced the Irgun into an even more radical stance. The Irgun had previously limited most of its attacks to Arab targets, but, with the extension of the mandate, it began to strike at the British. The object of Jabotinsky's strategy was to turn the Irgun into a military force and a genuine freedom movement to achieve independence from the British.

When World War II broke out, Irgun forces reduced their attacks against the British in the mandate. But most of their members refused to join the Jewish units under British command to fight in Europe; most of their leaders and members remained in Israel to organize. During the war, terrorist acts were carried out against the British by extremists in the Irgun. When the British did not respond, pressure grew on the Irgun to step up these attacks, and eventually the Irgun gave birth to a more radical group of terrorists, the Stern Gang. The basic goal of this new group was to maintain pressure on the British by continued military attacks. The Stern Gang became the most extreme of the terrorist radicals. Their view was that only through continuous military pressure could Israel achieve its independence from Britain.

The third group, a direct forerunner of the IDF, is the Palmach. During World War II, some thirty-two thousand Jews from Palestine volunteered for service with British units. Of these, five thousand were formed into the famous Jewish Brigade, which fought long and hard for Britain and acquired a reputation for bravery and daring. With considerable numbers being drawn away from Palestine into the British forces, the strength of the Haganah at home was depleted. The British therefore created a force of some three thousand full-time soldiers to defend Jewish settlements in Palestine. This group was known formally as the Palmach. Once World War II was over, the Palmach began a campaign, in concert with the Irgun and the Haganah, to renew military pressure on the British occupation forces to press for independence for Israel.[1]

It is important to understand that the Israeli Defense Force has its roots in organizations that by modern standards would be judged, depending on one's point of view, as either genuine freedom fighters or genuine terrorists. Each major force—the

Haganah, the Irgun, and the Palmach—had a political constituency within the Jewish population, and each had a political arm in the form of a political movement or political party. Each group differed radically in its ideology and in the way they viewed the tenor and nature of the emergent Jewish state for which they had all fought. The Palmach, for example, had strong pro-Soviet and socialist tendencies and saw itself as an organization of independent freedom fighters striking against the British. The Irgun was almost fascist and even today traces its heritage to the Likud Party. The Haganah was more moderate and tended to be strongly socialist in orientation, drawing heavily on the Russian background of many of its leaders.

A point of major concern once the State of Israel was established in 1948 was the fact that the early military leaders were *underground* military commanders, and also *political* commanders. Each of them and his following had a long history of clandestine operations against a hostile military force. It was often difficult for these leaders to separate military tactics from their overall political orientation and an essentially conspiratorial concept of military force. In short, the organizations which constitute the basis of the IDF were really private political armies, each with a different idea of what the new state should be, what form it should take, and, most important, what their role would be in the larger political context of the State of Israel.

A problem for the new nation was how to persuade these competing, politically oriented armed movements to disband and place their armed forces and leadership at the disposal of a central military command. The greater problem was how to place them under a stable political command where they would be willing to submerge their interests into the larger interest of the state. As independence approached, there were clashes among the three military organizations, and a number of leaders were assassinated. When independence came, Israel's first president, David Ben-Gurion, issued the famous Decree Number 4, on May 28, 1948, banning all military organizations within Israel. At the same time, he created the Israeli Defense Force as the sole military arm of the state. Initially, the Irgun and the Palmach refused to disband and there were violent clashes between them and the army of the new state. But with the Arab attack in May 1948, which began almost immediately after independence, these forces gradually pulled together. The Irgun was disbanded in June 1948, and the Palmach in October. The 1948 war, which came so rapidly after the declaration of independence, virtually cut the ground out from under these private military movements; they were forced to choose either to join the Israeli state or to lose whatever legitimacy and following they had. In any case, Ben-Gurion's consummate political skill was brought to bear, and he was able to bring the disbanded military forces together under one command.

The war in 1948 and the need to prepare and to fight five more wars since then has honed the structure of the Israeli Defense Force and kept it loyal to the state. The IDF has assumed the primary role for the survival of the State of Israel. Thirty-five years of recurring conflict or of preparing for conflict has submerged the divergent views of the three radically different politico-military groups into one. In time, as new generations came into service and as military service became conditioned more and more by individual military and political experiences, attachments to the private armies of pre-independence days weakened. In the early days, however, the country could easily have been plunged into civil war had it not been for Arab attacks and the political skill of David Ben-Gurion. Ben-Gurion's dictum of 1948 remains the basis of the IDF's role in the nation. Political parties must refrain from attempting to influence the IDF politically, and the IDF is expected to have no political connections with the political structure. The IDF in thirty-five years has moved from a situation of potential civil war growing out of conflicting partisan loyalties to where it is today—above politics, the bulwark of national security, and totally subservient to the will of the political leadership. This is no small accomplishment; there are any number of new states in the modern world whose military have failed to make the transition from underground military forces to a modern military organization subordinate to civilian leadership.

The present-day Israeli Defense Force is an integrated organization. There is no truly separate air force, navy, or army. Operational responsibility and command are located in the Chief of Staff and day-to-day operations are conducted by the General Staff. There are no separate chiefs of staff for the air force, army, or navy, and the commanders of the respective services act as advisors to the Chief. It is the Chief of Staff who has the overall operational and planning responsibility for the entire Israeli Defense Force. In this way, long-range planning, doctrine, and battlefield deployment can remain flexible but coordinated, and maximum combat power is ensured. It is interesting to note that most nations do not have integrated forces but separate military branches. The integrated services in the IDF are a reflection of its history, of the need to bring under political control competing military forces whose conflicts reach back to pre-independence days.

SOCIAL ROLE

The IDF is more than a military force; it is involved in a number of social roles that are no longer performed by most Western armies but, paradoxically, are still performed by the Russian army. Many of the founders and shapers of the Israeli state were immigrants from Russia and influenced by Russian socialist thought and the general Russian experience. A direct consequence is the tendency to view the military establishment as more than a military shield; rather, as a complete social institution with wider functions within the state. There are four basic roles in addition to military defense that are performed by the Israeli Defense Force.

Chief among these is nation building. Israel is a highly heterogeneous state. Its citizenry is drawn from sixty countries and speaks twenty different languages. In addition, the values of various ethnic groups within the Israeli state are often at odds. Although most commonly the distinction is drawn between the Ashkenazim and the Sephardim, in point of fact even within these major groups significant ethnic, racial, religious, and cultural differences exist. Yet Israelis must build a nation in a secular world that has common values extending to a common religious tradition. One way to achieve this, often practiced in underdeveloped countries, is to use national conscription and military service as an integrating mechanism to build a national identity. The Israeli army has done this very well. Based entirely on conscription, it brings together through a common experience members of every ethnic, racial, and religious group in the society. While in the army, everyone learns to speak Hebrew, and they all share common experiences.

A second social role of the IDF is the inculcation of democratic values. Many of the ethnic groups within Israel come from traditions that are not democratic. Indeed, the extreme Orthodox Jewish sects are so devout that they perceive the existence of a secular state as fundamentally blasphemous. Others are not as extreme, but groups from Morocco, Egypt, and Yemen, to name only three, have political traditions that are feudal and authoritarian. Israel must integrate these groups into a secular nation state, and ensure that democratic values and customs are inculcated and passed on. Again, universal military service serves a purpose here. While in the military, all individuals are treated equally; an enormous social leveling takes place that breaks down traditional social barriers. Promotion is rigorously determined by merit and bravery, and democratic values are openly praised and fostered.

A third major role of the Israeli army is education. The IDF is one of the largest educational institutions in Israel. It sends more people to more schools than almost any other establishment, save, of course, the formal education structure itself. Education is not only in military skills; the Israelis make great efforts to ensure that technical skills are taught which can be of use in the civilian economy. The IDF also finances higher education in civilian educational institutions by sending its regular officers to school. It also finances a range of programs in which reserve officers can continue their education at government expense. Perhaps among the IDF's more interesting educational programs are the remedial ones that rescue the marginally literate and bring them up to a literate standard. During the last few years, the IDF, under the prodding of Chief of Staff Rafael Eitan, initiated a program that is in some ways the equivalent of Project One Hundred Thousand, which the American army initiated during the sixties. The goal in both armies is to bring in individuals who do not qualify and to pace their training so as to educate them up to an acceptable level. The IDF has been careful not to allow this policy, as happened in the United States, to reduce the standards of education in the army as a whole.

A fourth function of the IDF is to accelerate upward mobility. Military service in Israel provides opportunities for a number of groups to advance rapidly in their social status. This applies most specifically to socioeconomic groups such as the Sephardim and Orientals, who are at a great disadvantage because of a lack of educational skills. A substantial number of poor and immigrant Jews see the military as a vehicle for advancement, therefore the military are scrupulous in ensuring that promotion is based on fairness, competence, and bravery. Many Israeli officers of high rank are, in fact, members of minority groups. A number, for example, are Yemenites and Druse, two groups which society often discriminates against. The IDF has been very successful in assisting in the general acculturation and assimilation process and in ensuring fairness; mobility for certain segments of the population is at least as fast and in many instances faster than in society at large.

Military service is so central to life in Israel that if someone does not perform adequately or honorably, his or her success in civilian life is almost impossible. Even obtaining employment is difficult in Israel without a proper and adequate service record. The IDF is virtually at the center of Israeli society, in that it is the one social institution with which every Israeli has some experience, and in most instances a very long and intimate experience.

THE ARMY

The ground forces of the IDF are the shield of Israel, and all military services exist to support it. Air tactics, naval tactics, and even the organizational configuration of the other services are determined to a large extent by the roles they play in support of the ground forces. The IDF is a conscript army and everyone who is physically fit enters military service at age eighteen. Most, by far, end up in the ground forces. Service is for a period of three years for men and twenty-four months for women. After leaving active service, men must serve in reserve units until they reach the age of fifty-four; women serve in reserve units until they are thirty-four. Reserve units are well equipped and well organized and train in a highly realistic fashion. They are called up for thirty to forty-five days twice a year. Israel is a true militia state, with almost 80 percent of its ground forces in reserve, ready for deployment at a moment's notice.

The Israeli Defense Force is quite large relative to the country's total population of four million people; almost 94 percent of the eligible population serves in active or reserve roles, a percentage that compares very favorably with the Soviet Union, which also has universal conscription and in which 92 percent of draft-age youth serve. The ground army has a standing strength of about 134,000, of which 110,000 are conscripts doing their three-year service. When mobilized, the force can expand to 450,000, with more than 100,000 coming into active duty in deployable units within twenty-four hours. Normally when reserve units are brought up, they conduct operational missions such as border patrols and crossing raids, and are thoroughly integrated into regular units. Each of the major divisions in the Israeli army, for example, has a reserve brigade permanently assigned to it, which is mobilized and attached to bring the regular unit up to full strength. The manpower distribution is relatively stable. Reserve officers are experienced and often have a higher IQ than active officers. In battlefield performance, Israeli reserve units often perform better than active-duty units. The reserve units constitute a militia of considerable size and capability. One study of military heroism which analyzed Israel's medal-of-honor winners indicates that a higher rate of heroism is to be found in reserve units than in active-service units.[2]

The Israeli army is a highly sophisticated military force equipped with modern tanks, artillery, armored personnel carriers, mobile guns, and small arms (see Table 1 in the Appendix). Official government releases indicate that the IDF can deploy eleven divisions within seventy-two hours. Intelligence estimates, however, suggest that it can actually deploy almost fifteen divisions. If that estimate is correct, it makes the IDF one of the largest deployable ground forces in the Western world. By comparison, the United States army is able to deploy some sixteen divisions, but it would take an enormous amount of time and effort to fill them out with sufficient manpower and equipment. According to one estimate, it would take 280 days for the United States army to fill out its full sixteen divisions with equipment and manpower and move them to the battlefield. By contrast, Israeli active and reserve units fully equipped and at full manpower strength can be mobilized and deployed within seventy-two hours.

The emphasis on speed is a consequence of the fact that Israel has no territory which it can trade for time. The ability of the Israeli army to mobilize rapidly is central to its ability to survive. In addition, Israeli combat formations are highly flexible. The basic Israeli combat unit is the *ugdah*, which is often translated as a division, but it is more accurately a German *Kampfgruppe*, or task force group. Israelis tailor their combat units to the task at hand. There are basic combat formations, but, as shown in Table 2 in the Appendix, manpower and equipment configurations are deployed to suit specific battlefield conditions.

SUSTAINABILITY

The Israeli Defense Force has the capability to fight a sustained battle for about twenty-eight days. It has supplies and stores to carry out a full-scale war, with all units engaged in battle and without significant resupply, for a period of almost a month, a condition which American forces in Europe have yet to attain. After twenty-eight days, the Israeli army's ability to continue sustained battle declines rapidly, which accounts for the Israelis' refusal to allow the enemy to fight a war of attrition. The need to be able to sustain a full-scale battle for a long period became evident in the 1973 war, when problems in the chain of supply, coupled with lack of equipment, due to dependence on foreign sources, made that war a very close thing. Today, almost all small-arms weaponry for the ground forces—including the Galile rifle, the Uzi machine gun, 81mm mortars, 106mm anti-tank guns, the 105mm tank cannon and fieldpiece, Katyusha rockets, RPG's, and almost all the ammunition for these weapons —is produced at home by a defense industry that has grown significantly since the 1973 war.[3] For weapons of larger caliber than 105mm, the IDF relies on the United States for the M-107, 175mm gun, and the M-110 203mm gun. Israel builds its own tank, the Merkava, which is among the best main battle tanks in the world. The IDF also has the ability to repair any tank the Soviets put in the field and can use captured Soviet guns and equipment. The air force is where the IDF is vulnerable due to lack of supplies. But even there, Israel has made rapid advances and now produces its own fighter and a number of air-to-surface weapons.

MANPOWER

Taken as a whole, the Israeli Defense Force is probably the best ground force in the world in the quality of its manpower. The Israelis are among the best-educated and best-trained people in the world. In an army that relies on conscription of all social levels, the quality of the soldiers called to active service represents the talent of the society at large. This does not apply in the United States army, of course, since it is an all-volunteer force, which tends to recruit disproportionately from the lower social levels. In addition to having excellent raw material, the Israeli army gives its soldiers excellent training. Another factor that contributes to the ability of the army to fight well is the quality of its officers, including its NCO ranks, which are among the best in the world due to a system that continually weeds out the marginal and selects the best for command. Finally, the combat experience of the Israeli officer corps, NCO, and soldier is probably the most extensive in the world. Eighty percent of the IDF ground forces is comprised of reserve units, and some of the men in these reserve units have fought in four or five wars. They have not only a high degree of unit attachment and cohesion but considerable combat experience and technical expertise. Thus, when General Israel Tal states that Israel must rely on "superior technology" to carry the day in battle, he means not only superior equipment and technical expertise but superior human material as well.[4] The Israeli Defense Force has managed to draw that material into the army, thus building a combat force which, for its size, is probably second to none in the world, and certainly second to none in the Middle East.

DEPLOYMENT DOCTRINE

Strategically, Israel finds itself confined by a number of politico-military realities that have shaped its military actions since 1948. These realities have been forced on Israel by geography and the nature of the enemy. First, Israel lacks strategic depth. In practice, this means that Israel cannot allow the enemy significantly to penetrate its small territory, for it would risk unacceptable damage or destruction of its population as well as its military reserves. Perhaps most important, trading territory for time would be self-defeating, because it would cripple Israel's ability to mobilize its reserves. It is an imperative of Israeli military strategy that it be able to mobilize its reserves totally and rapidly, and all reserve units must be at full strength and equipped for mobilization. The Israelis have therefore assigned to the air force the primary mission of keeping the skies clear of enemy aircraft, so there can be no disruption of mobilization. Moreover, it is imperative that the Israeli intelligence service function almost to perfection to prevent surprise attack. In 1973, there was a massive intelligence failure and Israeli forces were taken by surprise on two fronts. Enemy forces penetrated significantly and the result was a near-disaster.

A second major strategic premise is the fast-war doctrine. Israel realizes that its survival depends on quick and decisive victories; it cannot allow a war to drag on for any length of time. None of the five wars fought over its thirty-five-year history has brought permanent victory or peace. There have been only respites to prepare for the next war. One reason for this is that neither of the superpowers, the United States or the Soviet Union, is prepared to see its client states totally defeated. Whenever one state appears to be on the verge of a total victory or defeat, one or the other of the superpowers brings pressure to bear to bring the conflict to a halt. In all three major wars—1956, 1967, 1973—Israeli forces were advancing and were capable of destroying the enemy. In each instance, superpower pressure forced the Israeli advance to halt. One aspect of the war in Lebanon reflects this situation. The basis of the Israeli war plan was to achieve its objectives before the U.S. intervened and forced a halt to the fighting. Israel understands that its wars are not purely military but are fought in the larger political context of regional interests and great-power rivalry. The conclusion the Israelis have drawn is that it must achieve its battlefield goals rapidly and decisively before the great powers can intervene.

Israel's third major strategic premise is that it cannot ever truly defeat its combined Arab opponents in a final military sense. Arab manpower and the financial support that each country receives from other Arab states or the great powers make semi-permanent war the only real possibility in a purely military sense. Therefore, the Israeli application of military force is always directed toward the achievement of some political settlement. In practice, the Israelis see that the object of military force is to ensure that the enemy loses territory which can be traded for a political settlement. War must be the servant of political ends, as Clausewitz points out. In the operation in Lebanon, however, the Israelis may have forgotten this dictum, or at least failed to trade military gains for political concessions. But in the long run the Israelis understand that their enemies cannot be defeated militarily to the extent that they will no longer constitute a threat. Rather, military victories are to serve larger political goals.

A fourth major premise of Israeli strategic doctrine is that the effects of war are judged by their impact not only on the battle-field but on Israeli society. War is measured in terms of its economic, sociological, political, and psychological effect on the Israeli people. Israeli society has been in a state of war or preparation for war since 1948, and this "garrison state" has put tremendous pressure on Israeli society, its economy, and its political structure. The continued loss of soldiers increases emigration; it destabilizes the political leadership, and brings a tendency to blame military leadership for political errors. The investigations of the events at Sabra and Shatila in 1982 resulted in the removal of several high-ranking military and political officials. The same thing happened in 1973 when Israeli intelligence failed to provide adequate warning of an Arab attack. The point is that Israelis understand that war exacts a terrible sociological and psychological price. Given its nature, its heterogeneity, its size, and its memories of the Holocaust, the military and political leadership is acutely aware of the long-range effects of a continued war on its people; this concern helps to shape the strategy that guides the deployment of Israeli military forces.[5]

These four factors underlie Israeli strategic doctrine and lead to a number of basic sub-premises on how to employ the IDF in battle. The first of these is always to strike first. Surprise is never to be conceded to the enemy. When there is doubt, the IDF is to take the initiative and carry the war to the enemy. A second major application of defense doctrine is always to take the offensive. Israel is acutely aware that any attempt to fight a defensive war would quickly turn it into a war of attrition that would concede a maximum advantage to the superiority of her enemies' manpower. Therefore, the Israelis have an army that is continually on the move and rarely takes the defensive.

A third sub-premise of Israeli strategy is to achieve goals quickly before the great powers can prevent their achievement. The IDF doctrine seeks to minimize casualties by use of superior tactics and superior equipment, while maximizing enemy losses through surprise, initiative, and firepower. The Israelis are aware that they cannot afford to trade gun for gun, tank for tank, aircraft for aircraft, and, above all, soldier for soldier. They must deal the enemy a quick, decisive blow that cripples its ability to continue the war.

TACTICAL DOCTRINE[6]

How tactically to achieve Israel's goals has been a subject of debate within the IDF since 1948. And the debate tends to become more heated after each war. One can identify clear shifts in tactical emphasis which have occurred since 1948, representing responses to battlefield experiences as well as the development of weapons technology available to the Israelis and to its enemies. While strategic goals have remained relatively stable, the tactical means for achieving them have gone through four phases: (1) individual infantry; (2) mobile light vehicle; (3) pure tank; and (4) combined arms.

In the War for Independence, Israel faced an enemy superior in both manpower and weapons. The focus of military effort on both sides remained the infantryman and his weapons. Neither the crew-served weapon nor the tank had been in anything but a support role. Since Israel lacked tanks, equipment, and air power, and had only human motivation and endurance to compensate for Arab advantages, the IDF sought to carry the battle to the enemy by mobilizing morale, daring, initiative, and unconventional tactics. As a consequence, the tactical stress was on using infantry almost on its own, with very little support, because the IDF had very few crew weapons to deploy. The IDF, therefore, became masters of night attack and the ambush.

The basic thrust of IDF military tactics in the War for Independence was on small infantry units operating under excellent leadership, with officers who normally had total authority for the movement of their units. Individual firepower, bayonet, stealth, and unconventional tactics were the order of the day, instead of air, artillery, and tank support. Lacking almost any other resource, the Israelis turned to their soldiers, using them very effectively.

Between 1948 and 1956, the Israeli army went through a period of uncertainty. Efforts were made to create mobile light forces, but on balance, the IDF wasn't very successful. The Israelis continued to rely on the infantry-first doctrine, which had worked so well in 1948. Daring, individual bravery, and the best deployment of human resources continued to be stressed, but the Israeli military force between 1948 and the early 1950's declined in mobility, as evidenced by a number of unsuccessful military operations against Arab territory. Clearly, something was wrong; the IDF was having difficulties making the transition from a revolutionary army to a permanent one. And it was not until 1956 that most of these difficulties were solved and the Israelis began to operate with a modern military force.

In the 1956 Sinai campaign, Israel fought its first modern war, though by today's standards that war was relatively primitive in equipment and tactics. By 1956, much of the IDF was mounted on light vehicles such as half-tracks, jeeps, and trucks, and had some tanks. For the first time, the Israelis integrated crew-served weapons, especially artillery and tanks, and had air support, though from a relatively primitive air force.

During that war, the Israelis began to appreciate the value of mobility on the battlefield, especially when coupled with a sudden armored attack. In 1948, mobility had been severely limited by terrain, lack of vehicles, and the nature of infantry fighting. In 1956, the Israelis were fighting on a different battlefield, the open terrain of the Sinai Peninsula, on which tanks and vehicles could move very rapidly. Although some high-ranking staff were still skeptical of those tactics at the outbreak of the war, successful and daring tank operations which broke the back of the enemy proved to the military leadership that success on a modern battlefield could be achieved with a military force built around the tank. This led to Israeli tactical doctrine based on the use of tanks. It began in 1956 and ended rather suddenly in 1973.

The war in the Sinai convinced the IDF that the future lay in a configuration of its forces around the main battle tank. Everything was to be subordinated to the tank. All infantry was made mobile by mounting them on APC's so they could move as rapidly as the tank. Even air power was reconstituted to support ground operations as "flying artillery." Walking or light-mounted infantry operating as an independent force was virtually dispensed with. These forces were reconfigured to be able to move rapidly in armored vehicles in support of the tank. Artillery was neglected because it was not highly mobile and because the air support provided by the IAF would act as artillery sustaining the rapid movement of large armored formations. With the outbreak of the Six-Day War in 1967, with Israel's massive preemptive air strike and the collapse of the Arab armies in the face of large, rapidly moving armored forces, IDF planners were more convinced than ever that they had hit on the formula for modern war. As a consequence, between 1967 and 1973 the IDF became more and more tank-oriented, with decreasing emphasis on the infantry and still less on artillery. These developments proved disastrous in 1973.

Between 1968 and 1971, the Israelis engaged in a war of attrition mostly against the Egyptians on the Sinai front. During this time, the IDF gradually adopted a defensive posture by constructing the Bar Lev line along the Suez Canal. They used their airpower essentially for punitive strikes and occasionally in air-to-air engagements. The Israelis seemed not to understand what was happening in terms of the growth of battlefield technology. Israeli high-level officers paid scant attention to the growth of enemy infantry and the development of new weapons such as the rocket-propelled grenade and the antitank missile mounted on a jeep or fired from a fixed position. For reasons that are difficult to understand, few Israeli military planners appreciated the vulnerability of tanks and aircraft to these new weapons—despite the American experience in Vietnam with SAM missile screens.

The Yom Kippur War in 1973 saw a massive intelligence failure that allowed Egyptian and Syrian forces in a major attack to catch the Israelis completely unaware. More important, as the war developed, the Israelis attempted to apply their pure-tank strategy against entrenched infantry forces in the Sinai, with the result that hundreds of tanks were destroyed by enemy infantry firing missiles as tanks attacked fixed infantry positions with no supporting infantry of their own and no long-range artillery to suppress enemy fire. The IDF engaged in attritional tactics, using massed armor against infantry strongpoints, and suffered heavy losses to both tanks and armored vehicles. In time, the Israeli air force recouped air control of the battlefield, but the IAF's ability to deliver ground support was severely hindered by missile screens near the battle area. For the first three days of the war, IAF aircraft were knocked out of the skies in very high numbers by these screens. Eventually, the missiles were neutralized, not by air attacks, but by tanks which penetrated infantry positions and destroyed the missiles on the ground.

These battle experiences in 1973 led many ranking Israeli officials to question the pure-tank doctrine. As put into effect in 1973, it almost resulted in disaster. Moreover, experience showed that tanks operating in open country could not successfully operate independently of infantry and artillery to protect them from infantry attack. As Field Marshal Erwin Rommel pointed out in World War II, the greatest danger to the tank was still the armed infantryman. By 1973, that infantryman had acquired an arsenal of new weapons of great firepower, ranging from missiles to rocket-propelled grenades. In the Sinai campaign, even poorly trained Egyptian troops could function with devastating effectiveness.

The lessons learned in the Yom Kippur War caused the Israelis to shift from pure-tank strategy to a strategy based on combined arms. The army that went into Lebanon in 1982 was reconstituted along very different lines from the army of 1973. It still held that one of the most powerful weapons on a battlefield was the main battle tank. But it now understood that the main battle tank cannot operate alone. Moreover, with the reduced effectiveness of airpower as a result of the employment of missile screens, ground forces would have to protect the tank on the ground. This meant integrating mobile artillery and highly mobile infantry into armored combat formations to suppress antitank weaponry being used by enemy infantry in dug-in positions.

The new tactical doctrine forced the IDF to restructure itself radically. First, infantry forces were made totally mobile by placing them in armored personnel carriers. For a long time, Israeli infantry had been mobile, but it had not been structured so that it could be utilized as a screen for armor and to suppress infantry firing at tanks. The restructuring also affected the Israelis' use of artillery, which, historically, has been the forgotten branch in the IDF. Generally speaking, up to the 1973 war, the Israeli use of artillery was rather primitive. One reason seems to be that the IDF felt that the tank itself was an artillery piece. Further, it saw the air force as flying artillery. What artillery pieces it had were mostly towed rather than self-propelled. Beginning in 1973, then, the IDF began to create an entirely new branch of service for artillery, fully equipped with highly mobile artillery pieces that could keep pace, on the battlefield, with armor and infantry. Artillery became a full partner in the combined-arms team.

This tactical change required the restructuring of the air force to take into account its greater vulnerability to missiles and anti-aircraft fire over the battle area. The war of 1973 had shown that the use of the air force as flying artillery was severely limited by new technological developments. No longer could aircraft loiter for long periods over the battlefield, and no longer could ground forces rely on quick support strikes from the air force. Planes were extremely vulnerable to the new missiles. The air force would still cover the mobilization and ensure that Israel was not attacked by enemy aircraft. But on the battlefield its role had changed.

EXPANSION

The Israeli Defense Force expanded enormously since 1973 in manpower and in complexity. Just how much had changed in the IDF in ten years can be seen from the following figures. At the present time, the IDF is configured to fight on three fronts at the same time, with all its equipment in place, and with the capability of mobilizing one hundred percent of its reserves within seventy-two hours. It has truly become a modern army—a larger, more mobile, more heavily armored, more complex force than the army that fought in 1973. Consider the following data.[7]

- In 1973, the IDF had 75,000 men in its total standing forces, without reserves. In 1982, that number had increased 131 percent to 172,000.
- Regular army strength in 1973 was 11,500; this had increased to 25,000 by 1982. In 1973, it had 50,000 conscripts; by 1982, that number had increased to 110,000. In 1973, the entire Israeli army had a strength of 61,500 men; this increased 125 percent to 135,000.
- Mobilized reserves in 1973 were 275,000 for the total force deployed; in 1982, the army could mobilize in twenty-four hours a total ground force of 450,000, an increase in reserve forces of 63.5 percent.
- In 1973, the Israeli army had nineteen infantry brigades, eleven armored brigades, four paratroop brigades, and no artillery brigades. In 1982, it could field thirty-three armored brigades, ten mechanized infantry brigades, five paratroop brigades, twelve territorial infantry brigades, fifteen artillery brigades, and armor units organized into eleven armored divisions. It is important to note that its fifteen artillery brigades were all new and that the number of its armor brigades was doubled.
- In 1973, the Israelis could field 1,225 tanks; in 1982, the country was capable of deploying 3,825 tanks, an increase of 212 percent.
- In 1973, the Israeli Defense Force had 1,515 armored fighting vehicles; in 1983, that number had increased to 4,000, an increase of 164 percent.
- In 1973, the Israeli Defense Force had approximately 500 armored personnel carriers. In 1982, as a clear reflection of its desire to increase the mobility of its infantry forces, the IDF could field 4,800 armored personnel carriers, an increase of 900 percent.
- In 1973, the IDF had only 300-plus self-propelled artillery guns. In 1982 the number had increased to 958, or 219 percent. The caliber of the guns had also increased enormously.
- In 1973, of a gross national product of $5.4 billion, the military budget was allocated $1.48 billion, or 27.4 percent, an expenditure of $1,764 per capita. By 1982, the gross national product had increased to $23 billion and the military budget to $7.3 billion, or 31.9 percent of the GNP. This amounted to a per-capita expenditure of $1,835, in constant 1973 dollars.

These figures indicate a massive buildup of the Israeli armed forces between 1973 and 1982. They also reflect a changing attitude, with an increased emphasis on armored forces, an increased ability to move mechanized infantry, a reduction in the role played by "straight-leg" infantry, and a marked increase in artillery, in numbers, caliber, and mobility, with approximately two-thirds of all artillery made mobile. Most of the artillery is now self-propelled or mounted on tracked vehicles. Thus, the Israelis have reconstituted their forces so as to be able to fight a three-front war on a moment's notice, at a hundred percent of its strength. One of the paradoxes of the 1982 war is, however, that this massive military force was used for the first time in Lebanon, where the terrain and the nature of the war made it difficult if not impossible for the Israelis properly to apply their new combined-arms strategy. Yet no fact is more striking with regard to how much the IDF has changed since 1973 than that it could then deploy about six divisions whereas today it can deploy fifteen fully mobilized divisions in seventy-two hours.

PROBLEMS[8]

The Israelis have created a military force far larger than anything they had in the past and proportionately larger than any force maintained by a modern industrial state, including the United States. The expansion, however, has brought problems, which began to emerge in 1979, and which suggest that the complexity attendant to a large military force may impair its ability to function in a traditional manner with a heavy reliance on the quality of its manpower. Or, put another way, it may be that as Israel has moved into the modern military age its military structure has begun to show signs of the same difficulties encountered by other modern military structures such as those of the United States and of the Soviet Union. These problems may simply be attendant to any military force of a certain size and complexity.

One problem is how properly to utilize territorial commands. These commands established in 1967 were assigned very few resources; they seem mostly to have been organizational conveniences. But since 1973 these commands have grown, and their role has expanded. In addition to ground units specifically assigned to each territorial command, specific air squadrons have been attached to each. And each command now has its own intelligence assets, to avoid repeating the intelligence failures of 1973. As commands grow in size and complexity, they come to depend on modern facilities—centralized (C3) command, control, and communication links; and communication links may become overly centralized. There is the risk then of a loss of flexibility in combat command structures.

There is also concern among some IDF officers that each territorial command is beginning to develop doctrine specific to its own area. Moreover, the required integration of reserve units in each territorial command may result in these combat formations being not only doctrine-specific but overly specialized in their training as well. The Israelis are aware of this difficulty and have made efforts to ensure that each unit, especially reserve units, receives at least some training in the other territorial commands and in different battle environments. In practice, however, this does not always work well; as a rule, no more than 20 percent of a unit's training is outside its own area of responsibility. There is also the fear that not only will units become tailored to operate in a specific battle environment but their equipment mix will also become tailored. This is especially true of tanks. The Israelis deploy four basic types of tanks: the M-48, the Centurion, the Merkava and the M-60. Tank units are most often integrated in the reserves and since certain types of tank are better suited for specific environments and terrain, deploying them in different locales may adversely affect efficiency in battle and the ability to resupply them.

The expansion of the IDF has caused some concern that it may bring about a decline in the quality and intensity of training. Despite the expansion, the IDF ground army still maintains a regular force of only three standing combat divisions. In addition to these divisions, there is the elite Golani infantry brigade, augmented by five battalions. These few units comprise the standing Israeli ground force, and even they have to be augmented by at least one reserve component to fight at full strength.

These few units provide most of the training for all reserve units. They are responsible for training the equivalent of ten divisions. Their cadre also train reserve units that come on duty for periods of thirty to forty-five days; they train new officers and NCO's, much of whose training takes place in regular army units.

At least one battalion and often a brigade of each division spend at least three months each year training reserve troops or new troops. Each year, moreover, at least one third of all regular troops and almost 90 percent of the officers leave the regular force for reserve units as their conscript military duty ends. Finally, the troops in the regular units must keep their training up to standard, and attend career and training schools. Serious questions are being raised by Israeli officers about the ability of regular units to handle this tremendous burden of training. Can regular units handle the training load and still remain combat-ready?

As a result of the expansion of the IDF, there are increased pressures on the officer corps. The staggering death rate in 1973 was especially so for junior officers and combat leaders. One hundred fifty-three lieutenant colonels and majors were killed, and 350 were so badly wounded that they never returned to the military. There was a net shortage of 503 officers in just these two ranks alone. Two hundred and twenty captains and first lieutenants were killed, and six hundred were so badly wounded that they did not return, resulting in a net shortage of over eight hundred officers. Further, the number who left regular service at the end of their military service created a huge shortage of trained combat officers. Had the forces not been modernized or increased in size, normal replenishment would have brought the forces back to standard in three to five years.

Since the IDF expanded almost two and a half times in less than ten years, there was enormous need to recruit new officers and to retain veterans. A policy of accelerated promotion was implemented. However, a number of IDF officers are concerned about the quality of officers promoted too rapidly; they suggest that standards may also have declined.

An article written by Meir Pa'il, former commander of the IDF Central Officers School, notes that, because of the technological skills required, the air force and the navy tend to get recruits with the high IQ's and motivation, while the ground forces have what he calls a "mediocre quality of regular officers."[9] Moreover, since many of the best officers do not stay in the military, in time a gulf might widen between the young and excellent conscript officers and the selected group of regulars who choose to stay beyond their normal conscript service. Pa'il suggests that conscript officers have higher IQ's than regular officers and that their "spiritual level" may also be higher. Further, Pa'il contends that as regular officers remain on active duty they tend to put their careers first and to respond to the internal requirements of the bureaucratic system from which their promotions and advancements come. As a consequence, he fears, their daring, their initiative, and their strength as leaders may be sacrificed. In contrast, the conscript officers, who do not plan to make a career in the military, would tend to keep faith with themselves and their ideals, and be daring and take the initiative. In Pa'il's opinion, the young short-term conscripts are likely to make the best officers, whereas those who remain in the service are likely to decline in quality; and this may create a "spiritual" gulf between the two officer corps that may have grave consequences on the battlefield.

Moreover, there is a tendency for regular officers to be something of a guild. This is true in other large and complex armies such as those of the United States and the Soviet Union. Increased competition for promotion and command positions and the need for prior command as a prerequisite for promotion bring about a creeping careerism among the "survivors" of the system. To be sure, the careerist tendencies evident in the Israeli army are not nearly as severe or corrosive as they are in the United States army or, perhaps, in any other modern Western army. But the tendency is there and will develop further with the process of expansion and the need to recruit and retain more officers; the same factors generated similar pathologies in the U.S. army during the war in Vietnam.

As the IDF became larger, it necessarily became more complex. As a consequence, the fear is that there has been an increased reliance on technological fixes and use of firepower as substitutes for traditional qualities of leadership, daring, and initiative. Some stress on firepower and technology was a natural result of the development of the combined-arms strategy. Further, since the role of flying artillery has been diminished, the need to develop technological fixes to deal with the enemy's technology has inevitably increased. Has the emphasis on technology and firepower, then, undercut the traditional human qualities that have been so vital to Israeli success on the battlefield?

Another major development associated with a large, complex army is the need for officers and NCO's to master more sophisticated tasks of war. Officers, NCO's, and some troop elements now have shorter tours with their units. Officers and NCO's move in and out of positions at a faster rate in order to learn more and more about newer and newer skills. Officer turbulence is increasing in the Israeli army. In the past, an officer could count on spending about thirty-six months with his unit in a stabilized command tour. That time is down to about twenty-four months, which is more or less the same amount of time an American officer spends with his command unit. Increased rotational turbulence tends to reduce officers' attachments to their men and to reduce unit cohesion; at the same time, the administrative and technical aspects of command become increasingly important.

This is balanced by the fact that rotational turbulence is not found to the same degree at the lower combat levels. Rather, it tends to occur at the brigade and division level. At the platoon, company, and even battalion level, the leadership of lieutenants and captains remains highly stable. This is important because it is these units that do the fighting and it is in these units that individual attachment to one's men, unit cohesion, and leadership are most crucial.

It must also be remembered that the overwhelming majority of Israeli combat platoons, battalions, and companies are in the reserves. Reserve officers are assigned to their units for very long periods of time; indeed, often for life. It is not unusual, therefore, to see reserve units whose officers have held their commands for fifteen and even twenty years. The same is true of the reserve NCO leadership right down to the squad level. Thus, even if rotational turbulence is increasing in the IDF regular force, it is not increasing at the lower combat-unit level, and for at least 80 percent of the forces in the reserve, rotational turbulence has not increased at all.

Another problem is that the number of individuals who are asked to become officers and who accept—85 percent to 90 percent traditionally—has been dropping over the years. More and more individuals are refusing to accept the added responsibility of being officers and NCO's. Certainly one reason is that they don't want the extended year of service that is required of a commissioned officer. But it may also be indicative of a deeper social trend, war weariness, and a natural desire to get on with civilian life. Too, the fact that officers tend to die at excessively high rates relative to their numbers is hardly encouraging to young men to become officers. The general pool from which the regular IDF forces are able to draw their officers may be getting smaller, and that pool may no longer be made up of the best in Israeli society but rather of those who, in Pa'il's words, tend to be "mediocre in quality."

The educational level of most IDF career officers is far below that of their counterparts in the reserve. Indeed, it tends to be far below that of their counterparts in most Western armies, because the system is such that one cannot become an officer until one serves as a conscript. As a result, very few university graduates become officers, since the education of officers is delayed. Most IDF officers do not acquire a university degree or an advanced education for a very long time, and normally do it piecemeal. A substantial number of IDF officers, perhaps 25 percent, never obtain a university degree at all. The recently retired Chief of Staff, Rafael Eitan, does not have a university degree. Some would argue that a lack of a degree produces a narrow officer, a man who is well schooled in military and technical skills but not capable of grasping the bigger political picture.

It is difficult to accept this argument, given the past success of the Israeli Defense Force. Perhaps it is worth pointing out that the American officer corps is thoroughly educated, with master's degrees and Ph.D.'s, and yet its qualities of leadership in Vietnam were hardly testimony to the usefulness of advanced degrees in the military. The extent to which higher-level leadership talent is linked to education remains an open question, but that it is linked to some extent is clear enough. The fact that relatively few Israeli officers earn a university degree suggests that it may be difficult to create a general staff at the senior level which is educated well enough to grasp the import of military, political, and economic factors with which they must often deal.

A question of quality also applies to the NCO corps, which, like the officer corps, operates on a dual-tier system. Combat NCO's are selected from the best conscripts and are generally of excellent quality. But those who stay on as NCO's tend also to be below the traditionally high standards of the IDF. As a result, the same problem that Pa'il sees afflicting some elements of the officer corps also afflicts the NCO corps. On the other hand, the senior NCO corps in the IDF is used primarily in a staff or technical role. Fortunately, almost all NCO's in combat units are not long-term NCO's but conscripts, so that the impact of the quality of senior NCO corps on combat performance at the small-unit level is minimal.

In assessing the overall quality of the IDF officer, one must keep certain facts in mind. First, the performance of IDF officers in battle has historically been good, if not excellent. In every war since 1967, the Israeli officer corps has suffered 26 percent of the total casualties in battle; the death rate is three to four times higher than that of their men. The notion of leading from the front, of taking the initiative, of exercising daring, seems to be a condition and quality of IDF officers that is as strong today as it was in 1967. One would suggest of IDF officers that their bravery, initiative, daring, flexibility, and willingness to set the example for their men does not appear to have lessened significantly since 1973.

Whatever shortcomings IDF officers may have begun to develop are not likely to affect the small-unit level, in any case. In the battalion and below, officers and combat NCO's are conscripts, not career officers, and they are selected and promoted because they are the best the army has to offer. In this sense, "creeping careerism" and a lowering of the quality of IDF officers is likely to have little impact on combat units.

The basis for military service in Israel is, after all, conscription. This means that the "law of large numbers" is operative: the quality of recruits represents a cross section of the general citizenry. And the Israeli citizenry is among the best educated and healthiest in the world, so that the overall quality of raw recruit material is and will remain high. The problems that beset the American army, particularly drug abuse, poor discipline, desertion, etc., tend to be associated with the fact that an all-volunteer force draws disproportionately from the lowest strata of American society. These problems are almost unknown in the Israeli army.

The concern is not that the Israeli army suffers or will suffer from pathologies that undermine its ability to execute combat operations or affect the quality of its leadership and its unit cohesion. Rather, it is the fear that "creeping mediocrity" may in the future afflict its regular standing force. The reserve militia is likely to remain as good an army as it is today, but the standing force may decline in quality during peacetime. A mediocre regular force that produces mediocre officers at the top may, during periods of peace, generate inadequate tactical and strategic policies, may ignore technical innovations, and may become more concerned with promotion and advancement and the bureaucracy. There is, lastly, the fear that really capable younger officers may come increasingly to resent their seniors. To some extent, this condition exists in all armies, but because this has not been the case in the Israeli army, it is regarded perhaps as more of a threat than it is.

CONCLUSION

Since 1973, the Israeli Defense Force has become a modern army in every sense of the word. It has grown enormously in size, become highly technical in its equipment, and requires more manpower, more officers, and more resources. As it has grown, the initial signs of internal tensions associated with large modern forces are beginning to be seen. But on the eve of the Lebanon war the Israeli Defense Force mustered a military force capable of defeating any enemy in the region or any combination of enemies in the Middle East. Most certainly, it was in a position to deal severely with the PLO, a force of fifteen thousand stationed in southern Lebanon. The military outcome was virtually assured.

The IDF, of course, still enjoyed the almost total and unquestioned support of the political leadership and, more important, of the population at large. Public support—and its links with the public—has historically been one of the IDF's strongest assets. The military has always clearly explained its military actions and, in return, has received unquestioned public support. Because 80 percent of the army is militia in reserve units, a close relationship between the military and the population is crucial. A change in public opinion in Israel is likely to spread rapidly throughout the military structure—much more rapidly than it would in any other army in the West. The war in Lebanon for the first time raised the question of whether this linkage would remain strong in the future.

2

The PLO in Lebanon

Central to any attempt to understand the events in Lebanon are the nature and activities of the Palestinian Liberation Organization (PLO). The PLO is unique in that it is probably the best-financed guerrilla organization in history. Similar organizations in other states have had to lurch along from crisis to crisis, often robbing banks to finance themselves, or they have had to rely on their host enemy as a main source of arms. But the PLO has been financed to a total of $90 million to $100 million dollars a year by a number of Arab governments, including the confrontation states as well as the oil-producing states of the Saudi peninsula. One of the most interesting facts about the PLO is that it is not a national group. It is an international organization that maintains links with a number of other guerrilla and terrorist movements throughout the world. The organization cannot accurately be described as a true national liberation movement.

HISTORY

The PLO owes its existence to President Abdel Nasser of Egypt. In 1955, Nasser launched an initiative to create a pan-Arab movement whose goal was the destruction of Israel. How seriously Nasser accepted these goals is open to question. The formula proved irresistible, however, and by 1957 most Arab states were willing to join the anti-Israel cause. A number of guerrilla organizations sprang up in the next decade, none of which was of any military or political consequence. In a sense, they were opportunistic. Nasser offered them a chance to play at the game of national revolution and a chance to strike at Israel. Although many of the recruits came from Palestinian refugee camps, these organizations did not amount to much as military or political forces.

In 1964, the heads of the major Arab states met in Cairo and formally established the Palestinian Liberation Organization. They agreed to channel arms and financial support through the PLO, which was to act as an "umbrella organization" and bring all groups under one command to function as a common front. The largest of the groups was Al Fatah, which engaged in its first military attack on an Israeli village in December 1964. It would be Al Fatah, later headed by Yasir Arafat, which would form the nucleus of the PLO not only as a military force but, more important, as a political force to be reckoned with in the Middle East.

In 1967, two events changed the importance of the PLO. The first was the Six-Day War. In a lightning strike, Israel acquired the entire West Bank and the Gaza Strip, acquiring with it thousands of Palestinians who had been under Jordanian and Egyptian rule. In time, these populations began to look to the PLO as a means of freeing themselves from Israeli rule and of gaining revenge. The second decisive event was also military. Despite the Israelis' quick victory against the combined Arab armies, the PLO fought very well in a battle in the Jordanian village of Al Karamalf. The number of dead and wounded on either side is uncertain, but it does appear that the Israeli forces may have suffered a minor defeat. At the end of the war, the PLO emerged as the only Arab military force (as it defined itself) that did not suffer a complete and crushing defeat at the hands of the IDF. By means of excellent propaganda and with renewed support from the Soviet Union and other Arab states, the PLO began to cultivate an image as an elite and effective military force, and its credibility and support grew among Arab states, in the Soviet Union, and among the large Palestinian populations residing within Israeli borders.

For their part, having suffered a devastating defeat, the Arab states saw their public support of the PLO as a convenient inexpensive means to convince their own populations that they supported the extermination of Israel. For the Arab states, support of the PLO was a way of keeping the political pot boiling, as well as a way of playing off the United States, the primary supporter of Israel, against the Soviets. Moreover, this support could be provided without engaging their own forces and suffering another military defeat. By clever politics, the states of the region were able to extract considerable amounts of money, and political and military support, from both the United States and the Soviet Union. In 1969, Yasir Arafat, now head of Al Fatah, was recognized as the leader of the Palestinian Liberation Organization, and it was accepted as the "sole representative of the Palestinian people." The PLO had reached political maturity.

Whatever the image the PLO may have projected, the reality was considerably different. The PLO was, for instance, not an effective military force or even a guerrilla force of any quality. Indeed, it could barely carry out operations inside Israel even with the partial support of the Palestinian population residing there. Even when it was successful, and it almost always was not, it was clear to Palestinians residing within the Israeli borders that the PLO was not able to bring about a popular uprising of Palestinians on the West Bank, in Gaza, or anywhere else. Because of its inability to effect any kind of military solution to the conflict with Israel, its tactics shifted.

Between 1969 and the present, the PLO attempted to do several things, none of which was intended to achieve military victory. The first was to convince the Arab and Western states that it was a legitimate freedom fighters movement; this was done very successfully. Its program got a big boost when Arafat spoke before the United Nations in 1974. A second goal of the PLO, and central to its existence, was to ensure the continued financial support of the Arab countries; most specifically, the oil-producing states. This money was used to recruit new members, especially in the camps, where educational and economic opportunities were dismal. Cash was the primary means of keeping recruits and followers actively involved in PLO activities. Without Arab financial support, the PLO would long ago have withered on the vine. In return for financial support, the more traditional Arab countries, such as Saudi Arabia, Yemen, Muscat, and Oman, were making sure that the PLO would not incite unrest among their domestic populations.

A third element of PLO strategy was to engage in international terrorism, as opposed to national terrorism. The reason for this was simple. In the first place, the PLO lacked the military strength to engage in any significant military action against Israel. The PLO, in fact, has almost never struck at an Israeli military target inside Israel. When it has struck inside Israel, it has been against civilian targets. Incapable of striking effectively against the Israelis, the PLO set out to erode political support for Israel in other Western states by undertaking terrorist actions, and proclaiming that so long as the Western powers supported Israel, they would be subject to terrorism.

A fourth goal was to develop a small political and military force into a significant threat, great enough to inflict enough casualties on Israel to drive it to the bargaining table. Moreover, by increasing its own military forces, it would be in a position, if the need arose, to threaten the domestic stability of a number of Arab states, thus insuring their continued financial support. In order to achieve these basic objectives, the PLO had to acquire an autonomous base and the weapons to attack Israel. By 1970, the PLO had acquired that base in Jordan.

THE JORDANIAN CIVIL WAR

The tension between the PLO and Jordan, which had been growing for a long time, came to a head in 1970. The 1967 war was a disaster for Jordan that resulted in the loss of the entire West Bank and the headwaters of the Jordan River. As a consequence, the Jordanians were perhaps the least inclined of all Mideast states to become involved in a direct military confrontation with the Israelis. In addition, the PLO regarded Jordan as a Palestinian state. Comprised of the territory known during the British mandate as Transjordan, it contained large numbers of Palestinian refugees who arrived from Israel after the 1948 War for Independence. The Hashemite monarchy of King Hussein, while popular, has always feared its own population. The monarchy itself was transplanted from Saudi Arabia by the British, and to secure its throne has relied on a Bedouin army tied to the king by familial and blood ties of feudal loyalty. By 1970, Hussein feared that the PLO was becoming too independent, that it had developed to the point where it was in a position to threaten his hold over the government.

Events came to a head in 1970 after the PLO hijacked three airliners and flew them to a remote airfield in Jordan. After days of worldwide publicity in which the Jordanian government tried to act as intermediary, the PLO defied Jordan's request to release the airliners and blew them up. Shortly thereafter, a minister of Hussein's government was assassinated and a number of plots to kill Hussein were uncovered by Jordan's British-trained secret service. By September of 1970, King Hussein had reached the end of his patience and was prepared to destroy the PLO as an organized force within the Jordanian state.

In September 1970, which has become known as Black September to the PLO, Hussein turned his Bedouin army against them with the intention of destroying their forces. In eleven days of terrible sectarian fighting, the PLO suffered heavy losses. The Israeli intelligence service estimated that 30 percent of the key fighting soldiers and cadre of the PLO were slaughtered by the Jordanians. Hussein's forces were capable of destroying the entire movement, including its civilian supporters and the families of the PLO fighters, but he didn't go that far. PLO bases were closed, weapons confiscated, and almost 150,000 families, sympathizers, and fighters were driven into Syria.

Although the Syrians had been among the strongest supporters of the PLO and had even rushed an armored force to its defense against the Jordanians, they were under no illusions as to its true intentions. The Syrians were in reality no more trusting of the PLO than Hussein was. Moreover, having seen the PLO attempt to strike at Jordan, the Syrians were not about to allow a situation to develop where the PLO would be able to strike at the Syrian state. Pressure was brought to bear on Lebanon, therefore, to accept large numbers of PLO and its sympathizers who were driven out of Jordan. The Lebanese acquiesced, and large numbers of Palestinians and members of the PLO moved into Lebanon and settled there. The seeds of the future conflict in Lebanon were sown.

THE PLO

The PLO is an umbrella organization consisting of five major terrorist groups and several minor factions. The five major groups are Al Fatah, Al Saiqa, the PFLP, PDFLP, and the PFLP-GC. In principle, they have some representation on the Palestine National Council and are conjointly governed by the Executive Council chaired by Yasir Arafat. The Executive Council has the responsibility for devising strategy and tactics to be carried out in the name of the PLO. The PLO's military arm is the PLA, or Palestine Liberation Army, which has units in several countries. Arafat is its commander in chief, although its field general is a man known as Abu Jihad.

Of the PLO groups, Al Fatah is the oldest. It predates the 1967 war by almost three years. It is also the largest group and claims some eleven thousand members. Al Fatah dominates the coalition of the PLO insofar as it is generally able to determine the direction of the movement, although no faction wields control. The PLO is really a coalition of rival groups, nationalists and internationalists, some the instruments of other governments, who compete for money, power, and prestige. The groups comprising the PLO do not work together very well; they have fought among themselves at least as often as they have fought the Israelis. Ideologically, Al Fatah is nationalist rather than Marxist in orientation, as most others are. It is Al Fatah that most commonly poses as spokesman for the "national aspirations" of the Palestinian people. Moreover, Al Fatah, posing as a nationalist movement, has generally succeeded in giving the PLO and the factions within it an aura of legitimacy. It has convinced many observers and policymakers in the West that it is a genuine national liberation movement.

The second largest group is Al Saiqa. It is estimated to have between five thousand and seven thousand members. Al Saiqa was formed after the 1967 war. In theory, Al Saiqa is independent, with headquarters in Beirut and Damascus; in fact, it is controlled by the Syrian government and the Syrian army. Its arms, most of its money, and almost all its training are Syrian. Indeed, so close is the control of Al Saiqa that it has been called the "terrorist arm of the Syrian army." Ideologically, it is certainly pro-Syrian and follows the general lines of the Syrian

Ba'ath Party. Its independence and ideological position are limited by strong control and penetration at all levels by Syrian intelligence officers.

The third faction within the Palestine liberation front is the PFLP, or the Popular Front for the Liberation of Palestine. This, too, was formed after the 1967 war, and is led by a Christian doctor, George Habash. It has between 2,000 and 2,200 members. Although Habash is a Christian, he is also a dogmatic Marxist, and the organization's policies generally follow this orientation. Indeed, the PFLP cannot be seen as a nationalist movement in any sense. It tends to see the Palestinian problem, not as one of national aspirations, but as part of the larger conflict in the Middle East between capitalism, socialism, and imperialism. Accordingly, it is highly ideological, very radical, and consistently obstructionist in any kind of possible accommodation with Israel. In fact, a number of clashes have occurred within the PLO between George Habash and Yasir Arafat and have on several occasions involved attempted assassinations of one by the other. The personality of George Habash has lent considerable legitimacy to the PFLP in the Arab world.

Another of the organizations that constitute the PLO is the PFLP-GC, or the Popular Front of the Liberation of Palestine-General Command, formed by Ahmed Jebril. Based in Lebanon, it is a splinter group of Habash's group. It is strongly oriented toward Libya, but paradoxically it is noted for taking pro-Syrian positions. It is a small group, probably under a thousand, which has a reputation for conducting effective field operations and for mercilessly carrying out terrorist operations. Its financing appears to be adequate, since Libya has increasingly taken it under its protection. It was responsible for the infamous attack on a school bus in Avivim in 1970, and also for the slaughter of children in the nursery school in Ma'alot in 1974.

The PDFLP, the Popular Democratic Front for the Liberation of Palestine, is another major group within the PLO; it was created in 1969 as a splinter group from Habash's PFLP. Led by Nayef Hawatmeh, it, too, is Marxist in orientation but is to the left of the PFLP. It has about 1,500 members and maintains close ties to Syria and the Soviet Union.

There are a number of smaller groups, some to the left and

others to the right of the major PLO groups. By far the most significant of these lesser groups is another coalition, called the Rejectionist Front, which is comprised of the Arab Liberation Front and the Palestinian Liberation Front. Neither is likely to have more than seven hundred members, although exact data are difficult to come by, and both are supported by Iraq and support the more extreme policies of the Iraqi government. It was responsible, in league with the PFLP-GC, for the attack on the children's nursery in Misgav-Am in 1980.

The PLO likes to portray itself as a unified group of genuine Palestinian nationalists working toward a common cause: the liberation of the Palestinian people from the Israeli yoke and the creation of a Palestinian homeland. Moreover, the PLO like to characterize themselves as a genuine guerrilla movement, as a band of democratic radicals trying to liberate their people from foreign oppression. They portray themselves in the image of the guerrilla movements of the Sandinistas in Latin America or the Vietcong in Asia. This image is carefully cultivated. The very expensive propaganda to create it is financed largely by $90 million a year in Arab oil money. It also is not true.

The PLO is splintered. In point of fact, the PLO is not unified on anything, be it economic, social outlook, even on the existence of Israel. Each group pursues its selfish interests, governs in its own area, and often clashes violently with other groups of the PLO. In Lebanon, for example, groups often clash over the profits from illegal ports, the white slave trade, and smuggling. Clashes in the Bekaa are constantly occurring in jurisdictional disputes over the hashish-growing areas. The PLO lacks the unity or organizational strength to impose even a rough military control or ideological direction.

The leading personalities within these groups view each other with deep suspicion, each taking precautions against being killed by "dissident elements" in his own movement as well as in the other factions. They see themselves as competitors for power and riches and publicity. For some, especially the smaller groups, the PLO has become a business and a way of life, and its perpetuation has become an end in itself.

Only Al Fatah can be regarded as being even moderately nationalist. Al Fatah has consistently made it its goal to free the

Palestinians and set up a Palestinian state. None of the other groups shares this goal. They range from international Marxists, like the PFLP, to outright self-interested terrorists, such as the PFLP-GC and the Rejectionist Front, to organizations that are mere toadies of specific regimes, such as Al Saiqa, which does the bidding of Syrian intelligence.

To the extent that the PLO is a movement at all, it is one comprised of competitive factions headed by powerful warlords who are allowed to govern their factions as long as they protect the financial status, arms, and prestige of their members and are clever enough to avoid assassination by their competitors. They are more akin to Mafia groups in Sicily than they are to national liberation movements. In Lebanon, each group has carved for itself a share of the territory which it controls. Within their territories, the PLO factions make the law, enforce the law, share in the booty garnered through terrorizing the local population, and distribute among their members a share of the profits obtained from smuggling drugs, white slavery, and extortion. They are motivated far more by self-interest—power, prestige, and income—than by any definable ideological or political goal as would be the case with a true national liberation movement.

THE PLO MINI-STATE IN LEBANON

Lebanon, historically, has never been a secular state in the Western sense, where the power and values of the central government have been able to submerge and control confessional values and powerful groups within the state. In 1943, when Lebanon gained independence from France, the state was deliberately constructed on a confessional basis; that is, on the basis of ethnic and religious affiliation. There was clear recognition that each ethno-religious group should share proportionately in the power of the state, and complicated formulas were worked out so that the president of the state was always of one religion, the prime minister another, cabinet members represented other factions, army leaders still other factions, and every major group had a share in the government. That share was guaranteed on a confessional basis, regardless of the outcome of popular elections. The basic fact of Lebanese political life between 1943 and 1983 was the recognition by the central government of its limited power over the different religious and ethnic groups within the country.

From its inception, Lebanon has been an artificial geographic entity carved out by the French from what used to be Syria. It has always been composed of ethno-religious fiefdoms, and it still is. Map 1 shows the areas of the country occupied by major ethno-religious groups in 1982. Lebanon has been for most of its history a patchwork of confessional fiefdoms that view each other with suspicions rooted in animosities that go back centuries.

The key to understanding the confessional balance in Lebanon is the tension between the large Christian and Moslem communities. The last national census was taken in 1936, and it was used as the basis for dividing power among the various religious and ethnic entities in 1943. At that time, the census showed the Christians in a clear majority. As time passed, however, and certainly by 1970, the Moslems came to feel that they were in the majority and, in fact, probably were, although no new census has been taken. Moreover, the influx of over 240,000 Palestinians after 1948 and again after the Jordanian civil war in 1970 increased tensions, since for the most part the Palestinians were Moslems.

Since Lebanon's independence in 1943, Christians have come to dominate much of the social, political, and economic life of Lebanon. Their dominance is based on essentially pre-modern social organizations. Christian control, as well as the influence of the Druse and Moslems, is based on a number of strong Mafia-like families which share certain enterprises such as drugs, banking, the tourist trade, illegal ports (where smugglers can bribe officials), and prostitution. Among the Christians, the major families are the Gemayels, the Chamouns, and the Franjiehs; the major Druse family is the Jumblats. By 1970, most of the Moslems, especially those in urban areas, had begun to agitate for change, reform, and a larger share of social power. Until 1975, this agitation was generally aimed at reform. It was after 1975 that it turned increasingly violent and finally, in that year, resulted in civil war. The catalyst was the PLO.

The PLO has had bases in Beirut since 1968. Following their defeat in the Six-Day War, Egypt and the other Arab states

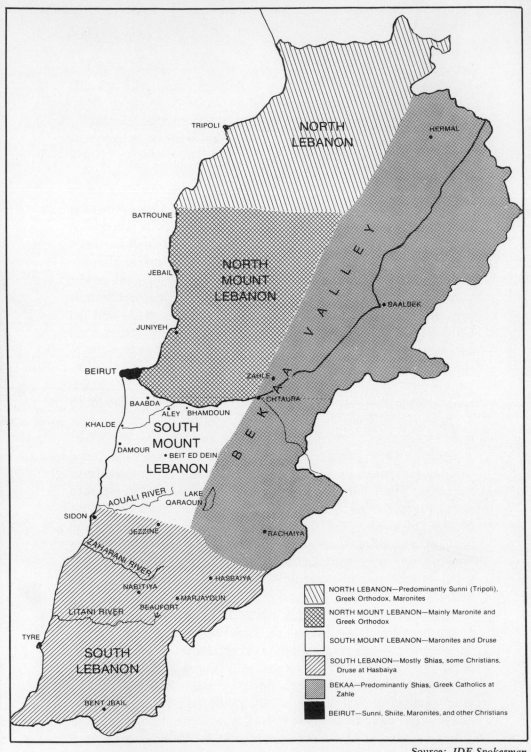

TRIPOLI

NORTH
LEBANON

HERMAL

BATROUNE

NORTH
MOUNT
LEBANON

JEBAIL

JUNIYEH

BAALBEK

BEIRUT

ZAHLE

BAABDA

CHTAURA

ALEY BHAMDOUN

KHALDE

SOUTH
MOUNT

DAMOUR

BEIT ED DEIN

LEBANON

AOUALI RIVER

LAKE
QARAOUN

SIDON

JEZZINE

RACHAIYA

ZAHARANI RIVER

HASBAIYA

NABITIYA

MARJAYOUN

LITANI RIVER

BEAUFORT

TYRE

SOUTH
LEBANON

BENT JBAIL

BEKAA VALLEY

NORTH LEBANON—Predominantly Sunni (Tripoli), Greek Orthodox, Maronites

NORTH MOUNT LEBANON—Mainly Maronite and Greek Orthodox

SOUTH MOUNT LEBANON—Maronites and Druse

SOUTH LEBANON—Mostly Shias, some Christians, Druse at Hasbaiya

BEKAA—Predominantly Shias, Greek Catholics at Zahle

BEIRUT—Sunni, Shiite, Maronites, and other Christians

Source: *IDF Spokesman*

Map 1. Ethnic/religious communities in Lebanon

tried to open up a "combat front" against Israel without putting themselves at risk. Pressure was brought to bear on Lebanon, which shares a border with Israel, to provide a base for PLO guerrilla activity against the Israelis, and since Lebanon had a weak government, it was eventually pressed into compliance. Finally, it served Syria's interest to weaken the Lebanese state. For the Syrians, Lebanon remains a legitimate part of Syria, from which it was removed by the French.

The Lebanese, for obvious reasons, resisted as long as they could. Syria then closed its borders with Lebanon and began to infiltrate troops under the guise of Al Saiqa guerrillas, which soon clashed openly with the Lebanese army. Iraq imposed economic sanctions, and Lebanon was denounced by every major Arab state in the region. Lebanon finally relented and reluctantly granted the PLO several areas, mostly in the largely agricultural southern part of the country. Whenever the PLO conducted attacks against Israel, the Lebanese feared counterattacks. As a result of Lebanese attempts to limit PLO activity against the Israelis, a number of armed clashes occurred between the Lebanese army and the PLO, and these clashes became an escalating feature of Lebanese life.

In 1969, Nasser pressured Lebanon into signing the Cairo Agreement, which formally granted the PLO areas of operation beyond effective control of the Lebanese government. In addition, it granted the PLO a number of extraterritorial rights, mostly in the refugee camps in the south. Finally, it freed the PLO from most of the restrictions placed on it to conduct operations against the Israelis. This legalization and creation of a "state-within-a-state" in Lebanon was the first step in the reduction and eventual destruction of the power of the central government.

After the brief civil war with Jordan in 1970, some 150,000 Palestinians were driven out of Jordan into Syria. The government of Lebanon came under renewed pressure from Syria and other Arab states to let the Palestinians enter Lebanon and settle there. The Lebanese government collapsed under the pressure and agreed. About 150,000 Palestinians settled in Lebanon as a result, many in the Beirut area, where their settlement patterns would take on great significance in the later civil war. Upward of 50,000 Palestinians, and most of the hard-core PLO driven from Jordan, settled in the Beirut area, while another 100,000 or so settled in the southern areas of Tyre and Sidon, joining another 200,000 or so Palestinians who had been living in southern Lebanon since 1948. With almost 500,000 Palestinians in Lebanon, and with the major part of the PLO's military arm located in and around Beirut, Lebanon became the primary base of operations for the PLO against Israel. Gradually, the PLO expanded its influence and pushed out from the areas granted to it in the Cairo Agreement. Clashes with the Lebanese army became more frequent and more violent.

In 1971 and 1972, the Syrians began to play a greater role in the struggle between the PLO and the Lebanese government. In 1971, in an effort to weaken Lebanon as a prelude to gaining the larger objective of reabsorbing Lebanon into greater Syria, Damascus stepped up its support of the PLO. It sent units of Al Saiqa into Lebanon in disguise, shipped arms to the PLO, and even disguised its own regular forces and sent them in. The message to the Lebanese was clear: Syria expected Lebanon to cooperate with Syrian policies. Faced with these threats, the Lebanese in May 1973 signed the Melkhart Agreement, which extended PLO influence beyond that already granted in the Cairo Agreement. The Melkhart Agreement, moreover, gave a semblance of legitimacy to the PLO's extraterritorial rights in Lebanon and marked the formal beginning of the PLO "ministate" in that country.

The growth of PLO power in Lebanon coincided with the increased restlessness of the Moslem population for greater participation in the Lebanese state. Much of the PLO's weakness in Jordan had been due to its failure to establish strong ties with the legitimate Moslem left in that country, so that, when confronted by the power of Hussein's army, it had few allies. The PLO was determined not to make the same mistake in Lebanon, and over the years it established close ties with the leftist and Moslem militias in the country. As it did so, it tried to radicalize the Moslem movement, control it and turn it away from reform toward a more violent solution. Fearing a PLO revolt backed by Syria, the Christians then began to arm. This forced other confessional groups to do likewise. By 1975, the country was an armed camp consisting of over twenty major private armies waiting for a spark to ignite a civil war.

CIVIL WAR IN LEBANON

In 1975, a Nasserite Moslem in Lebanon, Maraf Saad, leading one of a series of strike demonstrations, was shot by Lebanese police authorities. This touched off a series of confrontations, some of them violent, between the Moslem community and the government. The PLO joined the demonstrations, posing as the champion of Moslem communal justice within the confessional state.

The spark for the PLO–Christian civil war was set off on April 13, 1975. A busload of armed PLO soldiers traveling from Aley and bound for the Sabra camp detoured through the Christian neighborhood of Ain Rammanah, where Pierre Gemayel, chieftain of a major Christian family, was standing outside the church after a family baptism. A car approached and sprayed the party with gunfire, killing a bodyguard and wounding several others. To the Gemayels, it looked like an assassination attempt. At about the same time, the PLO bus came through the area, its soldiers firing into the air. The Christians fired at the bus, and the conflict escalated into a major battle with Moslems and the PLO in the Ain Rammanah area. The area, a principal connecting point between the camps of Karantina, Tal Zaatar, and other camps, is also the home of the Katibe Party, the major Christian political party in Lebanon, and is an important stronghold. Within a week, the area had become a battleground, with hundreds of buildings destroyed or damaged.

Within a few months after the clash, the Christians, now formed into a well-disciplined, armed militia of almost ten thousand men, moved against the Karantina PLO camp. They attacked and killed hundreds of PLO fighters and civilians. In retaliation, on January 21 and 22, 1976, the PLO, with help from Syrian artillery, attacked the Christian town of Damour on the main highway south of Beirut. Damour was a major Christian town with forty thousand inhabitants prior to the attack. When the attack was over, some ten thousand people had been killed and the remaining thirty thousand had been driven out. Many escaped on boats and sailed north to Juniyeh. The PLO took over the town and turned it into a redoubt controlling the road, under the command of the PFLP and George Habash.

The Christians, not to be outdone in brutality, responded in October 1976. The Christian army attacked the camp of Tal Zaatar, north of Beirut, and laid siege to it for fifty days. They used small arms and heavy weapons; thousands were killed and thousands driven out. The camp was destroyed and the area bulldozed. It was slaughter rivaling the slaughter carried out by the PLO at Damour. The civil war raged, and all the pent-up hatreds came to the surface; neither side gave any quarter.

As the conflict continued, PLO influence and control of territory grew. The PLO, allied with the Moslem left, was in a position to expand, and the Christians were in danger of being severely defeated. By 1976, the Syrians, fearful that events might get out of hand, joined the Lebanese government in an effort to end the civil war by reining in the PLO and the Moslem militias. Syria and Lebanon put together a joint proposal in February 1976, under the sponsorship of President Suleiman Franjieh. The plan, called the Franjieh Reforms, proposed to halt the civil war by granting Moslem demands for increased representation in the government generally—to some extent, at the expense of the Christians. Although the Lebanese Christians were hardly enthusiastic about the plan, they feared that they might be totally destroyed in the civil war.

By February 1976, the Christians, having fought bravely, were in retreat, and the PLO, with Moslem support, was winning. The PLO therefore rejected the Franjieh proposal. It was playing for larger stakes. The PLO reasoned that, if things continued to go their way, they would achieve their own national state. If they didn't control all of Lebanon, then certainly they could completely destroy the central government's ability to exercise control over southern Lebanon. From the Syrian perspective, this would be unacceptable. It would mean that a weakened Lebanese government would be replaced by an armed PLO force with strong support throughout the Arab world, which could be counted on to resist even more strongly Syrian pretensions to control of Lebanon. Accordingly, Syria responded with force. In June 1976, it intervened, sending in three divisions, which took up positions around Beirut and in southern Lebanon. It then directed its military operations against the PLO. Having intervened originally in support of the PLO, in less than a year, the Syrians had switched loyalties. They now came in on the side of the Christians, to keep the Lebanese government afloat. With Syrian forces planted between the Christians and the PLO armies, most hostilities had ceased by November 1976, with the country fragmented.

The consequences of the civil war were enormous. The PLO lost over three thousand killed, and some 20 percent of its combat leaders were killed or captured. The Christian losses were probably much higher, although exact figures are hard to come by. Over eighty thousand Lebanese of all groups died in the war, and three times that number were wounded.[1] Perhaps even more important, Lebanon, as an independent state, was finished. The country was split into a number of armed cantons. At least one hundred political groups, each with its private army, were ensconced all over the country, exercising their own authority in defiance of the government. The Lebanese army, which at the outset of the war joined the Christians, no longer existed as a government force, and Syrian armed forces were in control of a large part of the country. Political institutions ceased to function, and the economy came to a standstill.

Between 1976 and 1982, sporadic clashes between rival groups in Lebanon took another twenty thousand lives, leaving another sixty thousand wounded.[2] Each group took every opportunity to attack and massacre. The Syrians fought, alternately, with the Christians, then with the PLO, and then again with the Christians. When Egypt signed a peace treaty with Israel in 1980, Syrian–PLO relationships improved, and Syria abandoned its efforts to curtail PLO expansion and influence and left the Lebanese state to the tender mercies of the PLO. By 1980, Syria had withdrawn its troops from the coastal area between Sidon and Beirut and turned it over to the PLO. By 1981, most of Lebanon was either under the heel of Syrian forces or controlled by private militias. The balance of confessional forces and their respective areas of military occupation are shown on Map 2.

For the PLO, things could not have worked out better. It had certainly suffered losses, but its relationship with other Arab states was intact, and even Syria had come around to supporting it. Oil money continued to flow in, and for the first time the PLO had full control of its own area. Formalized by both the Cairo and the Melkhart agreements, and forged in the hostilities of civil war, most of southern Lebanon from Beirut to the

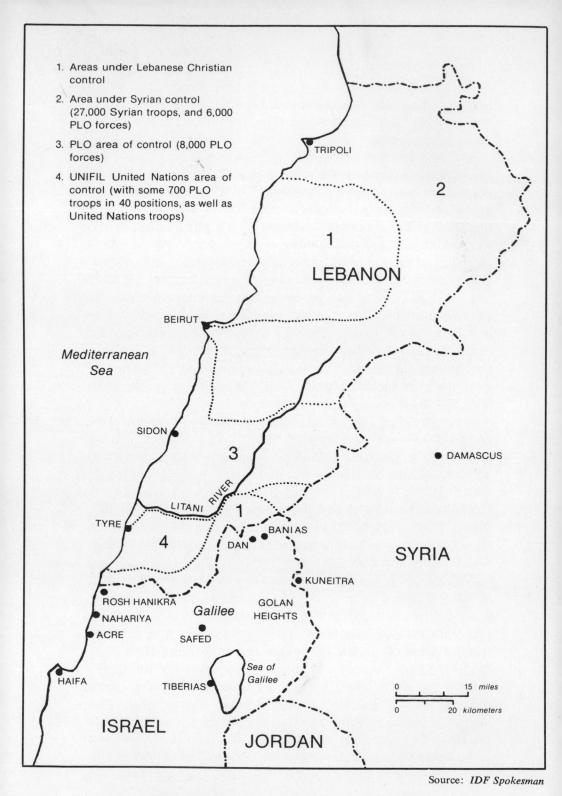

1. Areas under Lebanese Christian control

2. Area under Syrian control (27,000 Syrian troops, and 6,000 PLO forces)

3. PLO area of control (8,000 PLO forces)

4. UNIFIL United Nations area of control (with some 700 PLO troops in 40 positions, as well as United Nations troops)

TRIPOLI

2

1

LEBANON

BEIRUT

Mediterranean Sea

SIDON

3

DAMASCUS

LITANI RIVER

TYRE

1

4

DAN

BANIAS

SYRIA

KUNEITRA

ROSH HANIKRA

NAHARIYA

ACRE

Galilee

SAFED

GOLAN HEIGHTS

HAIFA

TIBERIAS

Sea of Galilee

0   15 *miles*

0   20 *kilometers*

ISRAEL

JORDAN

Source: *IDF Spokesman*

Map 2. Balance of forces in Lebanon, 1981

Israeli border was under the de facto control of the PLO. It was the only force capable of running the economy and the political structure in the area. With headquarters in Beirut, the PLO now had a free hand to deal with the mostly Moslem and Palestinian population under its control, and also to expand its forces, increase its weaponry, and stage the long-awaited military campaign against Israel from its own base. The mini-state which the PLO had sought for almost twenty years had become a reality, though at great cost to Lebanon.

PLO MILITARY FORCES

PLO military strength in Lebanon was largely deployed in an area ranging from Beirut south to the Israeli border and concentrating around the major cities along that coastal strip; namely, Beirut, Damour, Sidon, and Tyre. The number of Palestinians in the southern camps probably did not exceed 100,000. The largest Palestinian concentration was in Tyre. The city had about 40,000 Palestinians living in it. Approximately 5,000 Palestinians lived in the El Bass camp; 10,500 in the Bourj el Shamali camp; and 14,500 in the largest southern camp at Rachidiya. To the north, in Sidon, which had a population of 150,000, the largest PLO camp was Ein Hilwe, with a population of 24,000; a smaller satellite camp at Mija Mija held 3,500. The Beirut area itself, with a population of 1.7 million contained the three major camps of Sabra, Shatila, and Bourj el Barajneh, totaling between 20,000 and 24,000 Palestinians. Karantina and Tal Zaatar had been destroyed in the civil war.

The disposition of PLO military forces in southern Lebanon in 1982 is shown on Map 3. The total strength of PLO fighters from Beirut south to the border was about 15,000, with the main PLO strongholds located in the camps, most notably at Rachidiya and El Bass near Tyre, a town controlled completely by the PLO. In Sidon, the PLO had a major logistics and supply center. The city also contained the largest PLO camp in Lebanon, the Ein Hilwe camp, with a population of 24,000. In general, military positions had been well integrated with the civilian infrastructure, although the number and depth of these strongpoints were not nearly as great as the Israelis had anticipated.

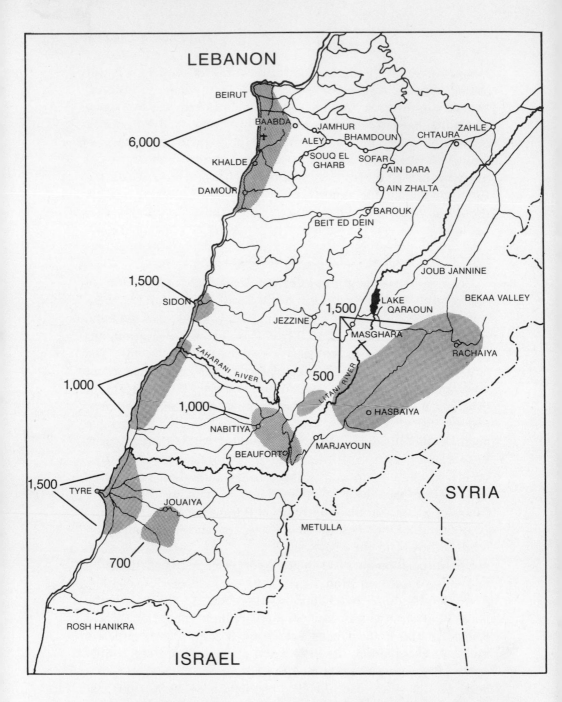

Map 3. PLO troop strength and dispositions

In addition to the major military installations deployed in the coastal cities, there were significant PLO military dispositions in four inland areas. The first, in the east, between Hasbaiya and Rachaiya, was known as Fatahland. PLO forces had been in this area for a number of years and had been generally integrated with and supported by Syrian military units deployed to the north. Syrian military strongpoints ran close to PLO lines, and a considerable interchange and interlinking of mutual defense positions was evident. The PLO in Fatahland was deployed in a conventional manner, having constructed a number of strongpoint installations, bunkers, firing pits, antitank positions, ammunition-storage bunkers, and communication trenches. About 1,500 PLO fighters, some with their families, were deployed in this area.

A second major PLO deployment was in the Achiye area, just north of the town of Marjayoun. It was held by about five hundred PLO fighters, but was heavily fortified with strongpoints and antitank positions. The deployment in this area was intended to create a blocking position for the main road junction controlling access north to Jezzine and the roads going east toward the Bekaa. The position is close to Nabatiya. This was a city of forty thousand when the PLO took over during the civil war. At the time of the Israeli invasion, that population had been reduced to about eight thousand, most of whom were PLO sympathizers or PLO support personnel. Moreover, Beaufort Castle is in the Nabatiya area; it is a major PLO strongpoint sitting on cliffs that rise seven hundred meters above sea level. From this point, the entire northern Israeli border could be attacked with artillery. It was an area constantly shelled by the PLO.

The fourth major inland military dispositions were in Jouaiya, an area known as the Iron Triangle. About seven hundred PLO were deployed here. The Iron Triangle was much more than a military strongpoint. It was located in the middle of the UNIFIL control zone, which had been established after Operation Litani in 1978, and which the UN was supposed to keep free of PLO forces. The PLO quickly established a number of military positions within the zone, however, and had complete freedom of movement to conduct operations against Israel. It also established a number of shelling pits and antitank positions—all in flagrant violation of UN regulations. The failure of the UN forces to curtail PLO activity in the zone represented a failure of the agreement reached in 1978, following Operation Litani.

PLO military dispositions included the camps, most of which were not heavily fortified. The term "camp" implies to the Western mind a military installation. In fact, a PLO camp is not a military camp at all. It is an urban neighborhood consisting of one- or two-story concrete-block buildings, in rectangular street patterns, separated by narrow streets and alleys. Moreover, the majority of individuals in these camps are not PLO fighters. PLO camps, for the most part, were not really good defensive positions as much as they were supply and logistical centers to support military positions in areas outside the camp.

The population of a camp is such that only a small percentage, perhaps one resident in eight, is actually a trained soldier. The fighters are younger men, often teenagers, with no family responsibilities. There are, of course, other men who are on the PLO payroll, who perform support, administrative, or clerical functions. These are called "trade unionists" by both the PLO and the IDF to indicate that, while they contribute to the PLO combat effort, they are not strictly speaking combat personnel. In any PLO camp, one must either work for some faction, fight for it, or at least openly support it. Otherwise, life is difficult and certainly dangerous. The instances in which Palestinians have been killed by PLO are too numerous and too well known to mention. On the other hand, PLO money provided a regular dole for its members. In an area where there were no real economic opportunities, the support for the PLO was more often based on economic grounds than on genuine political sympathy.

The PLO has never had much difficulty in obtaining weapons, largely because of the financial support of the Arab oil states. Before the war, the IDF estimated that the PLO possessed the following weapons, deployed in the area south of Beirut (not included are weapons deployed in Beirut). The PLO manned about eighty tanks, sixty of which were T-34's and twenty T-54's and T-55's. Most of the T-34's were dug in fixed positions and used as bunkers and strongpoints. Some didn't even run at all and had to be towed. The PLO could deploy forty-eight 130mm and 155mm long-range cannon, which were often used to shell Israeli civilian positions. In addition there were eighty BM-21

Katyusha rocket launchers; sixty 100mm and 160mm mortars and seventy-seven antitank cannons. The full inventory of weapons in Beirut was estimated to be double the above, in every category except tanks. It turned out, however, that the weapons actually captured in Beirut were considerably fewer than the IDF had estimated. The PLO had thousands of small-arms weapons, pistols, rocket-propelled grenades, and automatic weapons. In a country where a weapon is a major status symbol and often the only way to defend oneself from the hostile activities of other confessional groups or even other factions within one's own group, the ability of the PLO to distribute first-rate small arms clearly increased the perception of its legitimacy.

Equipment was never a problem for the PLO. The support received from both the Arab states and the Soviet Union made it possible for the PLO to purchase whatever it wanted. Often, the PLO seemed to purchase weapons simply to purchase weapons. In fact, PLO forces were never configured to use what weaponry they had. They never had any significant tank force, for example, and the tanks they had were used in fixed positions —the quickest way to get a tank killed. Even PLO artillery was used as harassing fire, and almost exclusively against civilian populations. The PLO had no capability for fire direction and control, nor could it sheave artillery on concentrated targets. It had almost no self-propelled guns, and its ability to move artillery once deployed was greatly limited. Even its Katyusha rockets, designed by the Soviets primarily as a support weapon for mass attack, could never be used in coordination with ground operations. The PLO simply lacked the ability to coordinate these types of operations: rocket launchers were used mostly in terror attacks against civilian targets. Although IDF forces would capture tons of equipment, mostly small arms and ammunition, only a small part of this equipment could have been used by the PLO at any given time. Even less of it could be used correctly, or be brought to bear against a conventional attack of the magnitude launched by the Israeli Defense Force.

It must be remembered that the PLO was configured as a guerrilla force rather than as a conventional army. They used the tactic of mixing with the civilian population to reduce the effectiveness of enemy fire, hoping that the IDF would withhold its massive firepower rather than kill civilians. As later analysis shows, this tactic worked very well. The IDF went out of its way in any number of instances to reduce civilian casualties, and thereby conceded to the enemy a degree of tactical surprise and even strategic advantage. In some instances, the IDF let the PLO escape rather than bring to bear firepower that would have endangered civilians. The PLO tactic of "being the fish that swims in the sea" and using civilian populations as a shield to forestall the Israeli military force worked rather effectively.

The PLO followed the guerrilla rule of never engaging an equal or superior force and never at a time and place of the enemy's choosing. Throughout its history, the PLO's only combat experience has been as a terrorist force. It has never fought a conventional battle of any size against any enemy. Indeed, in its attacks on Israel, the PLO rarely struck at military targets. As a guerrilla force it made good use of ambush and urban fighting until it was clear that it would be overwhelmed. The men would then take off their uniforms, abandon their weapons, and melt into the civilian population. Many simply passed through Israeli lines at night and traveled to Beirut or to the Bekaa. The fact that the terrain was heavily forested with citrus groves or was mountainous made it easy for the PLO to execute these tactics.

It seems clear that the PLO was completely surprised by both the size and the scope of the IDF incursion. Probably, the PLO thought the attack was going to be a repeat of the 1978 Operation Litani, in which the Israelis moved to a line about twenty-two kilometers inside Lebanon, cleared the area, and then withdrew. Although the Israelis announced that they would move forty kilometers into Lebanon, it is unlikely that the PLO felt there would be a systematic attempt to remain in Lebanon and to destroy its infrastructure. The PLO had every reason to withdraw in the face of the Israeli advance, therefore, and in most places that is what they did. The 15,000 PLO fighters in southern Lebanon were no match for the Israeli force of over 40,000 thrown against them in the western and central sectors. Since the PLO had a doctrine of never engaging a superior force, the leaders chose not to stand and fight. The PLO didn't always withdraw as units, but rather as individuals, often in their automobiles, with their families, back up the coast to Beirut or to

Syrian lines in the Bekaa. PLO fighting ability was not substantial, and so its troops did not take the field in any significant sense. Despite huge caches of arms, its ability to move supplies to the point of battle was almost nonexistent; it had neither the tracked vehicles nor the trucks to do so. Given the surprise and speed of the Israeli attack, most PLO units, which tend to be of company size or below, had to fight with what they had on hand—which was generally enough for a short battle but not enough to stop a large force. Also, no battle plan and no plan to coordinate units was in evidence. PLO units are a reflection of their political fiefdoms and cannot easily be coordinated in a true military sense. The divisive nature of the PLO's political components affected its ability to deploy and use military units. In the end, when the PLO fought, it fought in isolated groups.

SYRIAN FORCES IN LEBANON

The Syrians had been in Lebanon since their massive intervention with three divisions in June 1976 to separate the warring factions in the civil war. They had their own reasons for remaining; they kept almost thirty thousand men in Lebanon for almost eight years. One reason was to retain Syrian influence in Lebanese politics vis-à-vis the confessional struggle. Although the civil war had come to a tentative end in 1976, the struggle for power and influence continued among the various ethnic religious groups. Moreover, Syria had not abandoned her goal of bringing Lebanon back into greater Syria. The Syrian military forces in Lebanon were intended to achieve this long-term goal. Syria's deployment in the Bekaa was designed as a defense against any Israeli attack on Damascus. Since the Six-Day War, when the Israelis captured the Golan Heights, the military buildup on both sides of the Heights—Syrian and Israeli—was such that the defensive forces on each side had the advantage. Any Israeli attack on Damascus would have to come by one of two routes: either directly through Jordan, highly unlikely for political reasons; or through Lebanon in the Bekaa. Syrian forces were positioned along those routes in the Bekaa and dug in along Mount Hermon to block this avenue of attack.

Syrian forces were also deployed to protect the Beirut–Damascus highway, its major supply line to and from Syria. It had sizable units in Beirut and to the north and it was necessary to control the Beirut–Damascus highway to supply them. In the event of an attack against Israel, moreover, the highway would become a main axis of deployment or defense if things went badly. If the situation were reversed, the Syrians could no more attack through Jordan than could the Israelis. Thus, any attempt by Syria to attack Israel would have to come through the Bekaa Valley. Depending on one's perspective, the deployment of Syrian forces in the Bekaa can be viewed as a defensive move; but in Israel it was viewed as positioning forces for possible offensive moves against northern Israel.

The disposition of Syrian military forces is shown on Map 4. The complete order of battle of the Syrians in Lebanon, to the extent that it was identified by Israeli intelligence prior to the war, appears in Table 3 in the Appendix. It was this force of thirty thousand men, equipped with six hundred tanks and thirty commando battalions, which constituted the primary opposition the Israelis faced on the eastern front.

PROXIMATE CAUSES OF WAR

From 1970 through 1978, PLO forces operating from Lebanon carried out numerous terrorist attacks against Israel, as well as scores of artillery, mortar, and Katyusha rocket attacks. Israeli policy was to strike back with air raids whenever possible, and to conduct border raids and counter battery fire whenever feasible. Israel showed a tendency to adjust its response to the type of provocation it faced. However, the PLO rarely struck at military targets in Israel, or even at military personnel. On the few occasions when it did, it suffered summary defeat. The PLO attacked civilian targets, targets that often involved old people and children. Such an attack occurred in 1974, in Ma'alot, and twenty-four civilians, mostly children, were killed and nineteen others wounded.

In early 1978, the PLO attacked a bus on the Via Maris near the town of Zichron Ya'acov in Israel, capturing the bus and forcing its driver and passengers to drive to Tel Aviv, where it threatened to blow up the bus. Inevitably, there was military action and the PLO used hand grenades and shot the passengers,

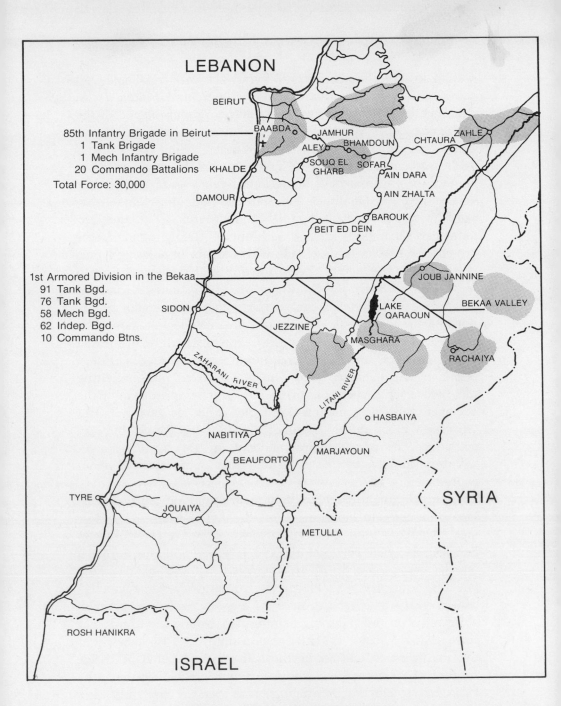

LEBANON

BEIRUT

85th Infantry Brigade in Beirut
 1 Tank Brigade
 1 Mech Infantry Brigade
 20 Commando Battalions
Total Force: 30,000

BAABDA
JAMHUR
ALEY
SOUQ EL
GHARB
BHAMDOUN
SOFAR
AIN DARA
CHTAURA
ZAHLE

KHALDE

DAMOUR

AIN ZHALTA

BAROUK

BEIT ED DEIN

1st Armored Division in the Bekaa
 91 Tank Bgd.
 76 Tank Bgd.
 58 Mech Bgd.
 62 Indep. Bgd.
 10 Commando Btns.

JOUB JANNINE

BEKAA VALLEY

SIDON

JEZZINE

LAKE
QARAOUN

MASGHARA

RACHAIYA

ZAHARANI RIVER

LITANI RIVER

HASBAIYA

NABITIYA

MARJAYOUN

BEAUFORT

TYRE

JOUAIYA

SYRIA

METULLA

ROSH HANIKRA

ISRAEL

Map 4. Syrian troop positions

with a loss of thirteen civilian lives. The IDF retaliated, yet the PLO kept up its attacks and shellings until March 1978, when the Israeli government finally acted. (From the end of the 1973 war until 1982, the PLO shelled northern Israeli settlements with artillery and rockets 1,548 times, killing 108 people.)

Pressure grew on the Israeli government to retaliate, more so since the government of Menachem Begin was decidedly more conservative, nationalistic, and hawkish than the Labor government which it defeated in 1977. In March 1978, the IDF launched Operation Litani. Substantial IDF ground forces crossed the border into Lebanon with the aim of creating a *cordon sanitaire* free of PLO activity from the Israeli border north to the Litani River. Syrian forces studiously avoided any involvement in the conflict and signaled that they would remain north of the Litani if the Israelis did not cross it. For their part, the Israelis stopped at the river. PLO forces withdrew before the Israeli advance, using their traditional guerrilla tactics. For a period of three months, IDF forces destroyed bunkers, firing pits, and arms caches. Terrorists who were trapped within the occupied zone were hunted down and killed or captured. But Operation Litani did not significantly affect the PLO's military activities. The overwhelming majority of the fighters simply withdrew in advance of the Israeli attack in order to avoid capture.

After three months, and under pressure from the United States, Israel consented to withdraw. The United Nations agreed to provide a United Nations Interim Force for Lebanon (UNIFIL) to garrison the area between the Litani River and the northern Israeli border. As charged by the United Nations mandate, the UNIFIL force was to confirm the withdrawal of the Israelis, restore peace and security in the area, and aid the Lebanese government in reestablishing its authority, which it had not had since 1975. A major UNIFIL responsibility was to ensure that the area was not used for hostile actions of any kind. A buffer zone of about twenty-five kilometers was created between the PLO forces and the Israeli border. To ensure that this zone remained intact, the United Nations deployed seven battalions of troops, about four thousand soldiers, comprised of Fijian, Ghanaian, Algerian, Dutch, Sengalese, and Irish units.

The PLO understood immediately that if the United Nations was allowed to carry out its mandate, it would be deprived of territory contiguous with Israel from which to launch its attacks. So the PLO set out to reverse the situation and reestablish its presence in the area. Within two months, in May 1978, a small PLO force clashed with UNIFIL soldiers in the city of Tyre. Three UNIFIL soldiers were killed and ten were wounded. With this simple act, the PLO showed that it was prepared to use force to reestablish itself in the UNIFIL zone. They literally cowed the UN and the UNIFIL soldiers into accepting a return of the PLO.

A year after the May 1978 clash, the PLO had repositioned at least seven hundred active fighters and their support units within the UNIFIL zone, mostly around the city of Jouaiya, in the Iron Triangle. More important, the PLO worked out a number of unofficial rules with the UN forces which allowed it to engage in attacks against Israel virtually unhindered. According to these rules, UN forces were not allowed to approach to within five hundred meters of PLO posts in the zone. Whenever PLO infiltrators were caught by UN soldiers, they were escorted to PLO headquarters in Tyre, and, by way of a PLO liaison officer, their weapons were turned over and the infiltrators were released. Between June and December 1980, sixty-nine military operations were conducted against Israel from within the UNIFIL zone. Whenever the IDF would pursue a PLO force back across the border, the PLO would surrender to UN forces, who then escorted them back to PLO headquarters in Tyre. No attempt was made by UN forces to interfere with PLO supply activities, and the PLO was granted a free hand in building up arms caches and supplies within the twenty-kilometer *cordon sanitaire* that the UN had guaranteed Israel.

In April 1981, fighting broke out between Christian and Syrian forces once again. The Syrians moved against the city of Zahle in the northern Bekaa. Zahle is a town of 200,000, and the largest Greek Catholic city in Lebanon. Syria laid siege to it for three months and carried out indiscriminate shelling and bombardment. Its purpose was to seize control of the city in order to secure its hold on the Beirut–Damascus highway.

In May 1981, the PLO escalated its attacks against Israel

with a major bombardment against the northern towns. From May to July, 1,230 rocket and artillery attacks had hit twenty-six northern Israeli towns, killing six and wounding fifty-nine civilians. The IDF hit back with bombing raids and even cross-border raids involving small numbers of troops. The United States, concerned that the fighting would escalate even further and result in another invasion of Lebanon, arranged a cease-fire on July 24, 1981. Violations of the cease-fire were immediate, and between July 1981 and June 1982 the PLO carried out 290 additional attacks against Israel, in which 29 people were killed and 271 wounded.

From July 1981 until the Israeli invasion in June 1982, the PLO added twenty tanks to its inventory, mostly T-54's and T-55's, and forty heavy Katyusha rocket launchers, doubling its number of launch positions in the south. It added ninety anti-tank cannons, which it also deployed in the south, in addition to one hundred 20mm and 160mm mortars, along with a large number of 14.5mm antitank guns. SA7-Strella antiaircraft missiles were also deployed in southern Lebanon.

The Israelis watched this buildup with unease, although in itself it presented no significant threat to Israeli security. But political pressure was building within the Israeli government, fostered by the appointment of Ariel Sharon and other hawks to positions of authority in the Defense Ministry. By 1982, they constituted a powerful faction in the Israeli government and consistently urged strong action against the PLO to settle the question once and for all. Twice before, Israel had massed troops on the Lebanese border only to stand down without taking any significant military action. Throughout April and May of 1982, the shellings and attacks on the towns continued; the Israeli air force carried out raids against PLO targets but was unable to stop the shelling from the north.

On the evening of June 3, 1982, Shlomo Argov, the Israeli ambassador in London, was shot in the head by three terrorists, at least one of whom turned out to be a Syrian intelligence officer. The next day the Israeli air force hit a number of PLO targets, including arms depots and headquarters buildings in Beirut, bringing the air war to the heart of the city. Arafat took this as a challenge and responded the same day with a twenty-four-hour artillery barrage against southern Lebanon, northern Galilee, and the Hadad Enclave. Thirty barrages hit twenty-three civilian settlements in a twenty-four-hour period in Israel alone. On the following day, Saturday, June 5, the cabinet met in full session and decided to attack. At eleven o'clock on Sunday morning, June 6, the Israeli Defense Force launched Operation Peace for Galilee and moved into Lebanon.

3

War in Lebanon:
The Campaign in the South

"No one starts a war, or rather, no one in his senses ought to do so, without first being clear in his mind what he intends to achieve by that war and how he intends to conduct it. The former is its political purpose; the latter, its operational objective." So said Karl von Clausewitz a hundred and fifty years ago in his famous dissertation on the nature of war. Although plans for the invasion of Lebanon, under the code name Pine Tree, were in preparation a year and a half before the event, and were completed, under the code name Peace for Galilee, almost six months before the attack, there is considerable doubt as to which plan was adopted by the cabinet and which was actually put into effect on the battlefield by the Defense Minister and members of the high-ranking military. This uncertainty has led to charges in the Israeli press and the Knesset that there was a serious disjunction between the goals and means of war of the military leaders and the Defense Minister, Ariel Sharon, and what the political leadership, led by Prime Minister Begin, thought the war was all about. For the first time in Israel's history, there was a grave divergence between the military leadership and the political leadership regarding a major military action undertaken by the IDF.

WAR PLAN

At least three war plans were circulated among the political and military leadership as early as five months before the war;

each was the subject of considerable discussion by both the military and the political decision-makers. The first plan called for an invasion of Lebanon to destroy the PLO in the south and stamp out artillery and terrorist attacks on Israeli border settlements. The war was to be fought only against the PLO; combat against the Syrians was to be avoided at all costs. The Israeli advance was to go no farther than the Aouali River, forty kilometers from the border as measured from the town of Rosh Hanikra. The Israelis would strike at the PLO as hard as possible, with no movement toward or into Beirut. This was to be an expanded incursion similar to Operation Litani, carried out by the Israeli army in 1978.

A second war plan also called for a strike against PLO forces without a war with the Syrians, but the IDF forces were to go as far north as Beirut. The Israelis were not to enter the city in force but to rely on their Phalangist allies to destroy the PLO left in the city. Once again, the forty-kilometer line was mentioned publicly, but this time measured from Metulla, Israel's northernmost border town, thus bringing IDF forces to a line even with the city of Beirut.

The third plan, known within the IDF as the "Big Plan," was the most ambitious and called for a war against both the PLO and the Syrians and for an advance up to and including Beirut. In Beirut, IDF forces were to be used only partially and in concert with Phalangist forces, with the latter bearing the brunt of the fighting. Here again, the forty-kilometer line was to be measured from Metulla. It was this war that was fought on the battlefield. The question is, however, whether this was the war the political leadership gave its assent to on the night of June 5.

Interviews with members of the Knesset suggest that no firm decision to invade, and no decision on how to conduct field operations, was made in advance of the Argov assassination on June 3, 1982. During the debates prior to the actual decision to invade, the cabinet tended to divide into a number of factions, each favoring a different plan. Prime Minister Begin and much of the civilian leadership favored the first plan, with a slight variation to bring the IDF closer to Beirut. The civilian leadership favored a war against the PLO with no war against the Syrians, with the advance stopping short of Beirut. Evidence gathered from these conversations indicates that the Defense

Minister, Ariel Sharon, and some high-ranking military leaders favored the much wider war outlined in the third plan.

With the assassination of Ambassador Argov on June 3, an Israeli counteraction was clearly in the offing. On Friday, June 4, the government ordered heavy air raids against PLO targets deep in Lebanon, striking military targets in and around Beirut— ammunition dumps, battlefield positions in the refugee camps around Beirut, the training camp in the sports stadium in the Fakhani district, and twenty-two other targets. At this point, no decision had been made to invade, and it appeared that the government was about to settle for the customary retaliatory air strikes.

On Saturday, June 5, the PLO replied with a heavy artillery bombardment all across the northern border of Israel. Twenty-three settlements were shelled almost continuously throughout the day. IDF air and artillery struck back. On the night of June 5, the cabinet met and the decision was taken to move into Lebanon in force. Which plan was approved by the political leadership still remains in question, however. From interviews, one gathers that Begin and the political leadership approved either the first plan or some variant of it that included moving past the Aouali River up to Beirut. The political leadership, including Begin, wanted a short, quick war against the PLO, with no attacks against the Syrians, and it refrained from committing the IDF to enter Beirut.

The Defense Minister and some of his supporters in the cabinet and in the military opposed this plan, and it may be that Sharon took actions which sabotaged the approved plan in order to put into effect his "more complete military solution of Israel's northern security problem." Having lost the battle in the cabinet to implement a larger version of the war, Sharon allowed the government to believe the war would be fought as the government had agreed. It would not be difficult, however, to orchestrate events to expand the war once the battle was joined. The rationale would be that a larger war was necessary to protect Israel's troops which were already engaged. This meant, of course, war with the Syrians.

One thing was clear: someone was in a hurry to invade Lebanon. On the average, the IDF needs twenty-four hours to mobilize its reserve and come to 60 percent strength, and forty-eight hours to come to full strength. Although a full-reserve mobilization was not required, the forces used were substantial and they had to be repositioned from their garrisons in the Jordan Valley and in the south. Of the IDF's three standing divisions which spearheaded the invasion, only the 36th division under Avigdor Kahalani was already in position on the Golan Heights. The 162nd had to be moved with its men and equipment, including over three hundred tanks and APC's, from the Jordan Valley, and Division 252 had to be moved from even farther south up to the coast. Though contingency plans exist and the Israeli army continually practices redeployment in all directions, its organic reserve units had to be mobilized and large support preparations made. The decision to attack was made on the evening of Saturday, June 5, and the IDF was expected to attack the following day. Briefings were conducted throughout the night, and the Chief of Staff, Rafael Eitan, asked for more time. He was told that speed was necessary to avoid the risk of the Americans pressuring Israel into taking no action at all. Eitan was told to commence the incursion as soon as possible, and the attack was set for twelve noon. As it turned out, the advance began at eleven o'clock in the morning, thus conceding fully six hours of daylight to the enemy and reducing the time available for daylight operations. There are indications that some units, especially in the east, moved out at less than full strength, with some having to borrow organic forces from neighboring units with less critical missions.

Given that someone in the government wanted a wider war, what was needed was some sort of provocation from the Syrians. In the course of military operations, Beirut would become involved; Sharon especially believed that, since he was convinced that the Phalangists would move eagerly against the PLO once the IDF appeared at the city's gate. Picking a war with the Syrians was not as easy as that. The Syrians seemed to be making every effort to avoid war. Politically, they were less than eager to come to the defense of the PLO. Yet it turned out that one of the gunmen who killed Argov was a colonel in Syrian intelligence. This suggests, especially to some analysts in the American intelligence community, that the attack on Argov was a "false flag" operation designed to place the blame on the PLO in order to provoke an Israeli attack on them. If so, the Syrians wanted an Israeli attack against the PLO but not a battle with the Israelis.

The Syrians had very good reasons for avoiding a war but allowing Israel a free hand in reducing the power of the PLO. In the first place, the relationship between Syria and the PLO has been stormy. There is a long history of armed clashes in Lebanon between PLO and Syrian forces over various prerogatives each wanted to exercise. In addition, Arafat and Habash are personally hated by President Assad of Syria, who feels that the PLO leadership has been responsible for encouraging the Moslem brotherhood in Syria in its several attempts to assassinate Assad and destroy his Alewite regime. Further, Syria sees the PLO as a competitor for influence in Lebanon. Any attempt by Syria to annex Lebanon as part of greater Syria would have to deal with the PLO in the long run and would probably mean war between them. In addition, the PLO has been less than supportive of Syrian foreign policy in a number of instances, especially with regard to the Iran–Iraq war. And Syria sees the PLO as a competitor for the role of protector of the Palestinians. The fundamental goals of the PLO and Syria are in the long run antithetical. It is logical that the Syrians would encourage an Israeli attack against the PLO, as long as it wasn't a fatal blow.

On the battlefield as well, the Syrians seemed to be doing their best to avoid war. Once the actual border crossing had begun, the Syrians almost immediately withdrew their forces from checkpoints in the southern tier—checkpoints as far south as Tyre and Sidon. They also moved their forces in the Shouf back from the main road to Beirut. Syrian forces stationed in Beirut did not deploy south to protect the approaches from Damour. In the Bekaa, they made no hostile moves against the main Israeli forces massed in front of them and advancing at their center. They didn't even defend the critical crossroads at Jezzine with much vigor, for which Arafat publicly condemned them. Their military moves showed every indication of a desire to consolidate forces in the east and to withdraw. To be sure, a few commando units were routinely integrated with the PLO in eastern Fatahland, but the main Syrian forces refused to engage even as the Israelis moved toward them.

The greatest number of IDF forces assembled for the war were deployed opposite the Syrian front, however, not opposite the PLO. The IDF deployed almost four divisions, with eight hundred tanks and thirty-eight thousand men, and adequate reserves, opposite Syrian positions in the east. The Syrians found themselves facing a force almost twice as large as their own. All the pronouncements out of Jerusalem were designed to convince them that the war was to be only against the PLO. Yet the Syrians saw the major IDF forces concentrating in front of them. The Syrians gave every political, diplomatic, and military indication of a desire to remain apart from the war; but those who wanted a wider war had to get the Syrians involved somehow.

PROVOKING A WAR

On June 6, the Israeli force slammed across the Lebanese border opposite the Syrian troops and began to advance with its main body aimed at the Syrian positions north of the Hasbaiya–Koukaba line, reaching that line easily by nightfall on the first day. At the same time, division-size units maneuvered to the right of the center along Wadi Cheba, aimed at Rachaiya in the foothills of Mount Hermon and threatening to outflank the entire Syrian force and cut off its retreat to Syria. Simultaneously, a major force moved on Jezzine and Masghara on the west flank, cutting the main road to the Syrian forces in the north and outflanking the Syrian 1st division from the west. Except for some harassing artillery fire and the one-battalion defense of the junction at Jezzine, the Syrians refused to engage. Israeli aircraft overflew the battle area, and Syrian missile sites did not engage. Then a curious thing happened: the Israeli advance at the Syrian center, at the mouth of the Bekaa Valley, stopped. It waited in place for almost seventy-two hours. The Israeli force continued its flanking movements to the east and west, however. With every hour, the Syrians were being outflanked and their military situation eroded. This was, in essence, the IDF's intent, so that the Syrians would give up the Bekaa Valley without a fight.

Why did the Israeli advance stop? In interviews given by Yitzhak Moda'i, minister without portfolio in the Begin government, he made the point that the Israeli advance halted because a number of diplomatic efforts were underway with the Syrians in an effort to get them to stay out of the war. The minister pointed out that there was diplomatic contact between Jerusalem and Damascus and the Israelis had every reason to believe the Syrians would agree because the Syrians had forbidden the terrorists to fire on Israel from Syrian territory.[1] The Syrians had called in Philip Habib to deliver their answer.

The true reason for the delay, which lasted two full days, until June 9, appears to be related to attempts by Sharon to convince the Begin government that now was the time to engage the Syrians. The cabinet viewed the IDF advance as a blocking force to protect the Israeli center. But Sharon argued strongly that he should be given the authority to strike at the Syrian center and drive them out of the Bekaa. The cabinet listened with interest, but no decision was taken to give Sharon additional authority. Time passed, and finally a conflict with the Syrians occurred.[2]

On the second day in the halt on the eastern front, divisional artillery began to catch up with the lead body at the Hasbaiya–Koukaba line. For the first time, six SAM missile batteries of the nineteen deployed behind the Syrian lines in the Bekaa came within range of Israeli mobile artillery. The Syrians faced a military dilemma. They watched the forces on their flanks continue to move while the center line was stopped; at the same time, Israeli artillery threatened their missile batteries, which stood between them and complete exposure of their ground forces to Israeli aircraft. Each hour weakened the Syrian position, as the Israeli flank attack kept moving. The Syrians apparently made a political decision to assume that the six batteries within range of Israeli artillery would be hit at some point. In an effort to compensate for this, Assad gave the order from Damascus to rush six more batteries into the northern Bekaa, to positions out of range of Israeli artillery but close enough to protect Syrian troops from air attack should the IDF strike.

Israeli intelligence picked up the movement of the missile batteries being deployed and passed the information to the military command, who passed it on to the Defense Minister. Sharon took the information to Begin and made the case that the Israeli air force would be in great danger if these missiles were allowed to deploy; the ability of the IDF to protect ground forces would also be severely hindered. Begin was reminded as well of his promise, made a year earlier, to remove the Syrian missiles in the Bekaa. Sharon argued for authority to hit the missiles and attack the Syrian forces. On June 9, the missiles were struck. IAF aircraft shot down twenty-nine MIG's, and seventeen of the nineteen missile batteries stationed in the Bekaa were destroyed. At the same time, the forces which had stopped at the Hasbaiya–Koukaba line began to move up the road toward the Bekaa Valley and Lake Qaraoun. War with the Syrians on the eastern front had begun.

An interview with Mordechai Gur, a member of the Opposition and former IDF Chief of Staff, hints very strongly that something went wrong inside the government. He notes that on the sixth of June Opposition leaders met with Prime Minister Begin and were told once again that the IDF would move no farther than forty kilometers into Lebanon and that the IDF would do everything they could to avoid a clash with the Syrians. Begin seems to be clearly on record with the Opposition that what he had in mind was an expanded Operation Litani that would avoid a war with the Syrians and avoid entry into Beirut. At that time, the Opposition agreed to support the government.[3] Two days later, on Tuesday, June 8, another meeting was held with the Opposition, and Begin once again promised that there would be no wider war and no contact with the Syrians.[4] What emerges from the interview with Gur is that until the eighth of June the political leadership had concluded that there was no need to engage the Syrians. But on the very next day, June 9, after Begin met in the evening with Sharon, who reported the deployment of new missiles and argued strongly for an expansion of the war, IDF forces attacked the Syrians and maintained the attack for four days. It was from this point, Gur says, that "the whole war simply unrolled."[5]

It seems clear, then, that war against the Syrians was not part of the original plan approved by the Begin cabinet. At best, it had been viewed as a contingency to be guarded against, and in fact avoided at all cost. The deployment of the IDF in the east near the Bekaa was seen essentially as a security move to guard the west and center thrusts of the Israeli attack and at the same time to signal to the Syrians that if they wanted to fight the IDF was ready. At the very least, the war against the Syrians may be regarded as an accident resulting from a collision of forces on the battlefield as a consequence of the IDF's continued flanking movements and the positioning of artillery that threatened Syrian missile cover for its troops. However, the decision to outflank the Syrians and to move artillery within range of their missiles may have been a deliberate attempt by Sharon and some of his supporters in the military to orchestrate events on the battlefield to bring IDF forces into collision with the Syrians in contravention of the agreement with the political leadership to avoid a wider war.

Part of the rationale for expanding the war against the Syrians is found in the fact, which a number of officials have noted, that the Defense Ministry had ordered a review of Israel's security status in 1981, which involved an assessment of long-range security threats posed by Syria. That report was prepared more than a year before the war began, and indicated Syria would probably attack Israel sometime in late 1983 or early 1984. As part of the attack, Syria would encourage the PLO to open a second front against Israel in the north, to tie down a number of Israeli divisions. Apparently, Sharon and other high-ranking military leaders had come to believe that the intelligence assessment was accurate and felt that an attack on the Syrians was necessary to preempt the planned Syrian attack. Thus, a war that had been justified to the Israeli public, at least by the political leadership, as having very limited goals was seen in a much wider context by some factions as being a strategic strike against the Syrians to preempt any attempt by Syria to make war against Israel in the future.

The IDF, then, found itself engaged in a two-front war, the objectives of each of which had no relation to the objectives or the outcome of the other. The IDF was given the simple enough mission of pushing the PLO back beyond the forty-kilometer artillery range of PLO guns and of destroying the infrastructure of the PLO in that area. Once the war with the Syrians began, however, the goals of the war were expanded to include the removal of Syrian forces from Lebanon, the creation of a new Lebanese governmental authority, and the securing of a peaceful northern border through a peace treaty between Israel and Lebanon. In short, the war became a strategic war instead of a tactical operation, and the IDF found itself engaged in a much larger conflict for which no clear-cut objectives or tactical goals had been developed.

FORTY-KILOMETER LINE

Considerable attention has been paid to the fact that throughout the war the Israeli government continued to make statements indicating that it did not intend to go farther into Lebanon than forty kilometers. Moreover, when Philip Habib telephoned Begin right after the invasion and asked him how much time he needed and how far he intended to go, Begin assured him that he needed no more than seventy-two hours and that the invasion would stop at forty kilometers. Even the Opposition was told by governmental sources on two separate occasions that the war would not go beyond forty kilometers. And yet the war went all the way to Beirut and engaged the Syrians. What place did all these announcements about the forty-kilometer line play in the actual development of events?

There are two possibilities, and both may in fact have been operating at the same time. If it is true that Begin initially did not want a larger war, as seems likely, then he was quite sincere in announcing the forty-kilometer line. He thereby publicly set limits to the war, which he hoped would deflect American pressure to restrict Israeli action, and at the same time would signal to the Syrians that he sought no wider war. He continued to maintain this until June 9, when the war was expanded to include the Syrians. At that point, holding to the forty-kilometer line was no longer a possibility.

If, on the other hand, it is assumed that the plan from the beginning was to go to Beirut and start a war with the Syrians, then the public statements that Israel would not move beyond the forty-kilometer line made considerable tactical sense. As noted, IDF planners have always known that their wars have to be won quickly; in every war, Israeli forces have been stopped from advancing by the pressure of the great powers to limit the fighting. Accordingly, if the plan was to go to Beirut and to attack the Syrians, some way had to be found to hold off this pressure until the IDF had gained the upper hand on the battlefield.

By announcing a "limited incursion" of only forty kilometers, leaving vague whether the line was to be measured from the border town of Rosh Hanikra in the west or from the eastern border town of Metulla, the Israelis gave the appearance of having limited objectives. By the time U.S. policymakers realized that IDF forces had a more comprehensive campaign in mind, it would take at least two days for them to react, by which time Israel would have reached the limits of its advance; namely, the Bekaa Valley and the outskirts of Beirut. The Israeli announcement of the forty-kilometer limit may have been a master stroke of disinformation designed to deceive not only the United States but the Soviets, the Syrians, and the PLO into thinking that the IDF was indeed engaging in a limited military operation. Deception would increase the element of surprise and give Israeli forces a significant advantage on the battlefield.

There is simply no way of knowing which of these situations was the case. In all probability, both were true to some degree. Menachem Begin's signal that this would be a limited war was probably sincere at least until June 9. On the other hand, these announcements played directly into the hands of the hawks, who wanted to expand the war. Whatever the original intention, the ultimate effect was to disinform and delay. Surely the PLO were convinced that the operation was a limited one, so that by the time Israeli forces had punched through to Damour, the PLO in Beirut were in such a state of disarray that, some Israeli officers have suggested, if the IDF had moved quickly into the city, it would have caught the PLO at a grave disadvantage.

BATTLE TERRAIN

One of the more important factors in the war was the terrain. Lebanon is a very small country. The war was fought in a rectangle extending roughly one hundred kilometers on each side by seventy-five kilometers at the top and bottom—about 7,500 square kilometers, a very small tactical box. The terrain is very hilly, and the distance between areas of engagement very short. Often, major engagements were fought within sight and sound of one another. (See Table 4 in the Appendix.) At no point, for example, did the Israeli advance extend more than 106 kilometers from its border. Map 5 provides a detailed overview of the Lebanese theater of operations, as well as noting the cities and towns where major engagements were fought or which were of tactical importance.

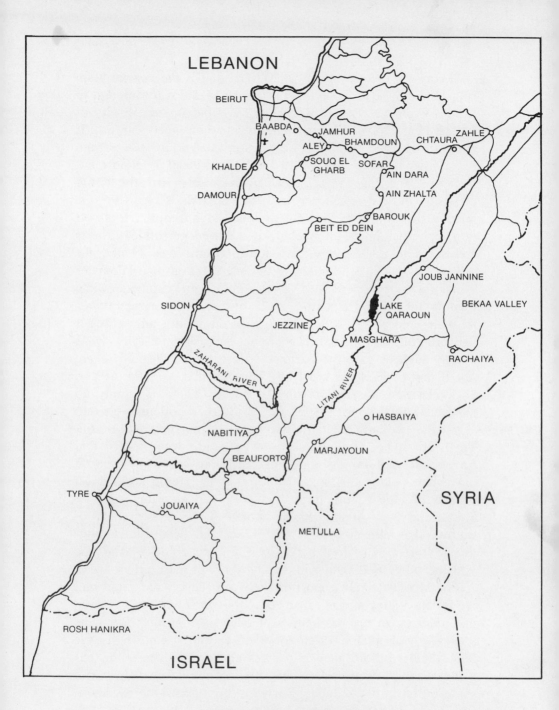

Map 5. Major battle sites

Lebanon has four terrain zones. The first is the coastal plain running from the Israeli border along the Mediterranean coast to Beirut. From the Israeli border to Tyre and on to the city of Sidon, there is only one road that an attacking army can use. It is a two-lane road, but in poor condition and barely wide enough for a tank; two-way traffic with military vehicles is almost impossible. This road is bounded on both sides for the entire distance from the Israeli border to Sidon by thick citrus groves, making the terrain perfect for ambush by antitank crews and infantry. It is almost impossible for armored personnel carriers and tanks to maneuver off the road. To the left, behind the orange groves, is the Mediterranean Sea, less than one kilometer away. To the right are citrus groves about one kilometer wide, planted right up to the steep foothills of the Lebanese mountains. At points, steep cliffs drop right against the road, sandwiching it between cliffs and the sea. It is perfect ambush country.

Any advance must be confined to the road itself. There are few if any parallel tracks of any consequence, and the area is pocked with wadis and ravines of basalt. There is simply no alternative to this road. After Sidon, the road widens a bit into a genuine two-lane artery to Damour and beyond into Beirut. There are some parallel roads, but they are very limited and traverse steep foothills and cliffs that prevent rapid vehicle movement. Along this coastal line of attack, three rivers must be crossed: the Litani, north of Tyre; the Zaharani, south of Sidon; and the Aouali, which is north of Sidon and south of Beirut. The main cities of Tyre, Sidon, and Damour are built astride the road. They make excellent roadblocks, and the Israelis had great difficulty in moving through these urban areas.

The second terrain zone runs between the coastal plain and the Bekaa Valley and is called the Lebanon ridge; the Lebanon mountain range reaches heights of over six thousand feet. The area of the Lebanon ridge south of Beirut is known as the Shouf and is full of small hill towns and deep ravines, and has a few narrow, steep roads. This ridge of mountains runs from south of Beirut to the Jabaal Barouk sub-range, which overlooks the Bekaa Valley to the east. Movement in this area is very difficult. The Shouf and Lebanese ridge is classic mountain terrain, characterized by narrow, steep, serpentine roads, either poorly paved or, more often, unpaved. The roads have very poor beds and collapse under the weight of a tank. North from Jezzine to Ain Zhalta, there is only one paved road; its serpentine nature and its numerous horseshoe bends overlooked by steep cliffs and strongpoints make the road a death trap.

The Lebanese ridge makes cross or flanking movements to the sea from the center very difficult. The Israelis were able to carry out a sweeping flanking movement across these mountains toward Sidon, but very special operational conditions made that possible. The terrain is obviously very poor for tanks and vehicles and gives the advantage to the defender, who from the high ground can ambush any force coming up the roads.

The third zone, running laterally from south to north from the Jabaal Barouk to the Anti-Lebanon ridge, is the Bekaa Valley. The valley is a broad flat plain on which it is very easy to maneuver. The difficulty for the Israelis was getting their armored vehicles to the valley floor so they could maneuver around the Syrians. The valley is easily covered by fire from positions on the west in the Jabaal Barouk and from the right in the high hills which form the foothills of Mount Hermon. Only two major roads lead to the east of the valley, one through the center and one to the left of Lake Qaraoun. To get to the valley, one has to cross the Litani River near Marjayoun under the guns of Beaufort Castle. And as one moves from Hasbaiya northeast toward the Bekaa, the roads leading to the valley are steep, narrow, and winding. The roads themselves make rapid mobile advances impossible.

The Anti-Lebanon ridge, another range of mountains, anchors the extreme east flank of the Bekaa Valley near Mount Hermon, and serves as a natural border between Israel and Syria. It is an effective barrier, and no military movement to or from Syria is possible unless one makes an end-run around the easternmost foothills near Yanta and Kfar Quoq. The area has almost no roads and is full of ravines and wadis, which makes cross-country travel very difficult. It was here, at Wadi Cheba, that the Israelis, in a brilliant engineering feat, cut a twelve-mile road in order to outflank the Syrian positions.

The terrain is ideally suited for defense, especially if the defenders deploy antitank weaponry and dismounted infantry armed with RPG's and missiles. The narrow, steep, serpentine roads in the center and eastern zones slow armored forces to a crawl. They also prevent attacking tanks from being deployed in the traditional fashion in rapid movement and shock action to dislodge infantry. More important, any attacker must stay on the roads (there is no alternative), thereby reducing any element of surprise.

These conditions were a great disadvantage for the Israeli Defense Force. As we have noted, the IDF is configured in heavy-armored formations designed to make rapid advances supported by mobile infantry. But here the IDF was consistently short of infantry. Moreover, it had no strategy or experience in using infantry as a screen to cover an armored advance. The Syrians broke up their armored units into smaller units of two and three tanks, spreading them in defensive positions supported by infantry commando groups armed with antitank guns, rocket-propelled grenades, and antitank missiles. As the Israeli forces worked their way up narrow roads, they were met by the Syrians in ambush and heavy casualties were inflicted, and then the Syrians would withdraw to the next position or to the next bend in the road and repeat the process. In this way, the Israeli advance was considerably slowed down in the east and center zones.

In the west, a better-positioned and braver force than the PLO put in the field could easily have inflicted ten times more casualties. In the opinion of the Deputy Director of Military Intelligence, Amos Gilboa, the PLO failed to take advantage of the terrain to the fullest extent, and the failure was greatest in the west.[6]

The nature of the terrain also prevented coordination between forces. As the main Israeli forces moved north, they were pretty much on their own. The IDF was able to move a division-size force from the center axis to the coastal plain to cut off the retreat of the PLO and open the road through Sidon, and this operation, under the command of Avigdor Kahalani, was executed successfully. But this advance moved on a well-built, main tourist road and three small auxiliary roads. In addition, the move from Nabitiya to Sidon was generally unopposed; it was, nevertheless, a textbook example of moving from alpine conditions to a coastal plain. This exception aside, each force, especially in the eastern sector, acted almost as an independent brigade. Israeli tactics center on the brigade as the basic maneuver element. In Lebanon, though whole divisions attacked with lead brigades, the roads, the steep terrain, and the limited avenues of advance quickly reduced the size of the maneuver elements that could advance—from a brigade to a company and at times to only a platoon. At times, a whole division was dependent on the ability of a single lead platoon to make its way through a particular road junction; and these platoons bore the brunt of the advance.

Probably no factor was more significant in the way battles were fought than the terrain. It was simply not possible, in Lebanon, to use heavily armored forces moving rapidly to strike deep into the enemy rear, or to bring maximum firepower to bear, because of the steep terrain and the poor roads. The Israelis built four hundred kilometers of new roads and paved old roads during the incursion, mainly during the first three months. In the end, the Israelis overcame the limitations of the terrain because the amount of men, tanks, and firepower they brought in was simply much larger than the enemy could resist. Had the forces been relatively equal, the terrain may well have given the defender an advantage significant enough to change the outcome.

ORDER OF BATTLE AND TACTICAL PLAN

The Israeli tactical plan divided the country into three operational zones. The zone immediately along the coast from the Israeli border to Beirut constituted the western sector; the central sector extended from Marjayoun north through Jezzine up through the Shouf and cut the Beirut–Damascus highway. The third zone, the eastern sector, extended through Hasbaiya toward Rachaiya east of Lake Qaraoun, striking through the center of the Bekaa Valley at Joub Jannine out toward Yanta. Each of the zones of operation had its own commander. For the first time in IDF history, a corps-level field command was established, under Major General Avigdor "Yanoosh" Ben Gal, who led the units in the east and in the Bekaa. The war in the center and west had no overall field commander, which left the division commanders pretty much on their own. They came under the normal command structure, which in the center and the west was the Northern Command Headquarters under Major General Amir Drori and his deputy, Major General Uri Simchoni. The establishment of a corps headquarters in the east reflected the need to create an interim headquarters between division and Northern Command to control the large force of approximately four divisions, 38,000 men, and 800 tanks.

The tactical plan in the western sector was to attack with a reinforced division along the coastal road: the IDF would strike rapidly and push toward Tyre and Sidon up to Damour. The plan called for Tyre and Sidon to be bypassed and sealed off with brigades to trap the PLO inside the cities and the camps. Highly mobile infantry forces in APC's would then dismount and clean out the camps and the cities. An armored spearhead, after reaching Damour, would fight its way to the outskirts of Beirut, where it would deploy. This plan of attack was typical of the IDF in its emphasis on rapid advance, heavy armor, and bypassing strong points of resistance and surprising the enemy in the rear.

Accomplishment of the mission in the west fell to two major units. Division 91, under the command of Yitzhak Mordechai, was a division-size unit initially deploying three brigades of mechanized infantry. The number of tanks in the division strike force was only a hundred, but it had more than its normal complement of APC's. In addition, Mordechai's Division 91 could call on a reserve of six brigades, mostly Nahal infantry and paratroops. As they moved toward Tyre and Sidon, they were allowed to draw on these reserves, which were deployed behind the Israel border. By the third day of the assault, Mordechai was able to add an additional paratrooper brigade, an armored brigade, and one infantry brigade to his force. The total force came almost to two divisions. As the operation continued, a brigade left Mordechai's command, passing under Amos Yaron's command; later, another passed under the command of Kahalani. The spearhead brigade that drove past Tyre and Sidon and advanced to Damour was the famous 211th brigade led by Colonel Eli Geva, on loan from Division 162.

A brigade force was to move from Bent Jbail toward Jouaiya, meeting forces from Tyre and trapping the PLO in the Iron Triangle. At the same time, Yaron was to lead a specially assembled force, centered on Division 96, on an amphibious assault behind Sidon, using a battalion as a blocking force and joining the spearhead moving north toward Damour. The amphibious landing was spearheaded by the 50th battalion of the 35th parachute brigade, a special reaction force under Colonel Yarir "Ya-Ya" Yarom. The mission was to land quickly behind Sidon and trap the PLO in a vise. Eventually, the forces deployed in the western sector totaled 22,000 men and 220 tanks.

The success of the plan for the center sector of operations hinged on the ability of a division-size force to move rapidly across the Litani River at two points, one south of Beaufort Castle and one north of the castle strongpoint, to capture the key road junction north of Nabitiya. The area north of Nabitiya is called the Arnoun Heights, and in the middle of it is the junction of five major roads, from which junction a road leads north to Jezzine and to the Beirut–Damascus highway. A road also leads to the Beirut Mountains, whose capture would be necessary to control the western ridge of the Bekaa. The major connecting road to the west also joins this intersection; any force that controls the intersection can strike in three or four directions, including to the west toward the coast. There the PLO forces could be trapped between Sidon and the Israelis coming up the coastal road. The plan involved an enormous tactical gamble. If for any reason the Israeli force was not able to seize the intersection, the tactical plan in the west and center would have to be revised on the spot or fail. The unit that had the responsibility for the capture of the Arnoun Heights was Division 36, under Brigadier General Kahalani—known as the best tank division in the Israeli army. It is normally comprised of three tank brigades, one brigade of mobile infantry and armored personnel carriers, and four battalions of artillery. But the 36th did not deploy with its full force. Instead, the 7th tank brigade was lent to Immanuel Sakel on the eastern front. When the 36th attacked, it was one brigade short of a full division and deployed 140 tanks.

The mission of the 36th division was to deploy from Metulla both east and west of Nabitiya, cross the Litani River over two bridges south and north of the Beaufort Castle, strike toward the Arnoun Heights, and open the road to Jezzine. Having captured the road and the intersection, Kahalani's force was to turn west along four roads and strike for the coast. There it was to link up with Yitzhak Mordechai's force on the coastal road at Zaharani Junction and move north to Sidon. The northernmost prong of the 36th division was to hit Sidon from the east, encircle the

Ein Hilwe PLO camp, and open the road north to Damour. It was crucial to open the road to allow the 211th spearhead, commanded by Eli Geva, to strike to Damour. On the way to Nabitiya, once Beaufort Castle had been encircled by the bypassing force, a brigade of Golani infantry was to break off from the main body and take the castle from the rear.

A second part of the central-sector force was Division 162, commanded by Brigadier General Menachem Einan. This force was smaller than a division and was comprised of a tank brigade, two battalions of infantry, and an artillery regiment. The force had been scaled down from a normal complement of two hundred tanks to fewer than a hundred tanks; the 211th brigade had been loaned to the 91st division. Einan's mission was to follow the 36th division up to Nabitiya. Once the intersection was captured and Kahalani had turned west to the coast, the 162nd was to move north on the Jezzine road. As Einan approached Jezzine, he would bypass it, swing left and cross the Besri River, go cross-country up the road to Beit ed Dein and move east on Barouk and on to Ain Zhalta. This was the major spearhead, whose mission was to outflank the Syrians and strike at the main position defending the Beirut–Damascus highway in the center. The total force in the center comprised approximately two divisions, with 220 tanks and 18,000 men.

By far the most crucial operation of the war, as it turned out, took place in the eastern sector. The idea initially was to block the Syrian forces in the center at the opening of the southern end of the Bekaa Valley by moving a large blocking force toward the towns of Hasbaiya and Koukaba. As this force moved to block Syrian forces in the center, two flanking movements would be carried out simultaneously. The first was a flanking movement to the east, or the right side of the Hasbaiya–Koukaba line, striking along the foothills of the Hermon mountain range toward Rachaiya, with the objective of cutting off the Syrian retreat toward Damascus. At the same time, forces in the center, with those attached to the eastern sector, would continue toward Jezzine along the Barouk ridge and control the Bekaa from peaks of the mountain range running along the west side of the valley. Still another force was to move north to take the Beirut–Damascus highway, though basically this force was deployed through the central sector. If it became necessary to engage the

Syrians, the central force would be in position to smash through the southern Bekaa near Lake Qaraoun and move toward Joub Jannine to take the Bekaa Valley. Even if the Syrian forces did not have to be engaged, the flanking movements to their east and west would put them at a severe disadvantage.

In command of the eastern sector was Major General Ben Gal, with a force comprised of five basic elements. The first, Division 252, commanded by Immanuel Sakel, was comprised of two tank brigades, one brigade of mobile infantry, and a full brigade of mobile artillery. The 460th tank brigade, normally stationed with Division 252, had been lent to Danni Vardi's force as an independent brigade for action near Jezzine. The mission of the 252nd was to attack out of the Golan Heights along two avenues of advance: along the foothills of Mount Hermon through Wadi Cheba on a twelve-kilometer road of its own making; and down through the valley toward Hasbaiya out along the road to Kfair and Rachaiya toward Kfar Quoq, in a wide flanking movement paralleling the Syrian border designed to outflank the Syrian forces and if necessary cut off their retreat to Damascus.

A second major force in the eastern sector was Division 90, commanded by General Giora Lev, a full-combat arms division whose mission was to attack in the center along the Micha Axis. It was to attack from Metulla through Marjayoun and hit the Syrian center at Lake Qaraoun; it also had a flanking force, under Colonel Micki Shachar, on the right. Joub Jannine was its ultimate target. The main blow was to fall on the right side of the lake at Joub Jannine, while Shachar's force moved along the right wing on the road and linked up with a battalion of Sakel's force at the approaches to the town of Yanta.

The third element of the eastern-sector task force was called the Vardi force, after its commander, Brigadier General Danni Vardi. This was a specially configured independent force comprised of two brigades. The centerpiece of the force was the 460th tank brigade, commanded by Colonel Hagai Cohen. The Vardi force was to move from the Nabitiya junction to capture Jezzine and open the road north. Moving along the narrow roads between Jezzine and Yohmor, it was to take the junction at Masghara, which served as a headquarters for the Syrian army. It was then to move north on the main road west of the lake, thus constituting one flank of a two-pronged attack along the sides of Lake Qaraoun.

The fourth element was the Special Maneuver Force, commanded by Brigadier General Yossi Peled, a specially configured force of two brigades. The Israelis have a penchant for configuring their units to carry out a particular mission. In this instance, the mission was to kill tanks and prevent armored reinforcement in the Bekaa Valley. The tank-killing force of paratroopers and infantry was outfitted with antitank weapons, TOW missiles, APC's, and helicopters. It was to move up the road past Jezzine, after the route had been opened by Hagai Cohen, toward the ridges of the Jabaal Barouk Mountains. It was then to move along secondary roads, climbing to Masser el Shouf as engineers cut roads, so that from the eastern slope of the Jabaal Barouk control of the Bekaa Valley could be established. Peled's special force would then overlook the main reinforcement road into the Bekaa and control both the west side of Lake Qaraoun and the Bekaa. It was to stop any attempt at reinforcement into the Bekaa, a job which it did remarkably well.

The final element of the eastern-zone task force was Division 880, commanded by Brigadier General Yom-Tov Tamir, a full combined-arms division deployed as the corps' strategic reserve; it saw little action. It deployed behind the rest of the forces, near the Micha Axis, and some of its units rescued forces ambushed at Soultan Yaaquoub, in the upper reaches of the Bekaa Valley.

The total force assembled in the eastern sector was approximately four divisions, comprising 800 tanks and 38,000 men. Not counted in this total, but clearly available should there be need, was the larger strategic reserve, located on the Golan Heights, under Brigadier General Bar Koch Bar, and consisting of two divisions of mobilized reservists plus one brigade gazetted from the 36th division. The role of this reserve was to place on the Golan Heights a force large enough to stop the Syrians should they attack across it to strike at the Israeli rear; its mission was to deter the Syrians from an attack through the Golan Heights.

The Israelis threw almost six and a half divisions into the Lebanon war. They were configured in various ways. Some divisions were light brigades, and others carried as many as two extra brigades. In addition, the IDF made use of independent brigade units that had specially tailored missions. This six-and-a-half-division force deployed between 75,000 and 78,000 men, 1,240 tanks, and 1,520 armored personnel carriers. The Israelis faced two Syrian divisions, but only one was fully deployed in the Bekaa at the start of the war; the second was not engaged until later, when it saw action in the Shouf and on the Beirut–Damascus highway. The IDF faced 15,000 PLO fighters, deployed mostly in the west, along the coast, though there were almost two thousand deployed in the center and eastern zones as well.

The tactical plan and the Israeli deployment of forces seemed generally sound. On closer analysis, however, it seems to have failed to take sufficient account of the terrain. The advances were much slower than expected, and, especially in the east, were far more costly in men and equipment than anticipated. The IDF had no experience in mountain warfare, and the tactics they brought to bear on this war—rapid advance, heavy-armor formations, and mounted infantry—were more suitable for open terrain and desert warfare. Equally important was the fact that the IDF was chronically short of infantry. Because of the value the Israelis place on the life of each soldier, the IDF has never developed the use of infantry screens as protection for armor. A more effective way of advancing on mountain roads would have been to pattern their tactics after the mountain campaigns fought by the American and British forces in Italy. In these campaigns, infantry was deployed in front of the tanks. Deployed in this manner, infantrymen are less susceptible to being killed by tank fire and force the enemy to disclose its ambush position. If the enemy chose not to engage, then the infantry could engage tank units, to the tanks' great disadvantage. In addition, the commando units which the Syrians deployed with the tanks could have been brought under infantry attack without risking Israeli tanks. IDF tactics in Lebanon clearly reflected its past experience. The IDF was not adequately prepared to fight a mountain campaign and to deal with the kind of resistance that it met.

Having assembled almost seven divisions on the Lebanese border, the Israelis were prepared to strike. At 11 a.m. on Sunday, June 6, three major assault groups crossed the border and attacked. Since the operation depended heavily on speed, especially to outflank and trap the PLO in the western zone, the decision to go at eleven in the morning may not have been tactically sound. An attack this late conceded six hours of daylight to the enemy. The reason for attacking at that time was of course political. The political leadership had calculated that if the Israelis did not move that day, pressure from the United States might be brought to bear that would prevent the Israelis from moving into Lebanon at all.

Sunday, June 6

On the coastal road in the western zone, a three-brigade force under Brigadier General Yitzhak Mordechai crossed the border at Rosh Hanikra. Additional forces continued to assemble just behind the border to press the advance on the road. Division 91 began to move toward Tyre, its first objective to bypass the city, surround the three major PLO camps there, and move up the coast toward Sidon to link up with the 36th division under Kahalani, which would be coming cross-country from the center zone on the Nabitiya road. The linkup, to be completed no later than the second day of the war, was at the Zaharani Junction, south of Sidon. Spearheading the assault was an armored brigade, the 211th, commanded by Colonel Geva, whose task was to bypass Tyre and Sidon and race to Damour, capture it, and move on toward Beirut. The objective was to deliver the enemy a rapid blow based on both strategic and tactical surprise.

The assault on the coastal road went slowly. It was preceded by an artillery bombardment which continued along the road as the Israelis advanced. Air strikes were conducted all along the coast against suspected PLO positions. Because the road is narrow, a monumental traffic jam developed which slowed the Israelis to a crawl. PLO forces lurking in the groves ambushed several armed personnel carriers and tanks. Some of the ambushes in which armored personnel carriers were struck by rocket-propelled grenades and antitank fire were horrible; the APC's aluminum skins caught fire and caused a number of terrible burn casualties. In reaction troops refused to ride in the APC's and began walking beside them or riding on top. Given the ability of the PLO to strike at them, General Mordechai slowed his advance deliberately, to minimize both his own casualties and those of the civilians in the area.

As Mordechai's units approached Tyre, a lead battalion was supposed to bypass the city and place its force in a blocking position. Tyre is on a peninsula, and the main road passes alongside the city and continues up the coast. By placing a blocking force in position where the peninsula meets the main road, the IDF could easily have trapped the PLO left on the peninsula. However, the lead battalion lost its way, and instead of bypassing the city and putting a blocking force in place, it stumbled right into the city and into a PLO ambush. Trying to back out, it stumbled into yet another ambush. The result was a number of casualties, and the battalion commander and an enlisted man taken prisoner; later they would be tortured and executed and their bodies thrown in a well. The ambush in Tyre slowed the entire column, except for Geva's brigade, which continued its rapid movement up the coast.

After a few hours, the situation outside Tyre began to stabilize as the ambushed forces extricated themselves. A brigade of the main force deployed into a blocking position, and another brigade, drawn against the reserves left behind the border, moved up to augment the main force. By 1600 hours, the lead elements of Mordechai's main force had spanned the Litani River with a Bailey bridge, erected to replace the Qasmiye Bridge, which had been destroyed by Israeli aircraft the day before. It had been bombed to prevent reinforcement by the PLO and their escape to the north. Mordechai's units poured across the Litani River; by eight o'clock that evening, his units were five kilometers north of Tyre. At the same time a brigade-size mixed battle group which had been deployed around the Rachidiya refugee camp prepared to enter the camp at dawn the next day.

In the center zone, the 36th division under Kahalani struck out from Metulla in a two-pronged attack, racing for Nabitiya and the Arnoun Heights. The first prong crossed the Khardali Bridge over the Litani just south of the Beaufort Castle and began the steep climb to the Arnoun Heights. The second prong crossed the Kakalet Bridge to the north of the castle, and climbed a narrow winding road up to the town of Nabitiya, all the while subject to antitank and artillery fire by PLO forces entrenched in the Beaufort Castle. Moving rapidly, both wings bypassed Nabitiya and moved to seize the key road junction one kilometer north of the city. At this point, a battalion-size force struck north toward Jezzine, to clear the road as far north as Jbaa, where Kahalani's forces would turn west and head for the coast. The operation was carried out swiftly and almost without casualties. Kahalani made excellent use of the element of speed, catching the PLO by surprise in Nabitiya and forcing most of them to withdraw north toward Jezzine or east toward the Bekaa Valley. Only a small force was left behind to try to delay the Israeli forces.

Part of the center force was comprised of a brigade of Golani infantry, the elite regular infantry force of the army. Beginning on the evening of June 6, Beaufort Castle, which had for years been a PLO strongpoint, came under artillery bombardment and air attack by the IDF. Once the Arnoun Heights were seized, the elite reconnaissance battalion of the Golani infantry brigade broke from the main assault force and launched an attack on the castle from the rear. An assault from the front is impossible, since the castle rises 750 meters above the Litani River gorge. Some serious thought had been given by the Israelis to utilizing special commando units to climb the steep cliffs in the evening, to strike at the castle from the front. But this plan was vetoed by Kahalani, who thought it the essence of stupidity. The rear approaches are narrow but gently sloping, and in the dark of June 6 the attack began. Fighting raged for six hours, and by early morning on June 7 Beaufort Castle had fallen, at a cost to the Israelis of eight dead.

Moving on Kahalani's right was a tank force slightly less than a division in size, commanded by Menachem Einan, which had eighty tanks and two battalions of paratroops with armored personnel carriers. Their job was to follow Kahalani up to Jbaa, move north and bypass Jezzine, and continue on toward Beit ed Dein and finally to Ain Zhalta. They moved quickly through the road junction and began the long climb up the steep hills toward the western outskirts of Jezzine.

In the eastern zone, Division 252, commanded by Immanuel Sakel, moved out in strength along two avenues of advance, to approach Syrian forces in the eastern Bekaa. The first attack was along the foothills of Mount Hermon, using poor secondary roads, through Wadi Cheba; Israeli engineers had to cut a twelve-mile strip through the wadi for their armor and artillery forces. The second attack moved across the valley and struck at Hasbaiya and Koukaba; gaining the main road, the attack turned right and struck along the road toward Rachaiya. Both advances constituted a wide-flanking movement on the Syrian left flank designed to cut off Syrian retreat to Damascus.

At the same time Division 90, commanded by Giora Lev, moved out from the town of Marjayoun, aiming directly at the road leading to Lake Qaraoun. Lev began to work his way toward the Lake Qaraoun area, to the right of the town of Masghara. A brigade under the command of Micki Shachar covered his right flank and moved on the major road toward the eastern Bekaa. Division 90 aimed directly at the Syrian center near Lake Qaraoun and reached the Hasbaiya–Koukaba line by early morning of June 7 and stopped. The two remaining forces of the eastern task force also deployed through Marjayoun. The first was the Vardi force, composed of three mixed brigades, whose task was to move up the road to Masghara while a brigade under the command of Hagai Cohen moved up the road toward Jezzine. Cohen's mission was to take Jezzine and move toward Masghara from the west, putting the town under attack from two directions. Another special force led by Yossi Peled, configured for tank killing, was to move through Jezzine once it was cleared by Cohen's brigade, take control of the mountain ridge of Jabaal Barouk, and move across it to control the approaches to the Bekaa Valley. Peled was to block any Syrian attempts at reinforcement and was to be in position should he be required to aid Menachem Einan as he moved toward Ain Zhalta. By the end of the first day of fighting, most IDF forces had achieved their objectives, although the advance in the west had gone slower than expected.

Monday, June 7

The day opened with Israeli jets bombing Beirut and other PLO strongpoints along the route of advance in the western zone. The Syrian air force rose to meet Israeli fighters over the Beirut area. The dogfight resulted in one MIG shot down and no losses for the Israelis. In the west, Mordechai continued to press toward Sidon, while the Israeli air force hit targets along the route from Tyre and Beirut. In Tyre, fighting continued as an infantry and armor brigade moved into the Rachidiya PLO camp. Fighting was moderately heavy, and the Israeli capture of the camp was more difficult because of their concern for Israeli and civilian casualties. Israeli units had strict instructions not to

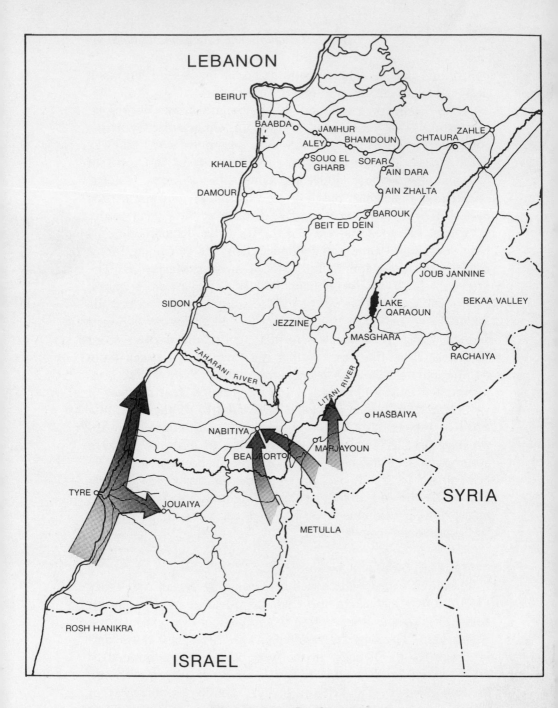

Map 6. Israeli advance
June 6
Day 1

use satchel charges or even hand grenades when entering buildings. This concern for civilian casualties marked almost all IDF operations throughout the war, especially in the areas of Tyre and Sidon, where it reduced the speed with which the Israelis were able to overcome enemy opposition.

By midday, elements of Mordechai's units were approaching the Zaharani Junction to link up with Kahalani's forces striking from the center zone, in order to make the assault on Sidon. The Zaharani Junction was chosen as the major linkup point for several reasons. First, it was the only place in the road between the border and Sidon wide enough to accommodate the assembling of a division-size force. Second, there was a petroleum refinery in the area, which the Israelis would be able to tap into. Third, the Zaharani Junction has an excellent port facility, which could be used for reinforcements, logistics, or evacuation of the wounded. As it happened, none of these contingencies arose. The linkup at the Zaharani went smoothly, and the big M-109 and M-110 self-propelled artillery pieces moved into position and began shelling Sidon.

Back across the border, a brigade now attached to Mordechai's forces struck across the Hadad Enclave from Bent Jbail toward the town of Jouaiya. At the same time, a battalion of troops broke off from the main force at Tyre, raced down the road, and linked up with Israeli forces at Jouaiya. This maneuver put the Israelis in complete control of the Iron Triangle, which, prior to the invasion, held some seven hundred terrorists. Israeli forces began mopping-up operations to root out the terrorists one by one, killing or capturing them and destroying their arms caches and infrastructure.

In the early morning hours of June 7, the Israeli navy carried out the largest amphibious landing in its history. The navy's task was to transport a mixed brigade comprised of elements of the 96th division, paratroopers, and naval commandos, along with its tanks and vehicles, and land them at a point north of Sidon near the mouth of the Aouali River. This force was to link up with Geva's advance brigade moving on Damour and at the same time move elements south toward Sidon, putting the city in a vise. The Israeli navy had approximately fourteen landing craft of various types capable of transporting men and tanks. Although the exact number of landing craft involved in the

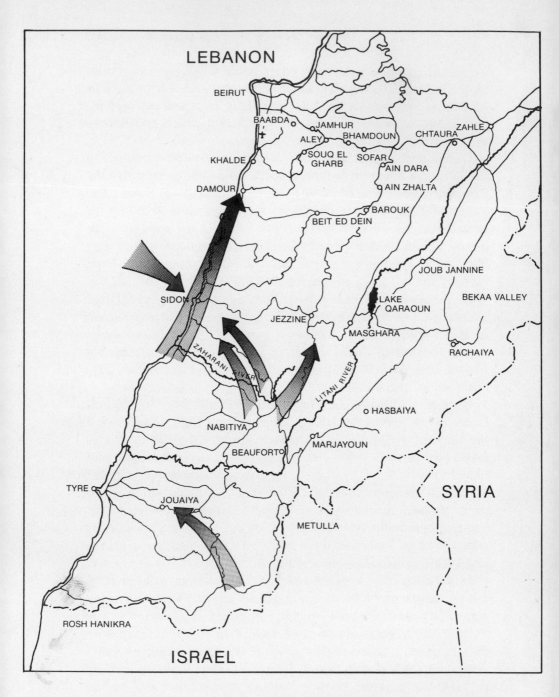

**Map 7. Israeli advance
June 7
Day 2**

operation remains classified, there is no doubt that the large majority of craft available was used. During the early morning of June 6, even before Israeli ground forces had crossed the border, elements of the 96th division were loaded aboard landing craft in the harbor at Ashdod. Ashdod, south of Tel Aviv, was chosen for the embarkation point because it is well out of visual and aircraft detection range by the enemy in Lebanon. The force sailed toward its landing point north of Sidon. The majority of the 96th division was not seaborne, however, but had been positioned in Nahariya, on the coast, just south of the Israeli–Lebanese border. Once the landing was carried out, these elements were shuttled to the landing area after the first wave went ashore.

In the early morning hours, the landing craft, with several battalions of troops and equipment, moved toward a point north of Sidon. The landing craft were escorted by missile boats and even submarines, while the air force flew cover to protect them from possible attack by Syrian aircraft. About five o'clock in the evening, the invasion force arrived opposite Sidon and began to land its forces near the estuary of the Aouali River.

The landing site, due north of the bridge over the Aouali, had been seized by naval commandos on the evening of June 6; they were soon joined by elements of the 50th parachute battalion of the 35th parachute brigade under the command of "Ya-Ya" Yarom. The overall operation was under the command of Amos Yaron. Close to midnight on June 6, the first landing craft reached the beach, and all night the beachhead was expanded as troops were put ashore and began to deploy inland. At 2:30 the next day, a second landing was carried out, and more troops and vehicles went ashore uneventfully. The Israeli navy shuttled its boats up and down the coast to Nahariya, where it picked up troops and deployed them to the beach. As a great traffic jam built up on the coastal road between Tyre and Sidon, CH-53 helicopters began picking up units off the road south of Sidon and moving them north of the city, where they could link up with the invasion force and continue their strike north.

The object of the invasion was to position a large force north of Sidon that could continue the assault toward Damour. The force which moved north comprised elements of the 96th division and elements of Kahalani's division that crossed over from

Nabitiya and was pressing Sidon from the south and east. In addition, Mordechai provided some troops that were airlifted around the city by helicopter. General Yaron had carried out his command brilliantly. The 211th independent brigade, commanded by Geva, continued the spearhead.

With the two landings, the navy put ashore almost four hundred vehicles, and by midday of June 7 Sidon was caught in a vise. Forces were pressing from the south under Mordechai, while additional forces arrived from the east under Kahalani, who joined up at two points, at the Zaharani Junction and also northeast of the city, where his troops engaged the PLO at the Ein Hilwe camp. At the same time, a major force was in position north of the city. Sidon was surrounded on three sides, and it was only a matter of time before the city fell.

Moving from the west, Kahalani's 36th division had struck cross-country and linked up with Mordechai's forces south of Sidon at the Zaharani Junction. The major task remaining was to open the main road through Sidon to allow Mordechai's forces to punch through. A brigade, commanded by Colonel Egoezzi, was cut loose from Mordechai's forces and ordered to join Kahalani's forces and open the road through Sidon. But Kahalani's forces, already short one brigade (lent to Sakel at the beginning of the invasion), ran into stiff resistance at the Ein Hilwe camp, outside Sidon. The 36th did not have sufficient forces to open the road on schedule. With the road still closed, Geva's spearhead brigade had to make the choice of either fighting its way through the city and opening the road or bypassing the city and continuing its thrust toward Damour. An argument ensued between Geva and Kahalani, but the decision was made by Kahalani to have Geva bypass Sidon and sustain his advance north.

Kahalani found himself in some difficulty. Having given forces to Mordechai at the Zaharani Junction and also some units to Geva to proceed north with the attack on Damour, and having at least two battalions tied down at the Ein Hilwe camp, Kahalani now had insufficient strength to open the road through Sidon. Fortunately, the special brigade under Egoezzi arrived on time. Within hours, the road through the center of the city was open for Mordechai's forces to deploy through the city. Mordechai's forces, in greater and greater numbers, began to arrive in and around Sidon, and the battle for the city and the Ein Hilwe camp began. Kahalani's forces were placed under the command of Yaron, as his main forces, led by Geva's spearhead, continued toward Damour.

In the center zone, Einan's force, which had followed in Kahalani's wake and moved north toward Jezzine after Kahalani turned off on the western road leading to the coast, approached the town of Jezzine. On the outskirts, on a very steep road with a horseshoe curve in it, a minor clash occurred with Syrian and PLO forces defending the area. Since Einan's mission was to strike north toward Beit ed Dein and eventually toward Ain Zhalta, he broke contact and continued to move north. At the same time, the 460th brigade under Hagai Cohen, moving behind Einan, struck toward Jezzine in an effort to clear it. Opposing Cohen's forces was a light Syrian battalion reinforced by a company of PLO. The battle did not last long, and when it was over, virtually every tank of the Syrian and PLO units had been destroyed. The rest of the Vardi force, of which the 460th brigade was a part, began to move on Masghara from the south, over poor, serpentine roads, hoping eventually to capture the Syrian headquarters town which commands the left-hand approach to Lake Qaraoun and the Bekaa Valley.

In the east, with the twin towns of Hasbaiya and Koukaba now under control, the main force under Lev came to a halt and simply waited. The right flank, under Sakel, moved down the road toward Rachaiya to outflank Syrian positions at Ain Ata and Kfair. In the center, the pressure on Jezzine was increased by Cohen's moves into the area and by Vardi's forces moving toward Masghara. The Syrian position was eroding rapidly in the center; although the main center force of the Israeli thrust had stopped, both wings continued to move in the east and west, outflanking Syrian positions. At this point, the heavy mobile artillery organic to an Israeli division began to pour into the area around Hasbaiya—guns with the power to bring six Syrian missile batteries stationed behind Syrian lines within range. The PLO had fled behind Syrian lines from Fatahland, so there was no longer any PLO buffer force between Israeli troops and the Syrians either in the center at Hasbaiya or on the left flank near

Jezzine and Masghara. Any further movement by the IDF toward Jezzine, Jabaal Barouk, Rachaiya, or Masghara would bring it into direct contact with Syrian forces.

At the end of the second day of fighting in the west, Sidon was completely surrounded and enough units had been brought in to seal it off. Tyre was blockaded by brigade-size forces, reinforced by their strategic reserve drawn from across the Israeli border. The Iron Triangle had been cut off by reserve brigades moved from Bent Jbail toward Tyre, linking up Jouaiya. A large force comprised of elements of Kahalani's units, Division 96, and those put ashore by the navy and led by Geva's spearhead began to move rapidly toward Damour. In the center, both Beaufort Castle and Jezzine had fallen, and Israeli forces continued up the narrow roads toward Beit ed Dein and the highway linking it to Ain Zhalta. In addition, elements of the Vardi force had moved into position around Masghara and Lake Qaraoun, while Lev's major force had come to a halt in the center. On the right flank, movement continued as Sakel's force proceeded toward Rachaiya, threatening to outflank the Syrians, and for the first time Syrian missile batteries were brought within range of ground artillery. The Syrian position was rapidly eroding, and the Syrians had to do something or lose the war by default.

Tuesday, June 8

On the third day, the fighting in the western zone continued, with battles in the refugee camp at Rachidiya; and the six-day siege of the Ein Hilwe camp outside Sidon began. Inside the city, the road was open, and as Mordechai's troops entered, they were confronted with sporadic but heavy fighting. North of Sidon, the combined force under Yaron continued to move rapidly on Damour. Heavy resistance was encountered south of Damour, at Saadiyat, but was overcome within hours. In the air, the IAF engaged Syrian jets over Beirut and southern Lebanon. Six Syrian aircraft were shot down, without a single Israeli loss. Throughout the day, the air force flew ground-support missions on all three fronts. It was careful not to strike at the Syrian missile batteries in the east, although its attacks around Jezzine and Lake Qaraoun and near Rachaiya brought it within missile range. The Syrians, although their tracking radars were turned on, did not engage Israeli aircraft with their missile batteries.

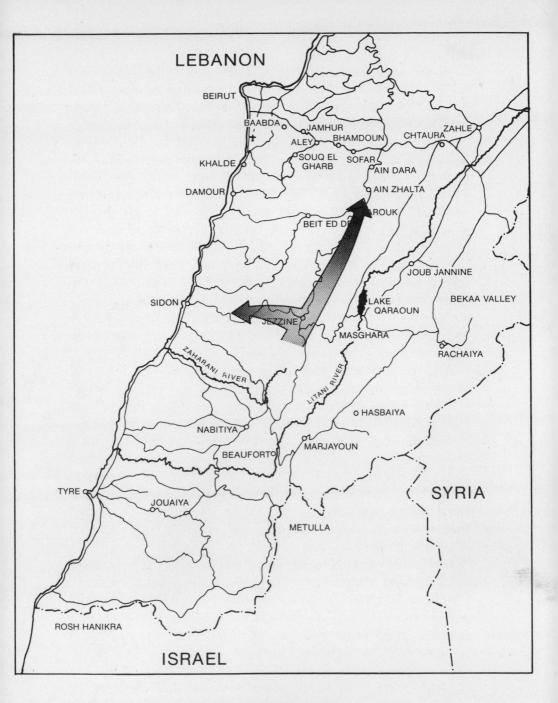

LEBANON

BEIRUT

BAABDA
JAMHUR
ALEY   BHAMDOUN   CHTAURA   ZAHLE
KHALDE   SOUQ EL   SOFAR
GHARB   AIN DARA
DAMOUR   AIN ZHALTA
BEIT ED DINE   AROUK

JOUB JANNINE   BEKAA VALLEY

SIDON   LAKE
QARAOUN
JEZZINE
ZAHARANI RIVER   MASGHARA
RACHAIYA

LITANI RIVER   HASBAIYA

NABITIYA
BEAUFORT   MARJAYOUN

SYRIA

TYRE
JOUAIYA
METULLA

ROSH HANIKRA

ISRAEL

Map 8. Israeli advance
June 8
Day 3

In the center, the 460th brigade engaged Syrian forces and the PLO around the town of Jezzine. Defending the town was a Syrian light battalion comprised of twenty-four tanks, some manned by PLO rather than Syrian regulars. Jezzine was a crucial crossroad and its capture would open all the roads to Masghara and the west side of the Bekaa, as well as the approaches to the Jabaal Barouk and the road to the left, which Einan had to take up to Ain Zhalta. Despite the strategic importance of the town, and the fact that its fall to the Israelis would outflank and drive a wedge between Syrian forces deployed in the Bekaa and those deployed to the north around Beirut and the highway, the Syrians did not fight very hard for it. After several hours, they left it to the IDF. As Cohen's force began to redeploy south of Jezzine to support Vardi's attack on Masghara, a tragic accident occurred which cost the lives of several Israelis and a number of tanks. As Cohen's force moved toward Masghara, one battalion, comprised of the armored officers' school unit, took the main road leading to Masghara. Another battalion, comprised of the tank commanders' school unit, moved farther south across very narrow roads to link up with the Vardi force moving toward the town. (In the Israeli army, groups that are in training, such as platoon leaders or tank commanders, deploy and fight as units.) As both battalions approached the crossroad of Ein Katina from opposite directions, they mistook each other for the enemy and engaged in armored combat. The battle raged for almost two hours before the mistake was discovered. By that time, there were a number of dead and wounded, and a number of tanks had been damaged.

By nightfall, the IDF in the center zone was poised for a major attack around Masghara and Lake Qaraoun if the need arose. Meanwhile, farther to the west, Yossi Peled's special tank-killing force continued its climb into the Jabaal Barouk Mountains along terrible roads in an effort to mount the peaks and position itself to command the roads leading into the Bekaa from the west.

Little action occurred on the eastern front. The center of the main attack remained halted at Hasbaiya and Koukaba awaiting further instructions. The Israelis continued to outflank Syrian forces to the west and east. Syrian troops began to move into positions to block the continued thrust of the Israelis toward

Rachaiya, so that, as the third day of fighting ended, IDF units in the east and center were facing Syrian forces only yards apart and a clash seemed inevitable. At the same time, Peled's men were moving rapidly along the Jabaal Barouk, extending the flank along the ridges of the Bekaa Valley and neutralizing the ability of Syrian forces in the Bekaa to communicate with and support Syrian forces on the Beirut–Damascus highway.

Wednesday, June 9

By midday, on the coastal road, only Damour had not fallen. George Habash's PFLP put up stiff resistance for control of the city. Although the town itself had been in ruins since the massacre of the Christians in 1976, the PLO had turned it into a redoubt and the main base of operations for the PFLP. Resistance was strong as the PLO fought from deep caves and from house to house. South of Damour, the IDF was in control of Sidon, but the siege of the Ein Hilwe camp went on. Some 120 PLO fighters continued to hold out, using civilians as shields and hostages. The siege of the camp lasted so long not because the Israelis were incapable of capturing it. Indeed, the concrete and tin shacks could easily have been reduced by air, artillery, and tank fire, or even house-to-house operations. However, the commander of the Israeli force, General Mordechai, had been deeply affected by the loss of his own unit in the '73 war; his sensitivity to casualties, military or civilian, was well known. He decided to treat the civilians and the PLO in the camps as hostages. For six days, IDF commanders conducted negotiations with PLO defenders and put their own troops under great restrictions regarding the use of firepower. In the end, the Israelis took the Ein Hilwe camp with very small loss of civilian life. The number of Israeli casualties, however, was considerably higher than it would have been had the IDF brought its firepower to bear. Tyre was subdued, with the main refugee camp at Rachidiya totally in Israeli hands.

In the center, the major armored force under Menachem Einan passed to the west of Jezzine and crossed the Besri River, gaining the major road at Gharife. It moved on to capture Beit ed Dein astride the major east-west road on the approaches to the Shouf Mountains and the city of Beirut. The advance continued until it made communications contact with the Vardi force mov-

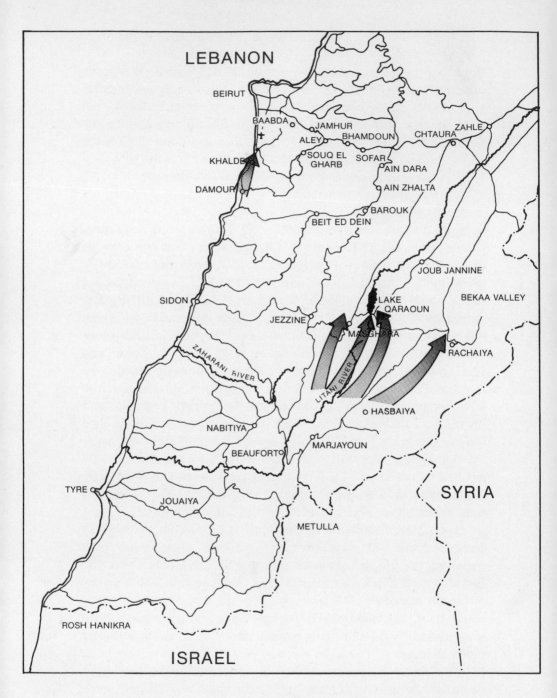

Map 9. Israeli advance
June 9
Day 4

ing along the Barouk ridge. Einan continued toward Ain Zhalta, which controlled the approaches to the Beirut–Damascus highway. The Syrians knew that the loss of Ain Zhalta would put them at a tactical disadvantage and they decided to fight.

On the approach to Ain Zhalta is a long horseshoe bend, which turned the road into a shooting gallery for antitank and missile crews deployed by the Syrians on the heights above it. Here Einan's force was ambushed, with considerable loss of tanks, APC's, and men. The ambush was so successful that the Israeli units were unable to continue their advance. The Israelis responded rapidly; they reinforced the area with a full battalion of troops ferried in by CH-53 helicopters. The troops were deployed as a blocking force behind the enemy, and after a significant armor and infantry engagement lasting several hours, Syrians tank units and their supporting commandos withdrew. The battle at Ain Zhalta, which stopped the Israeli advance some twelve kilometers short of the highway, bought time for the 68th and 85th Syrian brigades deployed along the highway and to the south in the Shouf to gather their forces and redeploy.

The situation in the east remained pretty much as it had been the night before, with IDF forces in the center striking along the Barouk Mountains, while those in the easternmost zone struck at Rachaiya. The main force in the center was still halted. The political situation changed on the ninth of June, however, and Prime Minister Begin finally authorized Defense Minister Sharon to neutralize the missiles in the Bekaa Valley. The Israelis decided on a preemptive strike against the missile batteries. A second part of the strategy was to draw Syrian aircraft into battle and destroy as many as possible in order to establish air superiority over the entire Lebanese battle zone.

On the afternoon of Wednesday, June 9, Israeli aircraft went into action, attacking the SAM missile batteries in the Bekaa Valley. At 2 p.m., ninety-six Israeli F-15 and F-16 jets attacked nineteen missile batteries in the Bekaa. The Syrian air force rose to the defense, and within hours twenty-two MIG's were shot down and seven more damaged. At 3:50 p.m., a second wave of ninety-two aircraft struck. Seventeen of the nineteen batteries were hit and destroyed or damaged. In discussing the destruction of the batteries, Sharon called the raid the "turning point of the war." With the missiles gone, the Israelis had complete air superiority; and all Syrian and PLO forces were exposed to air attack. In a single afternoon, the Israeli air force had cleared the skies and neutralized the batteries. The successful air attacks over the Bekaa had two dimensions, each so significant in itself that both deserve detailed consideration. First, the Israelis destroyed over ninety Syrian aircraft in three major air battles, with the loss of no aircraft to themselves. Second, in the raid on the SAM missile sites, the Israelis destroyed antiaircraft batteries of a very sophisticated nature. Both raids were superb military achievements and had a marked effect on other military operations.

The Bekaa missile raid was a textbook example of modern-day electronic warfare. The Israelis used remote-piloted vehicles (RPV) to a considerable degree. RPV's are pilotless drone aircraft which can be used in various ways. The Israelis had both Mastif and the Scout RPV's designed and built in Israel. The RPV's were first flown over the battlefield, emitting dummy signals designed to confuse the missile-tracking radar into thinking real aircraft were attacking. That set the Syrians to tracking the RPV's. The Mastifs which were being tracked then relayed the tracking signals to another Scout RPV out of range of the missiles. The Scout picked up the signals and relayed them to E2C Hawkeye AWACS aircraft orbiting off the coast. The Israelis used the RPV's to "excite" the electronic battlefield, and the data gathered were analyzed by the E2C Hawkeye AWACS aircraft and also by Boeing 707 ECM aircraft.

The Israelis then overflew the area, using Elta and other jamming radars to blind the missile-tracking radars. Data gathered from these operations were analyzed and relayed to air-force and ground artillery units. The ground artillery units which had been moved into position around Hasbaiya and Koukaba began to shell the missile batteries and radar locations that were in gun range to destroy them or to force them to move. At the same time, F-4 fighter-bombers and F-16's overflew the area, dropping flares and chaff to confuse and disorient the missile-tracking radar further. Behind the chaff and flares came the attacking aircraft homing in on the radar-tracking vans. Using laser target designators (smart bombs), they fired antiradiation missiles, both Israeli-made and U.S.-made Shrike missiles, and destroyed seventeen of the nineteen SAM missile batteries. SAM-8 and -9 mobile versions were better camouflaged and were able to move. But while they were being moved, they were unable to fire and were easily destroyed by conventional bombs dropped by F-16's on normal bombing runs. At least one SAM-8 was destroyed by an RPV configured with an ammunition payload.[7] The successful use of electronic warfare in the Bekaa represented a remarkable technological achievement for the Israelis. While American, Soviet, British, and most NATO armies have electronic warfare capability, this was the first time the capability had been deployed as effectively by a modern power on the battlefield. The lessons gained are eagerly sought by American and NATO intelligence agencies in the hope of improving their offensive and defensive capability.

No less important to the ability of Israeli ground forces to sustain the tempo of attack in the eastern front was the air battle between Syrian and Israeli aircraft that occurred on the ninth and tenth of June. Again using RPV's, the IAF positioned them over three major airfields deep within Syria to gather data on when and how many aircraft were taking off from Syrian airfields. This data was transmitted immediately from the RPV's to the E2C command aircraft responsible for guiding IAF planes to their targets. The Israelis also exploited a significant technological weakness of the MIG-21 and MIG-23 fighters. Both aircraft have only nose and tail alert threat warning radar systems; neither has side warning systems or look-up and look-down systems. Taking advantage of this, the Israelis jammed Syrian ground control radar and the ground control communications net, making it impossible for ground controllers to coordinate air attacks against Israeli aircraft. At the same time, the Israelis' ability to coordinate their own attacks remained unaffected. In addition, the E2C aircraft guided IAF aircraft into positions where they could attack from the side of Syrian aircraft so the pilots would have no warning at all. This placed the Syrian aircraft at an enormous disadvantage. They could not detect from what direction or from what altitude Israeli aircraft were coming. With their own ground control communications jammed, they had no information from ground radar to tell them the direction and size of the Israeli attack. The Syrian ground controllers were unable to direct aircraft toward incoming Israeli planes. And finally, the Israelis were attacking from the sides of the Syrian jets, so the pilots got no warning from their on-board radar receivers.[8]

The Israelis took even greater advantage of their technological skill when they employed their own version of the Sparrow missile as well as the U.S.-supplied "E" and "F" versions. These missiles can attack at speeds of Mach 3.5 at ranges of fourteen and twenty-five miles. The Syrians were being tracked and hit by missiles fired by aircraft that were not only outside radar range but outside visual range as well. The use of Sidewinder missiles with "head-on" capability at closer ranges also gave the Israelis a firepower advantage. As a result of these technological innovations employed by a first-rate fighter force, ninety Syrian aircraft were downed in three major air battles. These ninety Syrian MIG-21 and -23 aircraft represented about 15 percent of the entire Syrian air-force fleet and almost 25 percent of its first-line fighter fleet.[9] The significance of the air battle cannot be overemphasized. With the missiles and aircraft gone, Syrian ground forces in defensive positions were now altogether at the mercy of Israeli aircraft.

The Israeli ground forces now undertook a rapid assault, striking at the center. The Israeli blow fell all along the line but especially in the center, around the Lake Qaraoun area, striking toward the Bekaa Valley. Israeli forces also began to move toward Joub Jannine by attacking on both sides of the lake. The advance on the west side was covered by Yossi Peled, whose force had gained and now controlled the heights of Jabaal Barouk. Within two days, Israeli forces moved rapidly through Syrian positions, securing their objectives and inflicting heavy casualties. Lev's force, which was positioned in the center awaiting the political decision to move, began to move after the missile raid and struck toward its objectives in the Bekaa Valley. The course of the war in the east had clearly turned in favor of the Israelis.

Thursday, June 10

In the west, IDF forces continued to mop up in Tyre and Sidon and had the situation under control. The advancing spearhead continued toward the outskirts of Beirut. Israeli air strikes in the east made her intentions clear, so Syrian tank and commando units of the 85th and 62nd brigades began to deploy

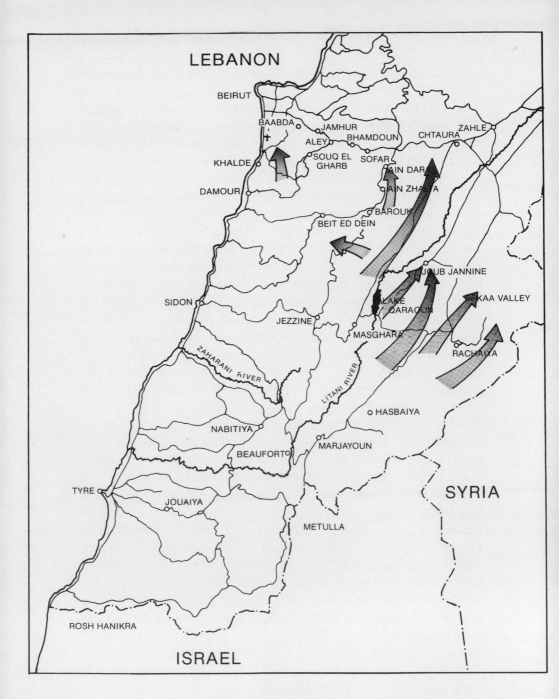

LEBANON

BEIRUT

BAABDA
JAMHUR
ALEY
BHAMDOUN
CHTAURA
ZAHLE

KHALDE
SOUQ EL
GHARB
SOFAR
AIN DARA

DAMOUR
AIN ZHALTA

BAROUK

BEIT ED DEIN

SIDON

JEZZINE
JOUB JANNINE

LAKE
QARAOUN
BEKAA VALLEY

MASGHARA
ZAHARANI RIVER
RACHAIYA

LITANI RIVER

HASBAIYA

NABITIYA

BEAUFORT
MARJAYOUN

SYRIA

TYRE

JOUAIYA

METULLA

ROSH HANIKRA

ISRAEL

Map 10. Israeli advance
June 10
Day 5

south of Beirut. The commando units of the 85th and 62nd infantry brigades began to fight alongside PLO units and the first Israeli clash with joint PLO–Syrian forces occurred in Kafr Sill, a suburb of the capital. This was a very difficult battle for the Israelis, and a significant number of casualties were taken. Kafr Sill would be the point of farthest IDF advance in the western zone for the time being.

In the center, reinforced IDF units renewed their attack on Ain Zhalta and captured it. The advance continued to move toward the outskirts of Ain Dara, a strongpoint overlooking the Beirut–Damascus highway. Although they did not enter the town, Israeli forces captured the heights overlooking it, and were in a position to take the town later. Near Ain Dara, along the road, IDF forces faced Syrian commando units supported by small tank detachments which took good advantage of the terrain. In an effort to break the logjam, the IDF called in air strikes and tank-killing helicopters. The helicopters took a comparatively high toll of Syrian tanks, their pilots taking full advantage of the terrain, which allows "nap of the earth" (NOE) approaches and flying into deep ravines below their targets. When helicopters approach through a ravine, the sound is diminished and they gain an element of surprise against their targets. By the end of the day, Israeli forces had deployed around Ain Dara and were positioned to strike at the highway.

In the east, pressure increased on Syrian forces all along the line as the Israelis struck along four main routes east toward Joub Jannine along both sides of the Qaraoun reservoir. The Syrians fought very well. They ambushed tanks with infantry armed with antitank weapons. The French Gazelle helicopter armed with the HOT missile was brought into play and proved deadly, striking terror in the hearts of IDF tankers. Once the valley floor was gained, however, IDF armor fanned out and the Syrians were forced to retreat. They retreated in disciplined fashion, giving as good as they got. These strategic withdrawals in the face of an advancing force earned the Syrians renewed respect from many Israeli commanders.

On the eastern approaches to the Bekaa, Sakel's troops captured the city of Rachaiya, moved through Kfar Quoq, and seized the outskirts of Yanta, only twenty-five kilometers from Damascus. The approach to Yanta was accomplished by link-

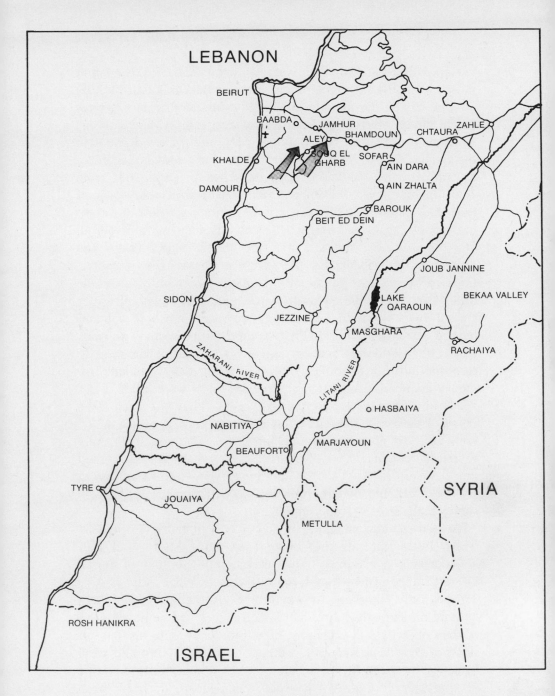

Map 11. Israeli advance
June 11
Day 6

ing up with a battalion of Lev's troops that had moved up into the area. In the meantime, Joub Jannine fell, and Peled's hold on the Jabaal Barouk Mountains guaranteed that the Syrians would not be able to reinforce on the west side of the reservoir.

At about this time, Israeli troops committed a major error in the Bekaa Valley, for which they paid dearly. An Israeli force of approximately battalion strength began to probe out from Joub Jannine, past the crossroads, toward the small town of Soultan Yaaquoub. Exercising proper military caution, the commander of the brigade sent his reconnaissance platoon out to determine whether the area was safe for the larger body. The platoon reported back that there were no significant concentrations of Syrian troops, and the brigade commander gave the order to continue the advance. A full battalion of Israeli armor started down the road toward Soultan Yaaquoub and was ambushed by Syrians thoroughly prepared with missiles, antitank guns, armor, and even artillery, which was poured on the Israelis, resulting in a considerable number of dead and wounded. Unofficial figures indicated that six to eight tanks were killed, damaged, or abandoned, and twenty-five to thirty-five men were killed or seriously injured, many of them burned as the M-60 tanks were set afire by the attacking forces. The Israelis brought in reinforcements and called artillery down on the ambushed unit in an effort to cover its withdrawal. After a battle of almost six hours, the Israeli force was able to extricate itself, but with significant loss of life and equipment.

Also in the eastern zone, another major air battle erupted, in which Israeli aircraft shot down twenty-five MIG's and four helicopters. Since Sunday, June 6, the total number of Syrian aircraft shot down by Israeli aircraft was sixty-five. The Israelis had lost only one plane to ground fire. By the end of the day's fighting on Thursday, June 10, Israeli forces had achieved most of their objectives in each zone of action. They were on the outskirts of Beirut, at Kafr Sill, although a strong Syrian and PLO force was between them and the city. All along the western line of approach, PLO forces had fled, been killed, or been taken prisoner. The camps around Tyre and Sidon, including Ein Hilwe, had been taken, with very small loss of life. In the center, Israeli forces were in command in the area around the southern Shouf as far north as Ain Dara and the Jabaal Barouk Mountains, which overlook and control the western half of the Bekaa Valley. In addition, the spearheads of the east force had pushed to Joub Jannine in the center of the Bekaa, and, on the eastern flank, as far out as Rachaiya, Kafr Quoq, and Yanta. The Syrians had withdrawn most of their forces northward and eastward in the Bekaa in a series of orderly withdrawals, still positioned in front of the Israelis, to protect the Beirut–Damascus highway. From a military perspective, the war in the south was almost over.

Friday, June 11

The Syrians and the Israelis announced that they had agreed to a cease-fire at noon of June 11 but that it would not include PLO forces. Just before the cease-fire took effect, however, the Syrians attempted to reinforce their forces in the Bekaa Valley by moving a column of T-72 tanks along the road from Chtaura down to Saghbine to counter the Israeli columns in the valley. This route was controlled by Yossi Peled's force on the heights of the Barouk ridge. As the Syrian column moved down the road, it was ambushed and nine T-72's were hit—not with Israeli tank cannon but with antitank missiles.

In the west, the town of Khalde fell on June 11, and there was frequent fighting with PLO and Syrian units as the IDF moved closer to the airport. Air strikes continued in Beirut against PLO positions. Skirmishes between Israeli tanks and Syrian commandos occurred very frequently and gradually the PLO's position grew worse. PLO troops were trapped in Beirut; the only way out was over the Beirut–Damascus highway. The eastern sector of the city was held by the Christian forces, and the IDF held the south. If the highway was cut, the PLO, along with the Syrian 85th brigade, would be trapped in the city. By June 11, Israeli forces were building up at Ain Dara and were ready to strike at the highway and trap the PLO.

Just before the cease-fire took effect, another major air battle occurred and eighteen more MIG's were shot down, bringing to 90 the total Syrian aircraft downed in the war. The Israelis announced that they would pursue a policy of "letaher," purifying the zone it occupied in southern Lebanon. Having driven

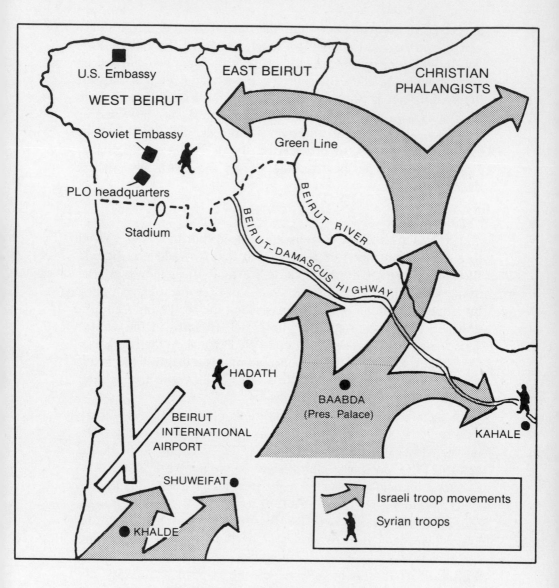

**Map 12. Renewed Israeli advance
June 13–14**

the PLO and the Syrians back, the Israelis would cleanse the area of any remaining PLO and destroy their infrastructure. Searches for arms caches began, as well as a systematic roundup of PLO suspects, who were arrested, screened, and taken to the Ansar detention camp on the Arnoun Heights. On Saturday, June 12, the cease-fire that had gone into effect between Syrian and Israeli forces the day before was extended to the PLO.

On Sunday, June 13, less than twelve hours after the cease-fire went into effect, it broke down, and very heavy fighting resumed around the city of Khalde, six miles south of Beirut on the coastal highway. Khalde was the last PLO position south of the airport. While the battle raged, an Israeli armored unit struck to the northeast in an attempt to bypass Khalde and make a run for Baabda. By Monday, June 14, the Syrians were deploying their units in the Khalde area—knowing that if Khalde fell there would be no major units between the Israelis and the airport. Syrian units of the 85th brigade in Beirut, and three commando battalions equipped with antitank missiles, moved south a few kilometers and took up a strong defensive position southwest of the airport to block any further Israeli advance. Units of Golani infantry and the 35th paratroop brigade under "Ya-Ya" Yarom —a battalion force, with tanks and APC's—attempted to flank these positions by moving off the road past Shuweifat up the narrow, winding, steep roads toward Baabda.

As the unit commander swung up the narrow road, he was ambushed by a commando battalion stationed at the roadside, waiting to meet the advance. The ambush occurred at very close range, sometimes as close as fifty meters, with the Syrians using rocket-propelled grenades and antitank missiles. The infantry dismounted and fought, calling in artillery at very close range. The battle raged up through Ain Aanoub and Souq el Gharb for fourteen hours, with considerable casualties on both sides. Unrelenting pressure from the IDF finally broke the Syrian positions on the road, and Israeli troops entered Baabda, a strategically important site because the presidential palace was there and it overlooked the airport and the three major refugee camps. Further, it could be used as a staging point to cut the Beirut–Damascus highway.

The IDF immediately reinforced the spearhead, so that by

midday on Monday, June 14, the force in Baabda was large enough for the Israelis to carry out further operations. Moreover, with the fall of Baabda, the Israelis could cut the highway very close to the city. IDF forces split into three small columns. One struck across the highway and entered the mountains northeast of the city in the Monte Verde area; one turned west toward Beirut and took up a blocking position in the steep hills; and one turned east toward Kahale, farther down the highway. By June 14, these were the most advanced IDF positions in the Beirut area. Most forces were still located south and east of the highway, in positions at Ain Dara and south, at Bhamdoun, Mansourieye, and Aley.

On Tuesday, June 15, Israel called for all Syrian troops to withdraw from Beirut east toward the Bekaa Valley and agreed to allow free passage if they would withdraw. Damascus refused and began to reinforce its units along the highway and a number of strongpoints north of the highway near Beirut. Both sides maneuvered into position for a major battle. To the south, the Israelis drove the PLO from Shuweifat, but no major confrontations occurred. By June 15, Israeli forces were confronting Syrian strongpoints, now reinforced by armor and artillery, all along the highway from Jamhur to Aley to the towns east, down to Ain Zhalta, where the center thrust of the Israeli advance had stalled.

Between Wednesday, June 16, and Tuesday, June 22, a number of artillery duels and small fire fights broke out between Syrian and Israeli forces, mostly in the Beirut area and on the highway north of the city, but there were no major confrontations. Both sides used the time to reinforce their units. The IDF used Baabda and Beit Meri in the Monte Verde region as major logistic and armored concentration points from which to launch further operations. To the south of the highway, Israeli forces continued to build up their reserves. The IDF had now firmly cut the Beirut–Damascus highway at Baabda, trapping the 85th Syrian brigade in Beirut. There was no longer any way out for either the Syrians or the PLO. On the other hand, there were no doubts that the Syrians would soon take action, nor did anyone believe that the Israelis would tolerate continued Syrian possession of most of the highway. It was only a question of time before the inevitable battle for the Beirut–Damascus highway would begin.

June 22–June 24
Battle for the Beirut–Damascus Highway

As long as the Israeli forces remained to the south of the highway and had to face strong Syrian forces commanding the towns on it and to the north, any Israeli plan to close the escape route of PLO and Syrian forces from Beirut would be in permanent jeopardy from a Syrian counterattack. Moreover, until the highway was clearly in Israeli hands, any future operations into Beirut itself would be subject to a Syrian flanking attack. A clear and safe transit to Christian East Beirut would be impossible, especially to the Monte Verde region, if Syrian forces remained in the area so close to East Beirut. The IDF decided, then, to clear the highway of major Syrian forces on Tuesday, June 22.

The Syrian forces consisted of two brigades augmented with ten commando battalions. They were also able to deploy 150 tanks in the battle and continually tried to reinforce with more. The attempts to reinforce were continually frustrated as the IAF flew interdiction missions over the battlefield, hitting Syrian strongpoints and disrupting any attempt to reinforce. In a single air strike, for example, the Israeli air force reported 130 "torches," a combination of tanks and vehicles destroyed. The Israeli aircraft attacked tank transporters, destroying the vehicles right on the transporters. At the same time, Israeli ground forces were able to reinforce without fear of attack from Syrian aircraft.

On Tuesday, June 22, the Israelis opened the offensive. The first move was to strike with very heavy air attacks, the only major air action in nine days, combined with artillery and armor. Fresh troops were rushed into position at Baabda, the major staging point for the offensive, and tanks fanned out from the town and headed east, paralleling the highway, and south of it into the Shouf hills. The objective was to drive the Syrians from the highway all the way back to Chtaura at the northern edge of the Bekaa. The Israelis attacked Syrian positions all along the highway, at Jamhur, Aley, and Bhamdoun. North of the high-

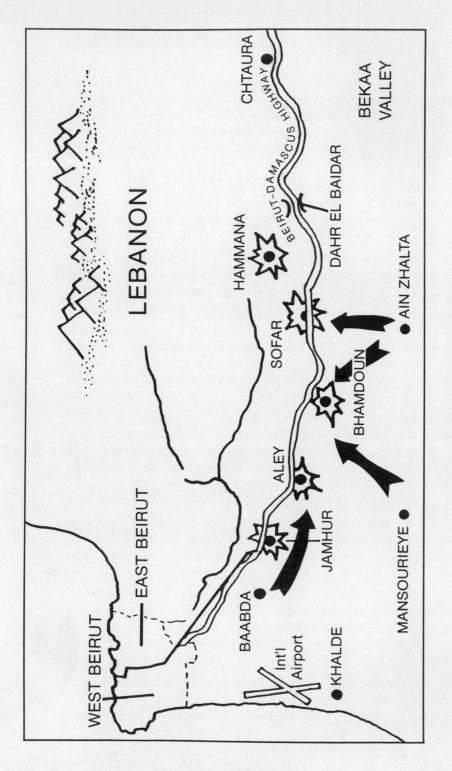

Map 13. Israeli–Syrian fighting
June 22–24

way, Syrian strongpoints at Abadia, Ras el Metn, and Hammana were hit by Israeli long-range artillery positioned in the Monte Verde hills. There was very heavy ground fighting on the highway and south of it; most of the air and artillery attacks were confined to targets north of the highway. By the end of the day, Israeli forces had made considerable headway, and the Syrians were clearly on the defensive, though putting up a stiff fight. At the request of the United States, the Israelis once again accepted a cease-fire and brought their assault to a stop.

On Wednesday, June 23, the cease-fire broke down and the Israelis resumed their attack on the highway strongpoints, using Ain Zhalta and Mansourieye as jumping-off points. The Israelis struck across the highway at Bhamdoun, trapping all Syrian forces between Bhamdoun and Jamhur. In one instance, at least ten Syrian tanks were captured intact as their crews abandoned them and surrendered. The Israelis took scores of prisoners as the Syrian defense began to crumble and for the first time in the war Syrian forces began to break and run. The battle for Aley was very heavy, however, probably because the troops defending it were Iranian volunteers sent by Khomeini to help their PLO Islamic brethren.

On Thursday, June 24, fighting continued farther down the highway. The Israelis attacked Sofar in strength, and began to shell the outskirts of Chtaura, at the northern mouth of the Bekaa and the headquarters of all Syrian forces there. If Chtaura fell, the road to Damascus would be wide open. Sofar, at 4,000 feet, was the last town of any size before Chtaura. Only the village of Dahr el Baidar, built on a mountain pass at 5,500 feet and overlooking Chtaura, remained unconquered. The Syrians fought hard to hold the pass at Dahr el Baidar; the Israeli advance halted. The Israelis seemed content to sit there and shell the outskirts of Chtaura; they were well aware that beyond Chtaura there were no major fortifications between them and Damascus. The Syrians understood that the loss of Chtaura would be a major blow and threw a number of additional units into the fighting. But the Israelis seemed content to allow the Syrians to hold Chtaura, and didn't press the attack but continued to harass with artillery fire.

By Friday, June 25, after four days of fighting, the Syrian positions on the highway and north of it were no longer tenable.

The Israelis controlled the highway from Baabda to Sofar and continued to shell Syrian positions at Dahr el Baidar and Chtaura. The Israeli forces allowed Syrian units in the Jamhur and Aley area to withdraw, as other Syrian forces north of the highway, elements of the 62nd brigade, also withdrew eastward toward Chtaura. For the first time since the battle around Shuweifat, Lebanese Christian militia entered Jamhur but did so without any resistance. The Israelis gradually pursued the Syrians and continued to harass them with artillery fire but stopped west of the Dahr el Baidar pass and went on shelling the approaches to Chtaura. In the Bekaa, the Syrians attempted to deploy a SAM-6 battery in the middle of the night, but Israeli intelligence noticed the movement and the missiles were destroyed by air attack. By the end of the day, a cease-fire was announced.

The IDF campaign in southern Lebanon came to a halt with the Israelis holding a final line extending from Beirut along the highway across the Bekaa Valley floor at Joub Jannine, anchoring at Kfar Quoq in the eastern end of the valley. In the south, the major territorial base of the PLO and its infrastructure were under Israeli military control. In addition, Syrian forces which had been in a position to guard any invasion of Syria through the Bekaa had been pushed back considerably closer to the Syrian border. The Syrians had also lost their hold on the Beirut–Damascus highway. Until Beirut had been dealt with, the success of the Israeli operation from a political as well as a military point of view could not be fully assessed.

ELUSIVE VICTORY

In a strict sense, the Israeli Defense Force certainly accomplished the limited military mission given to it at the outset of the war. It pushed back the PLO beyond artillery range of Israel's northern settlements and was systematically destroying the PLO infrastructure, which had taken more than a decade to create. Over a twelve-year period, the PLO had purchased vast amounts of weaponry, which it had stored throughout southern Lebanon. Following the campaign in the south, the Israeli army set about systematically searching for and uncovering arms caches. What they found exceeded even their wildest estimates.

According to IDF sources, the following equipment was taken by the Israelis in southern Lebanon.

- 4,670 tons of artillery and small-arms ammunition
- 1,077 combat vehicles, including 80 tanks of the T-34, T-55, and T-62 variety
- 28,304 small-arms weapons, rifles, and pistols
- 1,352 antitank weapons, including 1,099 rocket-propelled grenade launchers, 27 antitank missile launchers, 138 recoilless rifles, and 88 major antitank guns
- 202 mortars of various calibers, ranging from 81mm to 150mm
- 56 Katyusha rocket launchers of the 106mm and 122mm caliber
- 70 heavy-artillery pieces, ranging from 122mm to 130mm to 155mm
- 158 antiaircraft weapons, including 43 antiaircraft machine guns, 153 antiaircraft guns ranging from 20mm to 100mm
- 1,916 field communications pieces

What had taken the PLO almost twelve years to amass was now lost in less than twelve days. IDF estimates suggested that it would take the PLO at least two years to replace this weaponry.

Why did the PLO have such a vast cache of weapons? Enough matériel was captured in southern Lebanon to equip a military force at least five times as large as the force the PLO was able to field. Several possibilities suggest themselves. First, and probably most logical, is the fact that money was no object. The PLO was the richest guerrilla movement in history: it had some $90 million a year from Arab states. Moreover, its leaders often purchased weapons as a way of ingratiating themselves with other powers, notably the Soviet Union, and there is no doubt that some PLO members made a tidy commission on some of these sales. In addition, the stock of weapons was intended to increase PLO strength relative to other groups within the Lebanese state. This was especially important if, as the PLO had begun to believe, sooner or later there would be another showdown with the Christians. The PLO would be in a position to arm almost every Moslem in the country in the event of civil war with the Christians.

Whatever the reasons for the weaponry, its loss was a major blow. Yet the fact is that these weapons had not increased PLO military power. The PLO never had the manpower to employ the weapons, nor did it have the kind of training required to employ them in a conventional force configuration. The PLO remained essentially what it had always been: a small mobile guerrilla force quite incapable of mounting and sustaining conventional military operations against the Israelis or anyone else.

The IDF did strike an enormous blow against the infrastructure of the PLO. The Israelis captured the complete registration lists of the PLO in the south, so they were in a position to identify the "fighters" from the "trade unionists"—the administrative, clerical, and logistic personnel who had no direct combat role but who lived in the camps and were paid by the PLO. The Israelis systematically destroyed the bunkers and the arms caches and dynamited the homes of PLO leaders and military commanders in the camps. Camps in the south were systematically searched and generally flattened either during the war or after the war, when they were dynamited. Great regard was taken to hold down civilian casualties when these operations were carried out. By far the most important factor in destroying the infrastructure of the PLO was the roundup of almost ten thousand PLO suspects at the conclusion of hostilities; they were sent off to the detention camp at Ansar on the Arnoun Heights.

When the roundup began, no one in the IDF figured there would be so many suspects. Moreover, the roundup got completely out of hand and was routinely delegated to local commanders, who often exceeded their authority. As a result, children and old men and women were indiscriminately caught in its net. Often, suspects were rounded up on the pretext of having their identification cards checked. They were then screened against the list of PLO members which the IDF had captured. Those listed as leaders or in important positions were sent to Athlit prison in Israel for "serious interrogation." Others who appeared on the list or were suspected of being involved with the PLO were sent off to Ansar for detention and further processing.

The Ansar camp itself became a problem. A military intelligence advisor had suggested early on that, given the confessional nature of the Lebanese population, different camps be constructed, so that the PLO and other groups could be kept apart. This advice was rejected on the grounds that it would cost too much and require too much manpower. Also, no one believed that the detention of people at Ansar would involve such large numbers; in any case, it was felt that the processing would be swift and most people would be dealt with quickly. No one in the IDF foresaw the problem that Ansar would become.

In the early days, Ansar was a jerry-built barbed-wire enclosure situated on bare, windy, open terrain. It was too small and quickly became overcrowded, with less than adequate living conditions, water supplies, and sanitary facilities. After the siege of Beirut, when the Israelis could relax their military hold on the country, conditions were considerably improved. Interviews with scores of individuals who had been in the Ansar camp, as well as with Israeli prison guards, indicate that the Israelis deliberately set up the mukhtar system, creating communities of about two hundred. All contact between communities was through the head of the community, the mukhtar; food supplies were channeled through the mukhtar as well. The mukhtar system is common in the Middle East, and the Israelis adopted it to avoid aggravating confessional hatreds; the prisoners were allowed to govern themselves, prepare their own food, and punish their own. The result, however, was that the PLO came to dominate the camp's informal social structure and thus were able to extract tribute from non-PLO members. Brutal PLO discipline led to disturbances and riots by anti-PLO communities that demanded that the Israelis become more involved in the day-to-day operation of the camp to protect them from PLO retribution.

The central problem at Ansar was how to separate the PLO fighters from the larger population. By June 1983, there were 9,040 suspects being detained at Ansar; only 2,997 had been processed and released. Many religious communities in Lebanon wanted their people, whom they claimed were being brutalized by the PLO, to be released quickly. Their leaders complained to the Israelis that they had no right or purpose in holding them any longer.

In addition to the PLO, the suspected PLO, and innocent individuals rounded up, the Israelis identified about 1,800 foreign "mercenaries"; non-Arabs—Palestinians, Germans, Africans, among others—who had come to the PLO camps to be trained. They were never, in any sense, a serious fighting arm of the PLO, although clearly some of them had been involved in terrorist activities at home. The difficulty was in getting their governments to accept them, thus admitting that their nationals had been working for the PLO. In addition, many of the mercenaries realized that if they returned to their countries they would be executed. The problem was solved by placing them under Red Cross care and providing them with a plane ticket to wherever they wanted to go.

The Israelis still have problems with detainees who have no place to go or can't go home for fear of vengeance. Further, what are the Israelis to do with the real PLO fighters? Are they to be sent to prison or freed? It is a problem that the Israelis had not thought through at the beginning of the war and are now stuck with. Even if the Israelis were to leave Lebanon tomorrow, what would they do with almost seven thousand individuals still in the Ansar camp?

Although these problems exist, there is no doubt that the Israeli Defense Force has systematically destroyed the military, economic, political, and social infrastructure of the PLO in southern Lebanon. The military goals of the war have been achieved. However, if we ask to what degree PLO fighters— that is, actual combat-unit leaders, field commanders, and political leaders—were killed or captured, then it is clear that the Israeli operation in southern Lebanon was something less than a total success. If the object of the war was to kill and capture PLO fighters, then it could really be said to have been something of a military failure.

Rafael "Rafe" Eitan, the Prime Minister's advisor on terrorism,[10] in an interview conducted in Tel Aviv noted that the IDF estimated that there were 15,000 PLO fighters in southern Lebanon, including Beirut. Approximately 9,000 PLO fighters were deployed in the southern theater up to the beginning of the siege of Beirut. Unofficial figures obtained from Mossad and Shin Bet suggest that approximately one thousand PLO were captured or killed in the southern campaign, certainly no more than 1,400. In addition, about 1,700 PLO fighters have been screened out of the general population of the Ansar camp. Together, somewhere between 2,700 and 3,000 PLO in the south were either killed or captured. Simple subtraction suggests that of the 9,000 PLO deployed in the south, between 6,000 and 7,000 actually escaped capture and made their way either to Beirut or to the Bekaa Valley behind Syrian lines, where they were able to conduct operations throughout the siege of Beirut. The Israeli military operation simply failed to kill or capture a significant number of the PLO fighters deployed south of Beirut. Almost two-thirds of the PLO in the southern theater of operations managed to escape. Israeli special intelligence operations also failed to kill or capture any member of the PLO's top political and military leadership.

At least four special counterterror operational units are maintained by the Israelis. Two of these are located within the Israeli Defense Force itself and therefore have a military cast. One is run by Mossad, the Israeli equivalent of the CIA, and the other is run by Shin Bet, Israel's equivalent of the FBI. The tasks of these teams, the members of which speak Arabic, is counterterror—assassination, kidnapping, and the disruption of enemy operations. In principle, such teams operate in advance of military operations. They are trained to infiltrate enemy lines, assassinate top PLO leaders, kidnap them, or otherwise disrupt PLO activities. Given that none of the top seventeen PLO leaders on the Israeli "most-wanted list" was either killed or captured, and given, as well, that few of the second-echelon military commanders or political leaders were captured or killed, the question might be asked: what happened to the special operation teams and why did they fail?

The answer seems to be that these teams were simply not used during the war, and the reason can be traced to the decision by the Israeli political leadership to mount the invasion of Lebanon as quickly as it did. The decision to invade was made on Saturday evening, and Israeli forces were given until twelve o'clock the next day to begin the invasion. It was impossible to put special operation teams on the ground in time. These teams would have had to be placed a few days in advance of the invasion so they could position themselves to disrupt the PLO. However, the teams could not be deployed effectively on such short notice. The two special military teams saw limited action in the siege of Beirut, but they were used as shock squads rather than as special operations squads. Mossad had had a unit in

Beirut since 1975, where it had developed close contacts with the Christian Phalange. Mossad apparently had a rather high opinion of the Phalangists which was not shared either by Shin Bet or by military intelligence—a fact that came out quite clearly during the investigation of the Sabra and Shatila massacre. There was some suggestion that Mossad had developed such a high opinion of the Phalangists that special team operations were dispensed with in favor of using the Christians instead. Once the war was over, Shin Bet did mount a number of successful search-and-destroy campaigns in the liberated areas, where it hunted down and captured a number of PLO suspects. However, the explosion on November 12 which destroyed the military head-quarters in Tyre and killed some ninety military personnel also killed twelve of Shin Bet's best agents in southern Lebanon and reduced its ability to carry out special operations.

FIGHTING ABILITY: PLO AND SYRIANS

The PLO generally did not fight well; in most cases, it did not fight at all but withdrew before the Israeli advance. In the early days of the war, the PLO apparently believed that the Israeli advance would be like Operation Litani; that is to say, self-limiting. Rather than stand and fight, most Palestinian units which were cohesive chose to withdraw up the coast. Some even hid their weapons and tried to mingle with the population in Sidon and Tyre to avoid capture. In the Achiye region and in Fatahland, where the units were fairly well integrated and sup-ported by Syrian units, the PLO did put up resistance. But once it became clear that the Israeli advance had the force and power to continue, PLO units in the east withdrew along with the Syrian units in the face of Israeli pressure. In the center, mostly around Nabitiya and Beaufort Castle and up to Jezzine, the PLO had very little alternative except to withdraw or surrender. Most PLO units, after firing a few rounds to hold their positions, simply fled for fear of being cut off.

In the coastal region, PLO units in Tyre and Sidon used ambush tactics to inflict significant but not debilitating casual-ties on the Israeli forces. Both in the refugee camp at Rachidiya outside Tyre and in the Ein Hilwe camp in Sidon, the PLO stood and fought fairly well. In both instances, the number of PLO fighters did not exceed a hundred and fifty. They openly used civilians as shields and often fought from hospitals or ambushed from civilian areas. By far the overwhelming majority in Sidon and Tyre chose not to fight, instead putting their families in their Mercedes automobiles and fleeing north to Beirut or along the road to Jezzine and the Bekaa Valley. For the most part, those who stayed behind and fought in the camps were either single men without families or young boys and teenagers. Clearly, the major military commanders fled.

According to Amos Gilboa, the Deputy Director of Military Intelligence, the PLO did not exploit the terrain as well as they could have. This is certainly true with regard to the number of ambushes against Israeli forces moving on the narrow road from the border to Tyre and Sidon. There were ambushes, but not in significant numbers or sufficient intensity to slow the Israeli advance. Within the built-up areas, in the camps and cities, the PLO were able to fight from house to house, but the obstacles confronted by the IDF were essentially minor. "What we faced in the populated built-up areas," Gilboa has pointed out, "were minor tactical obstacles that were easily overcome."[11] The IDF, moreover, could have overcome these obstacles, especially in the Rachidiya and Ein Hilwe camps, much more rapidly by simply concentrating artillery and tank fire on the houses or at least using satchel charges, fire, and grenades as its troops went into doorways. But Israeli troops in these areas were under strong restrictions to minimize fire and civilian casualties. As a consequence, the PLO were often able to resist much longer than would normally have been the case.

In contrast to the PLO, Syrian units fought very well, especially in the east. There, Syrian units made maximum use of the terrain. Often, they broke up tank units into two or three tank elements and deployed them with antitank teams and commando units armed with rocket-propelled grenades and missiles. These units would then deploy along the route of advance in well-covered positions and use the terrain to maximum advantage by ambushing Israeli units coming up the narrow, winding roads. They would carry out an ambush, stay and fight until it was clear that they would be overwhelmed, and then conduct an orderly withdrawal to the next ambush point. The Syrians made maximum use of their tanks and commando infantry by reconfiguring their units to each situation.

Syrian units in most instances did not break or run as they had in past wars. It is true that some surrendered in the battle for the Beirut–Damascus highway when it became clear that their position was untenable. In general, though, Syrian forces conducted themselves well, their morale appeared high, their discipline excellent, and they demonstrated their ability to conduct orderly withdrawals while keeping their forces intact. Military analysts agree that it is most difficult to conduct an orderly withdrawal while keeping one's units intact. The Syrians did this consistently around the Lake Qaraoun area, on the road to Rachaiya, and up through Joub Jannine. In 1973, the Syrians were disappointed by the performance of their conscript infantry and since that time have moved away from regular conscript infantry, recruiting their best soldiers into elite commando infantry, whose morale, discipline, and reliability are very high. In the war with Israel in Lebanon this change paid off.

In the end, the destruction of the SAM missile batteries and the loss of sixty-two aircraft on June 9 and 10 meant that the Syrian forces in Lebanon, outnumbered and outmaneuvered, had to operate with a total lack of air cover that placed them at the mercy of Israeli aircraft and helicopter attacks. Moreover, Syrian forces in the Bekaa and along the Damascus highway couldn't reinforce their units without being spotted by Israeli intelligence and attacked on the way to the battle area. On a number of occasions, Syrian attempts to reinforce resulted in large numbers of tanks and APC's being destroyed while still on their transporters. Ariel Sharon was quite correct in calling the destruction of Syrian missiles the turning point of the war. After that point, the war against the Syrians was a foregone conclusion, as their forces were not only outnumbered but naked to their enemies from the sky.

The equipment and manpower losses of the Syrian forces in Lebanon, although substantial, were not crippling. In fact, most of the Syrian divisions were able to escape relatively intact with a goodly amount of their equipment. In terms of manpower, for example, less than 10 percent of total Syrian manpower deployed was killed or wounded. Units are normally considered combat ineffective when 30 percent of their troops are killed or wounded. The Syrians lost 1,200 dead, approximately 3,000 wounded, and 296 taken prisoner, out of a total force of 30,000. Equipment losses included 334 tanks (200 T-62's, 125 T-54's, 9 T-72's), of which about 60 were repairable. The Syrian army also lost 140 armored personnel carriers, 90 antitank guns, 75 to 80 artillery pieces, 90 aircraft, 6 Gazelle antitank helicopters, and 19 SAM-3, -6, and -8 missile batteries. Taken together, the damage done to the Syrian forces was more than enough to bring about military defeat. But by no stretch of the imagination can it be said that the Syrian divisions had been ground up and destroyed as in earlier conflicts with Israel. Quite the contrary. Israeli intelligence and field commanders make the point that the Syrians' performance in this war, especially their ability to integrate combined-arms teams, bring to bear the few helicopters they had, and maintain the soldiers' morale and discipline, was probably the best the Israelis had seen on the part of an Arab army. Both intelligence officers and military men have a new albeit grudging respect for the Syrian soldier and his leaders.

CIVILIAN CASUALTIES

One of the more urgent questions which emerged from press accounts concerned the number of civilians killed and wounded in the southern campaign, as well as estimates of the number of homeless and the damage done to civilian property. Estimates vary, but certainly the PLO figures of 10,000 dead and 600,000 homeless in the south is ridiculous. These estimates, provided by the Palestinian Red Crescent, are questionable because the head of that organization is Fahti Arafat, Yasir Arafat's brother. The PLO branch of the Red Crescent is clearly the handmaiden of the PLO's major political organization and is well financed and well able to conduct its own propaganda.

The *Time* Jerusalem bureau, which surveyed hospitals and battlefields and made spot checks in the south, suggests that the number of dead in the south was between 3,000 and 5,000, with 70,000 to 80,000 individuals left homeless.[12] Another estimate, offered by the Speaker of the Israeli Knesset, gave 800 dead and 40,000 homeless.[13] It is very difficult, if not impossible, to arrive at exact numbers of civilians killed or made homeless, but it certainly seems that the initial reports circulated by the PLO and so widely accepted in the press are simply too large.

According to official Israeli figures, there were 56 civilian dead and 95 wounded in the Tyre area, while in the area of Sidon 265 civilians were killed and 1,000 wounded. In the area of Nabitiya, Israeli sources reported 10 civilian dead and 15 hospitalized. The Israelis estimate that the homeless may number anywhere between 30,000 and 40,000, but this includes many who returned to the south and their homes once the PLO left.[14] One of the paradoxes of the war is that there are now more people residing in southern Lebanon, many of them returnees, than when the war started. One example is Damour, which was a Christian city of 40,000 before it was totally destroyed by the PLO in the civil war. The city was abandoned, but with the PLO gone, approximately 20,000 of the Christians who had left in 1976 have returned. Thus, in estimating the number of homeless, one has to be careful to identify those who are homeless as a consequence of the war and those who are homeless because they have returned to their former homes, where they are having difficulty finding adequate shelter.

Reports by fairly unbiased sources suggest that the initial estimates were exaggerated. Six American generals, all experienced combat officers, visited the war zone immediately after the fighting. Their report noted that the Israelis had taken great care to minimize civilian casualties and that the damage was relatively light. They also noted, and this was confirmed by my own experience, that much of the damage, especially in Sidon and Tyre, is old damage unrepaired from the civil war. Some damage is a consequence of fighting between confessional militias since the civil war.[15] In addition, the well-respected military historian T. N. Dupuy, who witnessed the bombing of Beirut, suggests that the reports in the press of actual fighting and bombing were grossly exaggerated, perhaps tenfold or a hundredfold on any given day.[16] Further, the Mayor of Beirut, in a press report in *An Nahar*, a respected Mideast newspaper published in Beirut, said that only 25 percent of the damage done to Lebanon was a consequence of the recent war. Most of it, he noted, was left over from the civil war; for a period of six years the

Lebanese government had been powerless to rebuild its water, lighting, and sewage systems and repair buildings and highways.[17]

The very nature of the war made it unlikely that large numbers of civilian casualties would result. In the first place, the IDF advance in the south was fairly rapid. Moreover, the initial stages of the advance bypassed the major cities of Tyre and Sidon; and its first major engagement in an urban battlefield took place in Damour, which was not a populated city but a stronghold of the PFLP.

When the IDF entered Tyre and Sidon, it took great care to avoid damage to civilian buildings and harm to civilians. The Israelis did not enter with massive military force. Rather, they had instructions to treat conflicts in the PLO camps as if they were hostage situations, to avoid killing civilians. For example, prior to the Israeli entrance into the major cities, maps and leaflets outlining safe areas were dropped to civilians, asking them to take refuge there. In Sidon, thousands left the city and moved to the beach on the northern outskirts, which was a totally protected zone. In addition, Israeli teams within the camps used loudspeakers to call for the surrender of Palestinian terrorists and in some instances even allowed them to escape. Israeli troops were given strict instructions not to fire until fired upon, and they were not allowed to enter houses firing. No use of satchel charges and grenades in houses as a way of flushing out suspected terrorists was allowed. Restrictions were also placed on the use of armor and artillery in certain areas. Although tanks were allowed to fire at specific targets after they had been fired upon at point-blank range, there was no use of heavy artillery shelling, or even heavy aerial bombardment, that could have taken a heavy toll of civilians. There were additional restrictions. The PLO often used civilians as shields, and fighting among a civilian population favored the tactic of shooting from the window of one house and then withdrawing to another. In many of these houses there were civilians. In the Ein Hilwe camp, the PLO staged military operations out of hospitals and put guns on their roofs. In most instances, the Israelis refrained from hitting these hospitals. Thus, when the Israelis moved into highly urbanized areas, more than reasonable care was taken to minimize the number of civilian dead and wounded, a policy that seems to have succeeded. In addition, with most of Israeli casualties being evacuated by helicopters, medical battalions were often free of the need to care for their own wounded, especially in the western zone. These battalions were turned to the task of helping out civilians who had been hurt or wounded, as well as wounded PLO fighters.

Another reason why the number of civilian casualties in the south was relatively low had to do with where the war was fought. In many areas, there was no significant civilian population at all. In the first days of the war, in the UNIFIL zone, there was no civilian population to speak of. On the assault on Jouaiya, which came on the second day of the war, the PLO dropped their weapons and melted through Israeli lines, putting up no significant resistance. In the center, around Achiye, a connecting belt of firing points and observation posts anchored at Beaufort Castle, there was no civilian population of any size. The same is true of Fatahland, although Hasbaiya and Koukaba are significantly large villages, but neither suffered any damage. In Hasbaiya the residents welcomed the Israelis with open arms, and in Koukaba the PLO did not put up a significant defense. In Nabitiya, the town itself was spared. Some civilians were killed, but the number was exceedingly small. The town's military governor, a reserve officer who is a professor, told me in our conversations that the Israeli officials were continually asking him for the number of civilian dead. Since he couldn't find any civilian dead, he made up the number of ten dead to satisfy the questions. But, he said, he had found no civilian dead at all. In the area between the Litani and Zaharani Rivers there are some seventy villages. But the IDF advance through this area was very rapid and met no serious opposition.

The war in the east against the Syrians was fought mostly as a classic military campaign, with few civilians in the battle area or used as shields. The Syrians had deployed outside the small villages and towns, using the terrain to maximum advantage. To be sure, battles were fought around a number of small villages, but in general the Syrian troops did not defend these towns from inside but occupied strategic strongpoints on their outskirts. As the Israeli advance moved forward, the Syrians withdrew in an organized military fashion. Thus, even in the eastern zone there were no considerable numbers of civilians in the battle area.

The same logic applies to damage. Since the IDF did not fight in built-up areas, except in the western zone, damage was fairly limited. Sidon and Tyre suffered the most. The commander in Sidon estimated that 30 percent of the buildings were destroyed, and a few hundred more damaged. The refugee camps were severely damaged. An assessment of the damage in Tyre by a Lebanese engineering concern indicated that 310 residences were destroyed and another 250 seriously damaged, a total loss of $70 million. On the other hand, only a month before this war, a battle broke out in the city of Sidon between the PLO and the Amal Moslem militia which caused an estimated $20 million in damage. One reason for the damage in the refugee camps and built-up areas was the curse of butane-gas cylinders. The most common fuel in Lebanon is butane, and it is stored in individual cylinders. Most houses have a number of containers, sometimes eight to ten, stored in the premises as a reserve supply. Often, when one of these containers was struck by a bullet or shrapnel, it exploded and set off the others, causing horrible burns and many secondary explosions.

On balance, then, though all estimates of actual dead and wounded and of damage are suspect, it seems likely that the war in the south did not result in a high number of civilian deaths. The number killed was probably under a thousand, and the number wounded probably did not exceed four thousand.

One thing seems clear, and that is that the Israelis lost the propaganda war. The PLO was much more adroit at getting out its side of the story to the world press and was much more effective in allowing media personnel into their area to photograph scenes which tended to support their point of view. The Israelis followed their traditional penchant for military censorship to protect their forces. As a consequence, a running war seemed to develop between media personnel and the Israelis which worked to the benefit of the PLO by substantiating in the minds of some media observers the PLO claims of thousands of dead and wounded.

CONCLUSION

There is little doubt that the Israelis achieved the military objectives they set for themselves in the south. The PLO were driven beyond artillery range of Israel's northern settlements, and its infrastructure was in the process of being destroyed. On the other hand, the PLO as a military force remained relatively intact, and despite the seizure of large arms caches, the amount of arms and ammunition in the positions the PLO held in Beirut and in the Bekaa Valley was significant enough for it to remain a credible military force. The Israelis had solved only half the problem. Intelligence officers were acutely aware that if the IDF withdrew from the gates of Beirut to the border, it would be a matter of months before the PLO reestablished itself in southern Lebanon. The Israelis had had a similar experience in the 1978 Litani campaign and were no longer disposed to trust UN assurances that it would not happen again. Their experience indicated that the UN forces were simply inadequate to the task of sustaining a *cordon sanitaire* in southern Lebanon that would satisfy Israel's security requirements.

Israeli forces were at the gates of Beirut. The military problem had been solved, but political goals, which at the start of the war had been secondary, now became paramount. By the beginning of August, the Israelis faced new dilemmas. The prospect of achieving their political goals was considerably diminished despite their military victory, and they were caught in a vise: if they withdrew, PLO forces would come back into the south; if they went into Beirut, they risked serious criticism at home and in much of the rest of the world as well.

4

The Siege of Beirut

The Israelis generally had been successful in the southern campaign. Their forces were at the outskirts of Beirut, but they faced the possibility of having to deal with PLO forces entrenched in the city. Furthermore, the Israeli government's war aims had changed significantly. Having achieved the minimum goal of driving the PLO back beyond artillery range and destroying its infrastructure, the Israeli government began to define new political goals to justify the war. The political dynamic got out of hand and broadened the goals to include a number of objectives which at the time seemed to be attainable. Among these was the normalization of relations with the Lebanese, the establishment of a central Lebanese government capable of extending its control over all the ethno-religious factions within the country, the removal of Syrian forces from Lebanon, and, finally, the extirpation or complete "expulsion" of the PLO from Beirut, a goal that was commonly referred to as "chopping the head off the snake."

The difficulty in achieving these political goals was compounded by two serious failures in the war plan as it developed on the battlefield. The first was the fact that most of the PLO fighters and commanders had escaped the grasp of the IDF and had fled either to Syrian lines in the Bekaa or to Beirut, where they joined an estimated six to seven thousand of their fellow PLO fighters already well dug in and prepared for a siege.

The PLO in fact was still very much intact and very well entrenched militarily and politically in Beirut. Over the years, it had taken great pains to establish a close relationship with other leftist militias, many of which were in the city and were prepared to fight in the service of the PLO. From the Israeli perspective, the PLO in Beirut had to be dealt with. Nobody in the Israeli cabinet wanted to face having invaded Lebanon and lost a considerable number of Israeli lives, only to have it all go for nothing if the PLO were left intact.

The second major difficulty confronting IDF planners was that the Israelis had almost no experience in urban fighting. Their experience was so limited that during the cease-fires during the siege of Beirut, Israeli paratroop forces practiced urban fighting in the captured town of Damour. The IDF had neither the strategy nor the experience nor the configuration of forces to fight and sustain a house-to-house campaign in Beirut. One of the classic shortcomings of the Israeli ground-force structure is its lack of sufficient infantry to conduct sustained operations. In terms of its force configuration, the Israelis were not prepared to fight a long house-to-house campaign in Beirut. Even more important, it was highly unlikely that the Israeli public would tolerate the high casualties that almost certainly would result from a long-drawn-out battle within the city. In addition, there was the increasing pressure on Israel from outside forces, most notably from the United States and other Western powers, to stop the fighting and not invade Beirut. So the Israelis found themselves at the gates of Beirut confronted with a greater problem than they had faced when the invasion began two weeks before.

One argument that Defense Minister Sharon had used to sell the concept of a wider war to the cabinet and to the Israeli public was that it would be possible to destroy the PLO even in Beirut if it became necessary, and at minimal cost. To achieve this, Sharon had to rely on a "cat's paw," someone who would be willing and able to do the job of driving the PLO from the camps of Beirut. Sharon's "cat's paw" was the Christian Phalangist army commanded by Bashir Gemayel. If the Phalangists, for whatever reason, refused to participate in the siege, Sharon would find one of the rationales for conducting the war completely eroded. Without a non-Israeli force to go into Beirut and absorb the human costs of driving out the PLO, even Sharon understood that the cabinet, the parliament, and the public would not sit still for a prolonged siege in which large numbers of IDF troops were killed. In short, the use of Phalangist forces in Beirut was crucial to the success of Sharon's plan to bring the war to a successful conclusion.

PHALANGISTS

The Phalangists are the fighting arm of the Christian Katibe Party. It is a conglomeration of various Christian groups hammered into an effective fighting force by the leadership of Bashir Gemayel. Originally, the Christian movement was dominated by three major families: the Chamouns, the Franjiehs, and the Gemayels. Each had its own private army and politico-economic organization. In addition, each had considerable income from business enterprises, some legal, many illegal. The situation was somewhat akin to the Mafia "families" that ruled New York from the forties to the sixties, each with its own army, its own leadership, deriving income from legal and illegal activities. In the early seventies, prior to the civil war, a series of Mafia-like wars broke out among the major Christian families in Lebanon for control of the Christian movement and to achieve political dominance over the state itself. The three Christian families were forcibly united under the leadership of Bashir Gemayel, who guided his family's fortunes through these wars; smaller groups within the Christian movement also generally gave their loyalty to Bashir Gemayel. Initially, this loyalty was tentative, but it was forged strong in the crucible of the 1975–76 civil wars, in which Bashir (which means lord in Lebanese) proved himself a tough and able commander. One important aspect of the relationship was the strong, personal, almost feudal attachment to Bashir Gemayel; this loyalty was difficult to shift to his older brother, Amin, when Bashir was killed in 1982.

Since 1976, close relationships had been established between the Christian movement and Israeli intelligence. Israeli military intelligence and Mossad had both established relationships with the Phalange, but Mossad established the closest ties, which persist to this day. Israeli support of the Phalange involved the training of Christian militiamen. Beginning in 1976 and continuing after the civil war, some 250 Christian officers and one thousand NCO's were trained by the IDF in special training camps in the Negev Desert in Israel. The Christian militia (now known as the Lebanese forces, not to be confused with the Lebanese army), absorbed by the Christian movement during the civil war, is a considerable military force. Interviews with political and military commanders of the Christian forces in 1982 indicate that the force has some 12,000 full-time, paid soldiers. This force, they claim, could be expanded to some 42,000 with the addition of its territorial reserve, essentially armed with small arms and deployed by automobile. Israeli intelligence sources indicate that the Christian force is not that large. The Christians, they feel, could probably mount somewhere between 8,000 and 10,000 regular-force troops, and with their territorial militia, which is highly unorganized, could probably field another fifteen or eighteen thousand. In any case, the Christian Phalange is a significant military force, armed with modern equipment and well trained. In addition, the Christian forces had a great deal of experience in urban warfare in Beirut during the civil war. Most of their commanders knew West Beirut and the camps very well. It was this force that the Israeli political leadership, or at least the Sharon faction within the government, counted on to expel the PLO from Beirut.

As Israeli forces approached the gates of Beirut, it became clear that a substantial PLO military and political organization was entrenched in the city. Israeli pressure on the Christians to engage in military action against the PLO began to increase. After a series of meetings, which included Sharon and Bashir Gemayel, it became apparent that the Christians were not about to be drawn into the fighting for the city. Throughout the war, and even before, they had provided some intelligence and logistical support for deep-penetration operations, but when forced to decide whether to commit their forces to drive the PLO out of Beirut, the Christian militia refused.

Their reasoning was simple and, from the point of view of Gemayel, very sound. Bashir Gemayel indicated several times in meetings with Sharon that, given the presence of some ninety private armies in Lebanon, most of them Moslem and Druse, and several of them sworn enemies of the Christians, a Christian attack on the PLO would galvanize the ninety private militias into opposition to the Christians and drive them into the arms of the PLO. This would make the military task, if not impossible, then certainly more difficult than the Christians could manage. Further, Gemayel was expecting to dominate the Lebanese political scene after the war. If he took pro-Israeli action which moved the rival militias into opposition against his forces, not only would their political dominance be threatened but their physical survival as well. The Christians recognized as clearly as the Israelis that any close collaboration with the IDF against a Moslem force in Beirut would make it impossible for the Christians to emerge as the dominant power. If they helped the IDF, the Christians would appear to be collaborating with a foreign occupying military power. This would undercut any claim that they truly represented Lebanese interests.

The game had changed. The Israelis were playing for the destruction of the PLO in Beirut and the establishment of some relationship with Lebanon that would guarantee their security. From the Christian point of view, the real game would begin after the PLO had been destroyed or had been forced out of Beirut. They saw it to their advantage not to help in any significant way. The Christian forces gambled that the Israelis could not leave the job unfinished and would sooner or later, with or without Christian help, deal with the PLO trapped in Beirut. Once that situation was resolved, the Christians and their militia would be in a dominant position to maneuver for legitimate control of Lebanon by seizing the major elective offices. Despite great pressure, including a number of personal pleas from Prime Minister Begin as well as Defense Minister Sharon, Bashir Gemayel refused to commit the Phalangists to battle the PLO in the streets of Beirut.

Sharon's hawks within the Israeli cabinet were on the horns of a dilemma. If the Israelis did not destroy the PLO, the war would appear to have been pointless, and the reaction at home might easily drive the Begin regime from power. Certainly, it would destabilize Sharon's position within the cabinet and could easily result in his dismissal. On the other hand, if the Israelis did undertake an attack on Beirut, without experience in urban warfare and without proper forces, the risk of high casualties and the prospect of a battle lasting several weeks would certainly increase the pressure on Israel from the United States and other Western nations. Moreover, high casualties might enrage public opinion, which could have the same result of driving the government from power or at least ousting Sharon and the hawks. The decision was made to remove the PLO from Beirut without engaging in direct battle. The Israelis would not try to take the city block by block; they would not fight within the city against an enemy to which they would have to concede a very great advantage. Instead, the IDF would lay siege to Beirut and force the PLO either to leave or to face the prospect of being destroyed where they stood.

PLO POSITION

From a military perspective, the PLO was not in a bad position at all. It had kept its command structure intact, and many of its heavy weapons were in Beirut, as were most of its major political and field commanders. The failure of the IDF to kill or capture large numbers of PLO fighters in the south meant that the PLO could marshal a force of between 12,000 and 14,000 soldiers. This force was augmented by what was left of a full brigade of Syrian soldiers stationed in the city. In addition, a number of Lebanese leftist militias and private armies that were also trapped in Beirut could be relied on to fight alongside the PLO. Equally important, the PLO knew the terrain and the camps far better than the Israelis did. The civilian neighborhoods were home to the PLO and had been for ten years. The major camps at Bourj el Barajneh, Sabra, and Shatila were honeycombed with strongpoints and ambush points, and a number of trenches and tunnels were dug that connected these points and the major PLO headquarters in the Fakhani district in West Beirut. This permitted considerable movement of forces and flexible logistics within the battle zone. A further advantage to the PLO was the presence of a relatively large civilian population in the battle area. This population, certainly friendly to the PLO, could be employed in several ways. It could be used as a shield behind which the PLO could conduct ambush operations. And whenever civilians were killed by Israeli air or artillery attack, the propaganda machine of the PLO could go into operation to undercut the moral position of the Israelis. Perhaps more important, the presence of large numbers of civilians led the PLO to gamble that the Israelis would not use their full air and artillery forces against the camps or even against military positions integrated within the camps. The experience of the PLO in the south, especially in Sidon and Tyre, indicated that the Israelis would limit their firepower against military targets whenever there were large numbers of civilians in the area.

The PLO units as small, lightly armed, and highly mobile groups were perfectly configured to fight an urban guerrilla war. Indeed, they were far better configured than the Israelis for urban war. Add to this the fact that the PLO stores of food, water, medical supplies, and ammunition, according to Israeli intelligence, were sufficient to sustain their forces for six months. The reduction of PLO forces in Beirut and their attendant expulsion would not be an easy task. If the Israelis tried to take the city house by house, they would pay dearly and would concede many military advantages to the defending force.

From a political perspective, the PLO was also in a relatively good position. Although it had taken some losses in the south, those losses had not significantly weakened its military credibility. They had not been badly beaten. If they could hold out in Beirut for at least a month under military pressure by the IDF, they might gain a great political victory. They could, as they had in 1967, show themselves to be a determined and effective fighting force and increase their weakened credibility with the Palestinian population. Moreover, their prestige with the Arab states and even with the West would rise considerably and perhaps give them a legitimacy they had lost as a consequence of their terrorist acts in the preceding five years. Equally important, Arafat reasoned that he could play the "great power card" at the appropriate time. Yasir Arafat understood that a prolonged siege would bring pressure on Israel from all Western nations, most particularly from the United States, and play into the hands of the Soviets, who, in more than one instance in the past, had offered to come to their rescue with support. By holding out for a considerable time, Arafat hoped to increase pressure on Israel to bring the war to an end, leaving the PLO in Beirut.

As a corollary, by denying Israel a quick victory in Beirut, the PLO could hope to increase domestic pressure on the Begin government for a negotiated settlement. Even before the siege had begun, a number of tentative peace movements had emerged within the Israeli public and even within the Israeli military. In addition, the PLO could point to the fact that the announced goals for which the Israelis had gone to war had already been achieved. A protracted siege might allow the PLO to achieve another goal that they had long sought—recognition as a political entity by the West and, most important, by the United States. If the war went on long enough and Arafat's prestige rose high enough and pressure from Arab governments grew strong enough, the U.S. might be willing to trade some sort of tacit recognition or perhaps even enter into direct negotiations with the PLO as a way of stopping the war.

In the final analysis, of course, the game in Beirut was zero-sum. The PLO understood that if it was driven from Beirut and from Lebanon and lost its territorial base contiguous with Israel, it would come to an end as a military if not a political force. Arafat was under no illusions that the loss of the war and the failure to come to a political settlement would mean the demise of the PLO as an effective force in Middle East politics. Thus, if it was true that the Israelis had chosen siege warfare as a way to achieve their military and political goals, it was equally true that their decision appealed to the PLO as the ideal way to achieve its goals. In the end, both antagonists mirrored one another in their choice of strategy, although for very different reasons.

SIEGE WARFARE

Fundamental to siege warfare as it is defined by international rules of war is that it involves the civilian population. It is the nature of such warfare to draw into the battle area large numbers of civilians, who may be wounded or killed. In medieval days, sieges involved starving out the defenders, including women and children; in modern warfare, where military pressure is brought to bear on the entire infrastructure of a besieged city (civilians, economy, water supply, industrial capacity, etc.), siege warfare integrally involves civilians. Civilians are involved not only in the tactics of the besieger but in the tactics of the defender, who, if he is to be successful, must marshal every available civilian to keep the city running and defensible. In any siege, great numbers of civilians are likely to be drawn into the battle area and will be killed, not only by accident, but quite deliberately, because their tasks, although civilian in nature, contribute directly to the military capacity of the defender. International law recognizes that in siege warfare the rules of engagement regarding civilians and noncombatants change.

Traditional sanctuaries, churches, hospitals, schools, and civilian population areas, still exist, but their status may be seriously modified. They remain sanctuaries only as long as neither side makes tactical use of them. This places a much greater responsibility on the defender, who has the choice of maintaining the sanctuary status of these places or converting them into military assets. By hiding ammunition in sanctuaries or placing antiaircraft guns on the roofs of churches or hospitals or quartering armed fighting troops in civilian areas and using them as staging areas, the defenders legally change such areas, which then become fair game; the civilian population within them also becomes subject to military action. Even in medieval law, it was the defender who had the greatest obligation to see to it that civilian casualties and damage to traditional places of sanctuary were minimized within the area of defense.

In Beirut, civilian casualties became inevitable. Once the Israelis and the PLO became involved in siege warfare as the means to achieve their military and political goals, the rules of engagement changed and civilians within the siege area became legitimate military targets even from the perspective of international law. Further, the very nature of the small PLO bands of highly mobile guerrillas required them to be thoroughly integrated into the civilian population within the camps. Conventional forces under siege conditions do not deploy their men outside civilian residences.

From the PLO perspective, siege conditions increased the probability that the Israeli sensitivity to civilian deaths would prohibit the full use of their air and artillery firepower. The IDF had operated this way throughout the war in the south. Indeed, in Sidon and Tyre the Israelis had even showed a willingness to accept additional casualties to their own forces rather than risk the charge of being insensitive to the safety of civilians. When civilians died and their homes were destroyed in Beirut, clever PLO propaganda was disseminated to outrage public opinion internationally and in Israel. Anyone who followed the war closely realized how successful the PLO was in propagating an image of Israelis indiscriminately bombing and killing civilians in residential areas.

The PLO understood that it was necessary to subordinate military goals to political goals. This was evident in the degree to which they constructed and utilized a first-rate propaganda operation, which was so effective that it virtually defeated the Israelis in the propaganda war. Even now that the siege of Beirut is long over, the Israelis are still the victims of that propaganda. The PLO relied on its ability to get its story out to the international press. For many years, it has been paying, seducing, and corrupting journalists in Beirut. Its techniques included granting exclusive interviews, making sure the press were well treated, and providing them with women and drugs, and sometimes making cash payments. Equally important, since 1975 in West Beirut, the PLO "licensed" selected journalists by providing them with PLO accreditation cards. With these cards, journalists were able to travel into various areas of Beirut to obtain news stories. During the siege, "unfriendly" journalists who over the years had refused PLO blandishments or who had tried to remain objective were openly threatened and forced to leave the city. In a number of cases, journalists were beaten, and in at least two instances they were killed. Only journalists licensed by the PLO could travel into PLO areas during the siege without risk of being shot. The PLO had selected these journalists over a period of years, screening them to assure that they were friendly. The Israelis got bogged down by restricting the movement of journalists and insisting on censorship, which in the end did nothing but concede a clear advantage to the PLO.

When the Israelis decided on siege warfare, the key to success was to convince the PLO leadership that if they insisted on remaining in the city they would die. It was perhaps even more important to convince the leadership of the PLO that, as long as they remained, the Israelis would not stay the hand of violence for fear of civilian deaths. The Israelis set out to convince the PLO, many of whom had families and relatives in the city, that the IDF would not only destroy them but would destroy their families and their property. The integration with the civilian population that the PLO had achieved was to be turned against them. Whether the Israelis would have carried out the threat is an open question. First, they had to convince the PLO and the civilian population that everyone was fair game, that the Israelis would not restrict the application of military force.

The Israeli tactical plan alternated force with incentive by presenting the PLO and the Syrians with every opportunity to disengage and leave the city. This took several forms. A complex psychological warfare campaign was conducted to convince the PLO and the civilian population that they had no alternative to leaving the city except death. The Israelis were very clear in not insisting on the surrender of the PLO, which would probably have forced the PLO to fight to the death. Faced with a choice between destruction and surrender, the PLO would have fought to the last man. A second major tactic was to allow civilians to leave the city whenever they wanted. Throughout the siege, the IDF kept open two major escape routes from the city to Syrian positions. Of the 500,000 people trapped in West Beirut, about 100,000 took advantage of the Israeli escape routes and did leave.

Another Israeli decision was to draw a distinction between the PLO areas and camps south of the Corniche Mazraa and the center of West Beirut proper, which ran north of the Corniche Mazraa. Bombing and military action in the area north of the Corniche Mazraa were extremely limited, so the civilians in the battle area could go there and be relatively safe. The object was to keep open the option of survival through withdrawal in order to encourage the PLO to withdraw when the military situation deteriorated. The Israelis also gave the Syrian regular units stationed within the city every opportunity to disengage and withdraw; it was hoped that the Syrian forces could in this way be separated from the PLO. For the most part, the Syrians did not leave the city, however. President Assad wanted to maintain a Syrian presence to increase his prestige in the Arab world. He could boast that the Syrians were the only people to fight alongside the PLO during the war. But Assad was clever enough to minimize the losses of his troops: Syrian regular units in Beirut did not take any serious part in the fighting. The Syrian PLO, Al Saiqa, did participate, however.

Having devised its political and psychological tactics for the siege, the IDF evolved a number of military tactics as well. The first was to make maximum use of air, naval, and artillery firepower, but to do so in a fairly discriminate way. Aerial photos ensured that pilots were able to hit only military targets. The IDF points out that in the area north of the Corniche Mazraa, Israeli aircraft struck at only forty targets, and those were military. The IDF also used highly accurate Maverick missiles in these raids. Artillery and naval shelling, much less precise than air strikes, could still be fairly accurate because the Israelis controlled the hills around the city.

A second tactic was to minimize the risks to its own troops. The IDF would keep up the ground pressure on PLO strongpoints, but only at the small-unit level, heavily supported by artillery and tank fire, often at point-blank range. There were no massive assaults against PLO strongpoints. The aim was, clearly, not to break through to the downtown areas, where the battle would become a free-for-all in which large numbers of casualties would be suffered. Rather, the intention was to engage the PLO at carefully selected strongpoints and break the PLO's will rather than forcing a military decision. The object was to compel the PLO to make the political decision to withdraw from Beirut.

The Israeli military force took considerable precautions to keep civilian casualties to the barest minimum. However, the IDF reserved the option of "disproportionate response," which meant the right to hit military targets in civilian areas and to do so regularly in retaliation for attacks against its forces. Although the Israelis would make every effort to avoid hitting civilian concentrations and the sanctuaries that were traditionally exempt from military action, they would not allow the integration of the PLO into civilian areas to reduce Israeli effectiveness. Attacks against military strongpoints integrated into civilian areas did result in civilian casualties, but this was necessary to convince the PLO that the IDF would not tie its hands in the fight for Beirut.

In the end, the battle was joined on terms that were mutually acceptable. Both sides had chosen siege warfare as the only alternative among the military options. The IDF simply had no other military or political choice. To the PLO, siege warfare seemed to offer the best chance of a political if not a military success. Engagements throughout the siege were far less military in nature than they were political. The IDF could easily have broken through any number of military positions garrisoned by the PLO if it had been prepared to pay the price in casualties. For the first time, the Israeli Defense Force found itself employing tactics and strategies dictated more by political considerations than by military expedience. The struggle for Beirut was far more a test of will, endurance, and politics than of military might. The IDF was engaged in a limited war fought for limited goals and objectives, something which it had never done before and which did not sit well with its officers, its men, and above all, with the populace back home.

SIEGE

The siege began officially on Thursday, the first of July. A cease-fire had been technically in effect for six days, since the Israelis had completed operations on the Beirut–Damascus highway, and had been punctuated by a number of violations. Some 12,000 to 14,000 PLO fighters and 500,000 civilians were located in the area of West Beirut, mostly in the camps of Sabra, Shatila, and Bourj el Barajneh. The PLO were dug in and prepared for a considerable attack. Diplomats, led by Philip Habib, the American negotiator, had been holding talks with the Lebanese and the PLO on and off for almost three weeks in an effort to find some kind of political solution. So far, they had failed. The Israelis began a concerted campaign of psychological warfare to convince the PLO that an assault was imminent and to prod them into coming to an agreement with Habib. The campaign consisted of leaflet drops warning the civilians to leave the city before the attack began. Helicopters and aircraft as well as ground vehicles mounted with loudspeakers issued the same message. Public statements were made by high-ranking Israeli political and military leaders that an attack could come at any minute. As if to underscore the point, at dusk on July 1, a score of Israeli aircraft conducted low-level passes over the city. They dropped flares, made mock bombing runs, and broke the sound barrier, sending shock waves over the city. Radio broadcasts in Arabic were beamed at the city, but no formal attacks took place. Negotiations continued on July 1, but it was clear that the PLO had taken a hard line and was in no mood to reach any agreement.

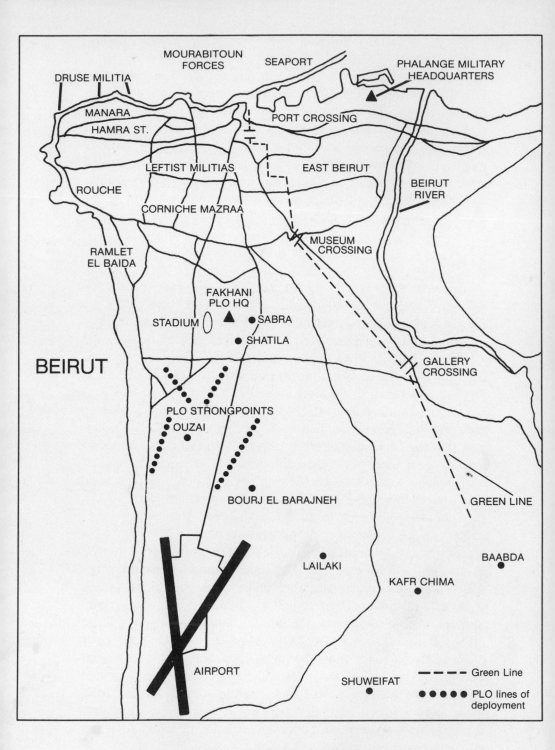

Map 14. Tactical map of Beirut

Friday, July 2

Habib openly announced that he was making no progress in the negotiations. As if to underscore its determination to stay in Beirut, the PLO issued a formal statement, which went out under the name of George Habash, commander of the PFLP, admitting that it was playing for time, to let the Israelis bear the onus of the siege. The Israeli Defense Minister, Ariel Sharon, visited Beirut and in a series of press statements pointed out that although the Israelis wanted a negotiated settlement, they did "not rule out the use of force." He went on: "Israel has resolved not to permit the maintenance of a terrorist infrastructure in Lebanon in the future." These statements were buttressed by General Rafael Eitan, the IDF Chief of Staff, who reiterated that the Israeli Defense Force would keep the pressure on Beirut and warned civilians to leave before the city was struck by air attacks. Civilians who left, he indicated, would be allowed to pass through Israeli lines and return to their homes in the south. Eitan also pointed out that the units of the 85th Syrian brigade which remained in Beirut had been reduced to one third their manpower because of losses suffered in the campaign south of the airport. Of the forty tanks originally attached to the brigade, only one was left, and only three of its original eighteen artillery pieces. General Amir Drori, chief of the Northern Command, issued a statement that the army was prepared for an assault on Beirut.

Saturday, July 3

On Saturday, the Israelis made the first move in the siege. Using units positioned in the area of Monte Verde, the Israelis moved up into the city proper and seized the Green Line, which had separated East and West Beirut since the 1975–76 civil war. At noon, tanks, armored personnel carriers, and reinforced infantry seized control of the Museum Crossing point on the Gallery Samaan. West Beirut was effectively sealed off from East Beirut.

After an eight-day lull in the fighting, the opposing forces conducted a series of artillery duels in the airport area. The PLO neighborhood of Lailaki and the Bourj el Barajneh camp were shelled by Israeli tank and artillery fire. Israeli armor moved up east at Aramun. Throughout the day, the air force flew mock bombing raids on the refugee camps and dropped flares and leaflets to maintain pressure on the military and civilian populations.

Sunday, July 4

Sunday became a crucial turning point in the political aspect of the siege. The Israelis were now in complete control of the line separating East and West Beirut. They shut off all food, water, and fuel into the city. Cars and trucks were searched, and only medical personnel were allowed to pass south of the city. Merkava tanks at Hadath continued to shell the town at Lailaki as well as the camp at Bourj el Barajneh. Infantry began to inch toward the city.

Monday, July 5

The blockade continued. At Beirut checkpoints, Christian Phalangists had now replaced Israeli troops in the stop-and-search operations. Israeli units remained discreetly in the background, with enough force evident to stop anyone trying to run the roadblocks. The policy of denying the siege area food, water, and fuel continued in force. At the same time, Golani infantry moved down from the town of Kafr and the Chima ridge and took the town of Hai es Salam, near the Lailaki camp. To the southeast, the Israelis launched a small operation at the town of Souq el Gharb and took the town. By this time, Israeli troops had positioned themselves on both sides of the high ground around Beirut, and the towns of Rihane and Hai es Salam were becoming staging points for further Israeli movements.

The blockade was maintained, and Israeli gunboats were off the coast to prevent the PLO from escaping by sea; these gunboats now began to shell the coast with their 76mm guns. Beginning Sunday night, July 4, and supported by ground artillery, the PLO camps were hit all night by artillery and naval barrages, including Gabriel missiles fired from the ships. The areas of Verdon and Corniche Mazraa were also hit. Farther to the south, in Hadath, Israeli tanks moved north toward the university campus and began their pressure on the airport. Here they encountered the first PLO resistance. Fighting from the rubble of destroyed buildings, the PLO hit a few tanks and caused some infantry casualties. This was a minor probe by the

Israelis; the IDF strategy seemed to be to maintain constant pressure on PLO military strongpoints without risking a major battle. They began the "salami strategy" of moving a few yards at a time, maximizing point-blank fire with tanks, and at the same time minimizing their own casualties. The blockade of the city and the artillery and naval bombardment continued for two days, through Wednesday, July 7.

Wednesday, July 7

On Wednesday, as a result of an urgent personal message from President Reagan, the Israelis turned electricity and water back on in West Beirut. Although the blockade continued for a fifth day, the artillery bombardment that had been going on for three days was reduced in pace. It had destroyed a great number of buildings, and fires raged in downtown West Beirut. To the south, Israeli artillery positions at Shuweifat and Khalde shelled the PLO neighborhoods in and around Lailaki and Hai es Salam. Once again, the Israelis moved a few yards closer to the PLO strongpoints, keeping up the pressure to get them to withdraw.

Thursday, July 8

On July 8, Major General Moshe Levy, Deputy Chief of Staff, stated publicly that Israeli forces were prepared to stay through the winter and were in fact making preparations to do so. Throughout Lebanon, the Israelis continued paving old roads and laying new ones; they had constructed or improved 400 kilometers of roads since the war began. They continued to install water pipes, fortify positions, and make battlefield adjustments to their deployments throughout the Bekaa, in the Shouf, and around Beirut. A new airstrip just north of Nabitiya was made into a permanent site. The improvements were justified to the public on the grounds that even if the PLO left Beirut, it would still take the IDF months to "sanitize" the area; the Israelis were simply preparing their forces for this. The bombardment and artillery fire on Beirut continued.

Friday, July 9

On Friday, fierce artillery and rocket exchanges broke out between the PLO and the Israelis; the PLO launched a considerable concentrated bombardment, using 130mm guns and

Katyusha rockets. The PLO areas were hit very hard in return, as the Israelis, using twenty-seven captured Katyusha rocket launchers and ammunition, turned around the captured equipment and rocketed the PLO positions in the same indiscriminate manner in which IDF positions were being hit. The PLO continued to fire on Israeli positions around Hadath, and the blockade of West Beirut continued. This pattern of intermittent rocket and artillery exchanges continued until Sunday, July 11.

Sunday, July 11

On Sunday, the Israelis continued pressure on PLO positions around the airport and the university, with fierce, day-long artillery and rocket bombardments and point-blank tank fire. The camps of Bourj el Barajneh, Sabra, and Shatila were hit as well. The Israelis probed the airport near the western runway and ran into expectedly fierce resistance. Two tanks were destroyed and several infantrymen killed and wounded. But the Israeli pressure continued, and the IDF moved a bit closer. At one point around the PLO strongpoints near the airport, Israeli shells were hitting PLO positions at the rate of thirty a minute.

At the same time, the PLO concentrated its return fire on Israeli positions from Hadath all the way east to Baabda, where in a three-minute period fifty-one shells landed near the president's palace. A direct hit was scored on Israeli positions there, killing three men and destroying five transport vehicles. The attack, with rockets hitting very rapidly, was probably carried out by a 122 Katyusha rocket launcher. Naval gunboats continued to pound the coastal areas, and for the first time a number of foreign embassies and luxury hotels on the coastal waterfront were hit by IDF fire. By the end of the day, the firing died down all along the line, probably as a consequence of darkness and the need for both sides to replenish their ammunition stocks.

Monday, July 12

The Israelis accused the PLO of stalling over the negotiations that had been going on for the better part of three weeks. The Israelis also charged that the PLO was using the delay to improve its positions. There is no doubt that the PLO had used the time to strengthen its strongpoints against what it believed to be an inevitable massive ground assault by Israeli forces. They plowed up roads with bulldozers, mined the most likely avenues of approach, and prepared booby traps to delay the attackers. The Israelis also charged that PLO forces were melting into the civilian population so they could stay behind should the PLO be defeated or be forced to withdraw. The Israelis increased their psychological warfare, using noise, leaflets, and mock raids to increase the level of stress on the besieged population to force them to leave. But the Israelis were coming to the conclusion that their psychological campaign was having no appreciable effect. Moreover, there was no movement in the talks; the Israelis began to feel that events might be slipping beyond their control.

Tuesday, July 13

A brief cease-fire was in effect for most of Tuesday while talks between the PLO and the Israelis continued. The Israelis used the time to reinforce their positions north of the city. They also moved an armored force of 3,500 men and a hundred tanks into position, reinforcing all along the line from the port section of East Beirut down to positions south of the city near the airport. General Sharon visited his officers and men and made a public statement again pointing out that although Israel preferred a negotiated settlement, it was quite prepared to drive the PLO out by force if necessary.

Within the city, the shortages of food, water, and fuel were having an effect on the civilian population. The Lebanese have historically been known for their skill at smuggling, and the siege seemed for many to present just another business opportunity. Food, water, and fuel were available, but the price was out of sight because of the Israeli blockade. There is some evidence that some of the available food was being marketed by PLO soldiers who were drawing it from their own stocks. In any event, it is doubtful that the PLO as a fighting force was being hurt by the blockade. According to Israeli intelligence, the PLO had a six-month supply of food, ammunition, and medical supplies.

The Israelis publicly called for a Syrian troop withdrawal and agreed to allow the Syrians free passage through Israeli lines to join their forces farther down the highway at Chtaura. Assad clearly understood what was at stake here. If he pulled out the

85th brigade, no matter how badly it had been mauled, he would give the impression throughout the Arab world that he had abandoned the Palestinians to the Israelis. Therefore, amid great ceremony, Assad refused to withdraw and vowed to keep the 85th brigade in Beirut throughout the siege to demonstrate Syrian resolve and support for the PLO.

The cease-fire which had been in effect from the evening of July 12 held throughout July 13 and on for almost a week, until Wednesday, July 21.

Wednesday, July 21

July 21 was a major turning point in the siege. PLO forces staged three attacks, striking behind Israeli lines and killing five soldiers and wounding three others. One of the attacks occurred in the Bekaa Valley, where, behind Syrian lines, substantial PLO forces remained in position. The Syrians were allowing the PLO to move through their lines, infiltrate Israeli positions, strike at the IDF, and then slip back through Syrian lines, where they were safe from attack. The Israelis had implemented a policy to avoid all conflict with the Syrians in the Bekaa. At the same time, a rocket attack took place on a bus carrying Israeli soldiers to Tyre. By far the most serious was a Katyusha rocket attack fired from positions in southern Lebanon which struck towns in northern Galilee. The attack itself was small but made the political point that the PLO was still capable of striking at Israeli border towns.

The Israelis used these three attacks as a reason to open a major drive against Beirut, which they had been preparing for almost five days. From the outset, the Israelis had indicated that they would respond to any PLO or Syrian provocation with what they called "disproportionate force." On July 22, a major attack on the city was launched.

Thursday, July 22

The Israelis announced that the attack was not the final assault on Beirut but retaliation for the PLO attacks of the day before. Israeli aircraft went into action for the first time since the June 25 cease-fire. They overflew the city for a period of thirty minutes, making low passes, dropping flares and leaflets.

After thirty minutes of these overflights, perhaps made to convince the defenders that the Israelis were not serious, Israeli aircraft suddenly attacked in earnest. All the major PLO camps in the southern part of the city were hit, as well as all the guerrilla strongpoints around the airport and the university. The IDF struck with aircraft firing Maverick missiles and with ground-based artillery and tank fire. The air raid on the city lasted ninety minutes in a bombing officially described as "moderately intense."

East of the city, along the Beirut–Damascus highway and in the Bekaa, Israeli forces engaged Syrian positions with artillery, air strikes, and tank fire. Syrian positions in the Bekaa were hit near Soultan Yaaquoub, Joub Jannine, and in the Shouf Mountains at Monsaura. Syrian barracks at Baalbek were hit hard, and the attack justified because there were some two thousand PLO deployed in the Wavel camp nearby. The Israelis maintained that it was these PLO forces that passed through Syrian lines to mine the roads and almost daily ambush Israeli units. The Syrians had formerly refused to restrict the PLO's actions, and the Israeli attack was intended to get them to enforce control. Syrian-controlled villages along the highway and north of it at Saad Nall, Taalabria, Taneiel, and Bar Elias were all struck by Israeli aircraft and artillery fire. At the end of the day the Israeli Defense Command announced that the air strikes against the Syrians had destroyed seven T-62 tanks, eighteen armored personnel carriers, two self-propelled guns, and nineteen other vehicles. This was the first major engagement between Syrian and Israeli forces since June 25, when the four-day battle for control of the Beirut–Damascus highway had ended. Since that battle, Syrian forces had been reinforced by almost 30,000 men, along with accompanying tanks and infantry. This brought the total Syrian forces in Lebanon close to 60,000 men.

Friday, July 23

Friday, July 23, was the second day of concentrated air and artillery strikes against Syrian and PLO positions. Most of the attacks in the Beirut area were against the PLO headquarters in the Fakhani district. Attacks continued into Saturday. On the evening of July 23, the Syrians had introduced three SAM-8 missile batteries in the Bekaa Valley. Israeli intelligence detected the movement, and on July 24 the IAF destroyed them all. In addition, Israel issued an official warning to the Syrians that they would not tolerate missiles of any type in the Bekaa Valley. In Beirut, PLO positions and the camps were hit again by artillery and air attacks for the third straight day. These attacks continued through Sunday evening, July 25.

Monday, July 26

Once again, Beirut was hit by air and artillery attacks. In the air north of the Corniche Mazraa, in the seafront area of Ramlet el Baida, Israeli aircraft struck a major ammunition dump in a field. Artillery, air bombardment, and naval gunfire continued against the major PLO camps and the Fakhani district, which housed the main PLO headquarters. The attack continued into the evening. The dust and smoke was so thick that it became impossible to direct fire. Israeli aircraft began dropping flares to illuminate targets to be shelled by naval gunfire. The city of Beirut had been subjected to five straight days of aerial, artillery, and naval bombardment.

Tuesday, July 27

On Tuesday, the air, naval, and artillery attacks continued for a sixth straight day with increased intensity. For the first time since the siege began, the Israelis hit populated non-PLO residential districts and caused heavy civilian casualties. On July 27, the newspaper *An Nahar* reported 120 dead and 230 wounded in the morning raids alone. This was the heaviest toll reported since the siege began. In the high-rent Rouche district near the city center, bombs and artillery shells rained down heavily. Ambassadorial residences were hit, and a nine-story apartment complex housing mostly staff serving at the American University Hospital was hit by an Israeli missile and the top six stories blown off. All the casualties were civilians.

In the south, artillery and rocket duels continued between Israeli and PLO forces around the airport and near the borders òf the Bourj el Barajneh camp. Israeli guns positioned at Shuweifat hit the PLO camps and the Corniche Mazraa, and the downtown area was brought under fire by artillery positions around Baabda. Naval ships continued to pound the coast, setting many fires in the port area.

Wednesday, July 28

The attack continued for the seventh straight day, mostly hitting the same targets. In response, the PLO unleashed a massive artillery bombardment which struck at IDF positions all along the line for almost six hours. Both sides seemed to be making more of a political point in these exchanges than a military point. The Israelis were keeping the pressure on while the PLO was demonstrating its military will to strengthen its position at the negotiating table. In any case, both sides continued fighting, and the camps of Bourj el Barajneh, Sabra, and Shatila and civilian neighborhoods were hit again.

South of the city, artillery and tank fire continued to shell PLO neighborhoods and strongpoints in the Ouzai district, as naval gunfire continued to hit targets along the seafront districts of Ramlet el Baida, Bain Militaire, and Manara. The result was a series of large fires that slowly began to burn out of control. Around the airport, the PLO remained under constant pressure as the Israelis continued their point-blank tank and artillery fire. Infantry and armor maneuvered gradually to press back the PLO. As the Israelis advanced a few yards at a time near the airport, the PLO began to give ground.

Thursday, July 29

In an attempt to sustain the morale of the PLO, Yasir Arafat, surrounded by media crews, openly toured West Beirut as the bombing attacks continued. PLO strongpoints were mostly sandbagged positions dug in the rubble. By both Israeli intelligence and media accounts, the morale of the PLO was high. Food, medical supplies, water, and military supplies were adequate. The Ouzai district and its large number of factories had been reduced to ruins; but its defensive positions were proudly displayed to the media by Arafat to convince everyone that the PLO was prepared to fight to the last man.

On the political front, for the first time the Arab League formally endorsed the latest peace proposal to emerge from the talks. Perhaps more significantly, the PLO representative was reported to have initialed the agreement as well. The essence of the Arab League's proposal was for the PLO to withdraw from Beirut under the protection of a foreign force and for them to be settled in other Arab countries. The PLO appeared to be serious about considering the proposal but renewed its demand for recognition as a political entity by Israel and the United States. The air attacks on the city continued for the eighth day.

Friday, July 30
As the talks continued, they appeared to be getting serious. On Friday, Israeli forces attacked by sea, air, and land. Using artillery, armor, and air attacks for the ninth straight day, the IDF hit all the major PLO camps, in addition to the Fakhani district and the race-track area, which was being used as a PLO training center. Various media people on the ground as well as local newspapers and police reports indicated high civilian casualties as artillery shelling continued to strike the camps and PLO positions south of the city. At the end of the day, a new cease-fire went into effect and for the first time the PLO offered a plan of its own. Some progress appeared to be made in the negotiations, and on the next day, Saturday, July 31, there were no attacks by either side. A brief lull settled over the city.

Sunday, August 1
On the evening of July 31, the Lebanese Foreign Ministry announced that talks arranging for a PLO withdrawal were "entering the final phase." In the early morning hours of Sunday, August 1, the Israelis mounted a major attack on the city. Shelling began at 3 a.m. and ended at 5 p.m. For fourteen straight hours, Beirut was subjected to heavy air, naval, and artillery bombardment.

Early-morning artillery attacks concentrated on the area south of the airport as Israeli armor moved against PLO strongpoints near the airport. A two-pronged attack was launched, the first column striking the western end of the airport runway and driving across to take the terminal building. The attack then moved on to positions a few hundred yards from the PLO camp at Bourj el Barajneh, the largest camp in the city. A second force moved up the coastal road toward the Ouzai district to outflank the camp to the west. Both operations were carried out by a combination of elite Golani infantry and paratroop units supported by tanks. By mid-afternoon, the Israelis had captured the airport and pushed PLO forces back to the outskirts of the camp. The Israelis apparently wanted to control the airport before any peace agreement froze their forces in place. With the airport in their hands, the Israelis had a major logistic asset that could be used to evacuate their wounded and bring in reinforcements. The action on Sunday was the first major ground action around Beirut since the first cease-fire on June 11.

Monday, August 2

The Israelis kept a slow and steady pressure on the coastal road in the Ouzai district, deploying additional units in the area to reinforce their paratroops and infantry. In the Ouzai area, they began to capture and destroy PLO strongpoints manned by T-62, T-55, and T-34 tanks as well as 130mm artillery and anti-tank guns. West of the airport, the Israelis continued to put pressure on the borders of the Bourj el Barajneh camp; they also made tactical improvements in their positions around the airport, and invited small clashes with the PLO. Although there had been an intense battle in the Ouzai district, the Israelis pushed the PLO back into the camp, occupying all but its northern border and sealing the camp off. They had no intention of entering it.

The real military action was occurring in the downtown area. Over two hundred tanks were redeployed along the Green Line, which the Israelis had seized almost a week and a half before. Israeli armor moved into place to control the major access roads at the Museum Crossing, the Port Crossing, and the Gallery Crossing. At the Museum Crossing alone, there were eighty tanks and armored personnel carriers and a number of 155mm self-propelled guns deployed in nearby side streets. At the Port Crossing to the north, IDF forces were also reinforced. The crossing points were only two miles from PLO headquarters in the Fakhani district, and the Israelis appeared to be preparing for a final assault at PLO headquarters to bring the siege to an end. On Tuesday, August 3, reinforcement around the crossing points continued, but no major military action was undertaken.

Wednesday, August 4

After a day of intense negotiations on August 3 in which all sides seemed close to agreement, negotiations suddenly began to stall. On the morning of August 4, the Israelis launched an intense artillery barrage that struck completely around West Beirut, ranging from the port area all the way south of the city out to the airport. Naval gunfire was intense, and the coastal areas from the port and south through the Ouzai district were heavily shelled. For the first time, the IDF used white phosphorus shells against targets, and many targets in residential areas, as well as the port, caught fire.

Having spent two days reinforcing their positions around the major crossing points into West Beirut, the Israelis launched a three-pronged attack supported by armor and artillery. The first attack occurred at the Port Crossing south of the Green Line in the seaport area. The attack moved only five hundred yards into West Beirut and was stopped by Syrian elements of the PLO, the famous "pink panthers," so called because of their light-red uniforms. The Israeli advance in the port area appeared serious; then it seemed to be a feint to ensure that PLO forces in the north of the city were tied down. The main thrust fell in the center at the Museum Crossing and was aimed directly at PLO headquarters in the Fakhani district. This attack across the Museum Crossing was comprised of tanks, along with paratroop infantry, and was led by engineers and bulldozers. The PLO had been expecting an attack and had created a number of strongpoints and sandbag positions in the rubble from which to ambush Israeli troops. The aim of the attack in the center was to strike at the Fakhani district and capture the Hippodrome. Its ultimate objective was to move down the main street of the Corniche Mazraa and link up with Israeli troops cutting through the Ouzai district from the south. The PLO fought extremely well and the Israeli advance was slow and costly. By nightfall, it began to bog down and eventually stopped.

The third prong of the attack came along the coastal highway, moving through the Ouzai district. The district, full of small factories and buildings, was virtually in shambles, which gave the PLO an excellent opportunity to fight from prepared positions carved out of the rubble. The PLO fought very well with their RPG's and machine guns and inflicted heavy casualties with their antitank guns and small-arms fire. The Israelis continued to press into Ouzai. Once through it, they fanned out from Cocadi Junction north across the golf course near the Chehab barracks. By

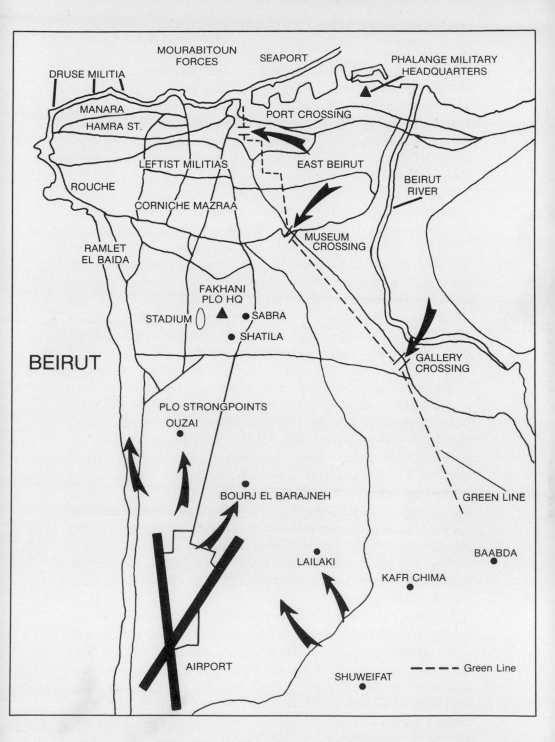

Map 15. Israeli advances in Beirut
August 4

afternoon, using close air support, the IDF had pressed north to the Bir Hanan-Kuwait embassy junction, the last major PLO strongpoint on the approach to the Sabra and Shatila camps. By evening, although fighting went on around the Museum Crossing and at the Hippodrome, the Israelis had outflanked the three major PLO camps. The camps were surrounded on at least three sides.

August 4 was a day of considerable cost to the IDF, a day which showed that combat against entrenched urban guerrillas is not easy. Indeed, this day was typical of what the Israelis could have anticipated had they gone into Beirut in force. It proved how expensive a house-to-house attack could be. It was the single most costly day of the war for the IDF. Nineteen soldiers were killed, and sixty-four wounded, attempting to cross into West Beirut. Whatever else both sides had learned, the lesson was very clear to the Israelis that any attempt to take Beirut house-by-house would be extremely costly.

Thursday, August 5

The reaction of the United States to the Israeli thrust into West Beirut was one of extreme anger, expressed by the personal outrage of President Reagan at what he regarded as the violation of earlier assurances given him through diplomatic channels that the Israelis would not invade West Beirut. Moreover, the Americans believed that all parties were very close to reaching an agreement. In the American view, the Israeli incursion into West Beirut might have derailed the diplomatic efforts to bring the siege to an end. In order to show its displeasure and the even-handedness of its policy, the United States publicly called for Israel to withdraw behind the Green Line, a request which the Israelis publicly refused.

Elsewhere in the city, skirmishes continued between IDF and PLO forces. The Israelis continued to make slow, steady, and costly progress toward the Hippodrome and the Fakhani PLO headquarters. Although there was some minor skirmishing in the south, for the most part the Israelis adjusted their lines to make them more defensible. Both sides seemed to be trying to minimize casualties. Signals from the negotiations continued to suggest that all parties were very close to agreement.

Friday, August 6

The day saw a major diplomatic breakthrough. Lebanese officials publicly announced that the American negotiating team, led by Philip Habib, and the PLO had reached agreement "on all major points." Real progress seemed to have been made and the PLO publicly stated that if all things continue to go well, the PLO forces could be withdrawn by "the middle of next week." Indeed, there were signs in the streets that the PLO was in fact preparing to leave, as some PLO units disengaged and began to return to their families. Merchants were doing a thriving business as PLO soldiers bought luggage. The United States publicly pledged to throw its "full weight" behind the proposal and to convince the Israelis that they ought to accept the agreement and allow the PLO to leave. On all sides, optimism was high. Minor skirmishing broke out on the Green Line, but there was no significant ground action. Two Israeli aircraft demolished two apartment buildings housing PLO arms caches; unfortunately, a number of civilians were killed in the attack. On Saturday, August 7, and Sunday, August 8, a general quiet descended on the city, while the Israeli cabinet studied the proposal.

Monday, August 9

On Monday, the Israeli government was formally presented with the Habib plan; informally it had had it for almost twenty-four hours. But early in the morning Israeli planes struck the city and the hills east of it. Other air strikes hit PLO positions behind Syrian lines near the highway nineteen miles east of the city at the towns of Tarekeesh and Jabil Knessa. There were minor skirmishes at the crossing points and other areas of confrontation south of the city, but no major battles erupted. Israeli aircraft staged mock attacks over Beirut and made low passes on the PLO camps, breaking the sound barrier and dropping flares, but there were no actual attacks on the camps.

Tuesday, August 10

In the early morning hours of Tuesday, August 10, as the PLO was preparing to leave, Israeli jets hit PLO camps with bombs and rockets. Their main targets were Sabra, Shatila, and Bourj el Barajneh. The air strikes at the camps seemed designed to level them so they could not be used again by the PLO. Naval gunfire, artillery, and air strikes began the night before and lasted through Tuesday.

While bombardment and air strikes were going on, Israel publicly accepted Habib's plan "in principle" but raised two significant objections. The Israelis insisted that the PLO withdraw before the arrival of any multi-national force. Throughout the negotiations this had been a major point for the Israelis, who feared that, once the multi-national force was put in place between the forces, the PLO would either renege on their agreement to withdraw or begin to delay. If this were to happen, the Israelis believed, they would not be able to renew the military pressure on the PLO, since they would have to move through the lines of the multi-national force to do so. The Israelis wanted assurances that the multi-national force would not become a buffer between its forces and the PLO. A second point that the Israelis wanted to be sure of was that all PLO were to be out of the city; none were to be left behind. They demanded a list of the guerrillas to be withdrawn, by name, and insisted that the men withdrawn must equal in number the names on the list. The Israelis had an advantage here because they had captured a complete list of the PLO at their headquarters in Sidon. With the list they now demanded, the Israelis could verify that all PLO forces left the city and that the individuals who left were fighters rather than administrative personnel. The Israelis wanted no significant fighting force left behind. As things turned out, however, six months after the PLO withdrawal was completed, there were still some two thousand PLO of various factional allegiances left in the city.

Wednesday, August 11

By Wednesday, the PLO had yet to agree to the Israeli demands made the day before, and the Israelis continued to maintain military pressure on the city. Israeli planes and artillery intensified their shelling and bombing of the PLO areas, hitting both military strongpoints and the camps. Naval gunfire continued all night long, and the port areas at Ain Muraisa were badly hit. Israeli attempts to advance troops along the Corniche Mazraa met fierce PLO resistance and bogged down. The attempt to cut the northern suburbs off from the PLO camps had essentially failed.

North of the city, however, Israeli tanks began to move in strength. Forty tanks moved up the coastal highway past Juniyeh toward Byblos and east along the Metun River into the Lagluk ski area east of Byblos. The region is full of wadis and ravines, and Israeli engineers once again cleared the way for the advance by means of sophisticated bridge equipment. An Israeli force of almost brigade size was now in position to prevent anyone from reinforcing the city from the north. There was a force of almost ten thousand PLO and Syrian troops stationed around Tripoli. By moving a brigade into a blocking position, the Israelis not only could foil any attempt on the part of the guerrillas in Beirut to escape to the north but made it impossible for Syrian and PLO forces in Tripoli to reinforce Beirut. Further, this setup put Israeli forces in an excellent position to move against the PLO in Tripoli once the siege was over. The Israelis were quick to point out that the evacuation agreement worked out with the PLO addressed only forces in Beirut and not those in Tripoli. The Begin government still insisted on the matter of the timing of the PLO withdrawal and the need for a complete list of PLO fighters. Despite these obstacles, everyone involved in the diplomatic process was convinced that within a few days an agreement was not only possible but inevitable.

Thursday, August 12

On Thursday, for reasons that appeared inexplicable, the Israelis began a massive aerial bombardment against Beirut. The air attack began at six o'clock in the morning and went on uninterrupted until five-thirty that afternoon, causing 128 dead and 400 wounded, most of whom were civilians. The major targets of this staggering air, artillery, and naval bombardment were the PLO camps and their military positions in West Beirut and all areas south of the Corniche Mazraa. Air attacks were also carried out against Syrian–PLO positions in the area of Manara. Undoubtedly by accident, even hospitals were hit. In the north, Israeli armor moved closer to Byblos and secured the mountain village of Aqura, the high point in the area controlling access to Byblos and the road about ten miles south of Tripoli. The Israelis had now positioned sufficient forces to move on Tripoli if they chose to do so.

The bombing campaign seemed designed to terrorize and level PLO neighborhoods within Beirut so completely so that they could never be lived in again. And it seemed a deliberate, lasting reminder of both the ability and the willingness of the IDF to strike at its enemy no matter what the cost. With the Israelis and the PLO so close to an agreement, such a massive attack threatened to derail the peace process. The question is: why was the attack undertaken?

Although the evidence is somewhat unclear, it seemed certain that the attack was ordered on the authority of Defense Minister Sharon. The reaction to the attack within the Israeli cabinet was anger. Most of the cabinet, even Sharon's supporters, concluded that he had exceeded his authority by ordering the attack. Its intensity seemed almost gratuitous in its attempt to crush the remaining PLO force of West Beirut. Sharon defended himself by pointing out that he had been given complete authority to run the war and to make the kind of battlefield decisions commanders have to make. As the result of this argument, the cabinet rescinded the earlier grant of authority to him. Henceforward, military engagements ordered by the Defense Minister had to be approved by the cabinet and the Prime Minister himself.

The day-long intensive bombardment did not significantly change the military situation, but it angered the United States and cast Israel in a poor light. By five-thirty that evening, at the order of the Prime Minister, a cease-fire settled over Beirut. The siege of Beirut seemed to have come to an end.

The day-long bombardment of August 12 appears to have frightened even the Israeli cabinet, which felt that the events of this day could well have derailed the peace process and prolonged the war, something it certainly did not want. Once the cease-fire began on August 12, then, events moved very rapidly. The following day the talks continued; ground forces began to disengage as some Israeli troops actually moved back a few yards to give the PLO breathing room. On the following day, August 14, the Syrians publicly announced that they would pull their troops out of Beirut as soon as they were given the opportunity to do so. Less than a week later, on August 19, the Israelis gave their final approval to the withdrawal plan for the PLO, and on

August 21 lead elements of the multi-national force had arrived and took up positions in Beirut. A day later, Sunday, August 22, the first PLO contingent of 379 men departed Beirut for camps in Arab countries. The siege was over.

AFTERMATH

The more pressing questions concern the physical damage and the number of civilian casualties caused by the thirty-three-day siege. A second question, which in the long run is of greater importance, concerns the capability of the PLO to mount military operations in the future, and its ability to survive as a political entity. Answers are often clouded by observers of television coverage, which tended to give the impression that the IDF attacked targets indiscriminately and caused massive damage. A greater concern, reinforced by the same media impressions, is the perception that IDF forces caused large numbers of civilian casualties during the siege. In addition to media coverage, there was a constant flow of PLO press releases and video tapes, as well as a number of absolutely false statements by the PLO, which had the effect of projecting the image of innocent women and children being ruthlessly destroyed. A careful investigation of the battle provides a more balanced assessment of the damage done to the city and the number of civilian casualties actually caused by hostile action.

With regard to civilian casualties, it must be remembered that Israeli tactics were deliberately designed to minimize civilian losses. No pitched battles occurred within the city or even at its outskirts once the siege began. The constant pressure that was applied against the area's strongpoints around the airport involved movement of no more than a few hundred feet at a time. Even the attacks at the Gallery Crossing and Museum Crossing were essentially minor skirmish operations when compared to some of the actions of the rest of the war. Military movement within the city was limited to only a few hundred feet or a few hundred meters at a time. When tank fire was brought to bear, it was often at point-blank range against identifiable and well-defended military strongpoints. There were no significant numbers of civilians in the Ouzai district; most of them had long since moved into the camps or withdrawn north of the Corniche Mazraa into West Beirut. The closeness of the forces, the nature of the battle, and the general absence of civilians in most of the ground-battle areas acted to reduce the numbers of civilian casualties in unit-to-unit ground action.

In addition, IDF forces never entered any PLO camp until well after the battle for Beirut ended. Israeli tactics were designed to press the PLO back against the borders of the camps, and Israeli forces at no time entered any of the camps or moved from house to house, clearing them of PLO fighters. Thus, IDF ground forces were likely to have killed only a small number of civilians, if any, during their skirmishes with the PLO. In those few areas where the IDF had to clear out buildings, they were under strict limitations on how to do it. IDF forces, as in Sidon and Tyre, were not allowed to enter buildings firing or to use grenades or satchel charges in advance. It is quite clear, therefore, that the number of civilian casualties that could possibly have occurred as a consequence of IDF ground-force action in Beirut was very low.

As to aerial bombardment: from the early days of the war, beginning with the battle for Sidon and Tyre, the IAF set up a complicated double-check process to decide when and how to hit urban targets from the air. The process was deliberately designed to reduce damage to civilian buildings and civilian populations. Whenever urban areas were under attack, the Israeli air force used either small-charge iron bombs or, more commonly, Maverick optically guided missiles, to minimize death and destruction. The Maverick was the ideal weapon to choose; it carries a comparatively small payload and produces limited damage. Because it is deadly accurate, it is ideal for hitting selected military targets within urban areas, especially when they are sandwiched between alleys or urban apartments. The Maverick missile's warhead is small enough to destroy one floor of a high-rise building without significant damage to the rest.

The system worked well in the south, especially in the built-up areas of Sidon and Tyre, and it was enforced throughout the siege of Beirut. There were areas in Beirut, however, where these restrictions did not apply. When the siege began, the Israeli air force originally concentrated on military targets, mostly located north of the Corniche Mazraa. In order to guide its bombing policy in a more precise manner, the IAF divided the city into two zones. The downtown area of West Beirut, from the Corniche Mazraa north to the sea, and its main commercial center, formed one zone. The area south of the Corniche Mazraa, running south to the airport, which included all the major PLO camps and the Ouzai industrial district, as well as most of the PLO strongpoints, comprised the other zone. Bombing policy and the conduct of bombing operations were radically different for each.

In the zone north of the Corniche Mazraa—that is, downtown West Beirut—the IDF struck only at "clear" targets, military gun positions, Katyusha rocket trucks, ammo dumps, and other easily identifiable military positions. In fact, the number of military targets struck by the air force north of the Corniche Mazraa did not exceed forty throughout the entire siege. It hit them with pinpoint precision, using small iron bombs and Maverick missiles. An analysis of scores of aerial photos made available to me shows clearly the pinpoint accuracy with which Israeli pilots were able to deliver their munitions on target, a result made easier by the fact that the PLO could mount no significant missile or conventional antiaircraft defense against the bombing runs. In the northern zone, pilots flew with pictures of their targets in their cockpits and were not given the authority to hit secondary targets or even targets of opportunity if they could not hit their first target. The control and discipline of Israeli airforce sorties flown north of the Corniche Mazraa were excellent; this limited damage and produced only a small number of civilian casualties. One reason for this control was that many PLO positions in the northern zone were close to foreign embassies; also, many civilians in the camps had fled to the downtown area of West Beirut.

In the second zone—that is, the area south of the Corniche Mazraa—circumstances were quite different. Because the PLO military positions were so thoroughly integrated within the camps, and because siege strategy required pressuring those parts of the population which supported the combatants, the camps became targets. The air force used Maverick missiles and small iron bombs and tried to limit the damage to civilian housing and to people in the area, but the camps were hit far less discriminately than targets in the northern zone. Part of the campaign in the southern zone included numerous low-level flyovers, dropping flares, and sonic booms, all intended to frighten the population and break its will to resist. The intention was also to convince the PLO that they would lose the battle, and that if they continued the fight the possibilities were very good that members of their families would also be destroyed.

Despite these facts, there was no systematic terror bombing as reported in the press. To numerous reporters who watched the bombing, as well as many individuals who were in the camps, it is clear that there was no carpet bombing of civilian areas. In the first place, the Israelis did not have the aircraft to carry out that kind of bombing, and second, the type of aircraft they did have did not lend itself to massive bombing of whole city areas. In the southern zone, military targets were more loosely defined and considerably less care was taken to be as precise when bombing raids were undertaken. There is no doubt that these conditions bothered some pilots. Near the end of the siege, especially during the large-scale attack on August 12 against the camps, a number of IDF pilots returned to the bases with bombs still on board; others dropped them in the sea rather than attack the camps, where they felt they were endangering civilians. There is no official count of how many pilots refused to drop their bombs, but this occurred in significant numbers; eight cases have been verified. These were essentially the decisions of individual pilots, of course, made on personal and ethical grounds. At no point, however, were there enough pilots who refused to drop their bombs to threaten the military effort.

Thus, although aerial bombing certainly did kill civilians and no doubt killed a large number of them in the camps, especially in the latter days of the siege, the image, so carefully cultivated in the West by PLO propaganda, that the IDF carried out carpet bombing of civilian targets or concentrated terror campaigns is simply inaccurate. Indeed, an analysis of the way individuals died in Beirut shows that the greatest number of civilian casualties during the siege was not due to ground action or aerial bombardment at all.

The real killer of civilians and destroyer of property was artillery fire. Part of the damage done by artillery can be traced to Israeli policy, announced at the beginning of the siege, of "disproportionate response." In practice, this meant that the Israelis reserved the right to respond to any PLO attack or provocation with a degree of firepower that was greater than that by which they had been attacked. This policy found its true expression in the use of artillery during the siege, with the consequence that high numbers of civilian casualties and a great deal of damage resulted. The PLO had a considerable number of antitank weapons, antiaircraft weapons, howitzers, field artillery pieces, and Katyusha rocket launchers within Beirut, most of which could be easily moved either on truck beds or towed behind other vehicles; the PLO also had a six-month supply of ammunition. When the PLO employed artillery, it did so with very good effect against the IDF, as evidenced by the fact that more artillery casualties were suffered by Israeli ground forces in the siege than during the entire war in the south, including the battles against the Syrians.[1]

A common technique employed by PLO artillery was to back a truck carrying a mortar on its flatbed or a Katyusha rocket truck out from an alley or garage. It would take up a position and fire on Israeli troops and then quickly move out of the area or back into the garage or alley. In response, the Israeli forces began sheaving their artillery—a technique that allows a large number of guns to be fired at once against the same target, with all their shells hitting at about the same time. This produces devastating area barrages in which the shells land on target within seconds of one another. The shelling may last anywhere from thirty to forty seconds to two minutes, and is especially devastating in urban areas where the houses are constructed of concrete and cinder blocks and built close together. As many as five to seven houses can be destroyed in a single barrage.

The Israelis controlled the heights around the city, especially near Baabda, and from these high points Israeli gunners could use heavy, self-propelled artillery pieces to snipe at PLO targets. This tactic of firing heavy artillery rounds point-blank into apartment complexes from which the Israelis had taken fire resulted often in several floors collapsing at the same time; in some instances, destroying complete high-rise buildings. Tank fire into PLO areas was also very effective. In a new wrinkle, the Israelis mounted a 20mm Vulcan cannon atop the M-113 Zelda APC and fired point-blank into buildings. At times, the Israelis brought additional artillery fire to bear from the navy, with its 76mm guns mounted on patrol boats, and at times also Gabriel missiles.

Most of the destruction in the camps, therefore, especially in the zone south of the Corniche Mazraa, was due primarily to artillery fire, often in response to a PLO attack, rather than being caused either by ground forces throwing satchel charges or grenades into houses or even less so by Israeli bombing runs. A significant number of civilian casualties and heavy property damage did result, but it is simply inaccurate to attribute this either to undisciplined ground-force actions or to indiscriminate air-force bombing. Generally speaking, it was a consequence of massed sheaved artillery employed within narrow urban zones.

CIVILIAN CASUALTIES

It is a curious aspect of the siege that neither the Israelis nor the PLO have been willing to provide an estimate of the number of civilian dead as a result of military action during the siege. In the war in the south, on the other hand, both sides competed for credibility by publishing their different accounts of the number of dead and wounded. After the battle for Beirut, however, no such figures were published. Thus any estimate of the dead is fraught with the risk of inaccuracy. Yet it seems possible to arrive at at least a close reckoning of the number of civilians killed and wounded in the siege.

On September 1, 1982, after the siege ended and the PLO had withdrawn, *An Nahar*, the well-respected Lebanese newspaper published in Beirut, noted in an article that the total number of all military personnel and civilians killed during the entire war was 17,825. It estimated that 30,103 were wounded.[2] The number of dead and wounded counts all parties in all zones of combat in all theaters of operations, including the siege of Beirut. The estimates were compiled by the Lebanese Ministry of the Interior and were the results of a two-week survey of hospitals, morgues, and police reports. It remains the only public estimate made available by even a moderately reliable source.

If the figure of 17,825 is used as a base line, and we subtract the number of Israeli, PLO, and Syrian dead in the southern campaign, we arrive at an approximate number of civilians dead in the siege of Beirut. If we subtract the 2,000 known Syrian dead, the 1,400 PLO dead in the south, the estimated 1,000 PLO killed in the siege (a figure to be confirmed in a later section of this chapter), the 1,000 to 3,000 civilians dead in the south

(IDF or *Time* bureau figures cited earlier), and the 368 IDF soldiers killed, we are left with a total of civilians dead due to the siege of between 10,000 and 12,000. Even the lesser is a number of some magnitude, given the limited nature of the war. If it can be assumed that the American doctors in Beirut are correct who stated both privately and publicly that 80 percent of the casualties they treated throughout the siege were civilian casualties and not PLO fighters, and, further, that they are wrong by a factor of 50 percent, we are still left with a figure of almost 8,000 civilian dead as a result of military action by all sides in the siege. When this figure was presented to various informed sources in Lebanon, including Israeli military intelligence, military leaders of the Phalange, PLO leaders, leaders of the Moslem militia, and journalists who were in Beirut during the war—in short, to a relatively large number of observers who were in a position to make a reasonable estimate—most suggested that 8,000 to 10,000 civilian dead might be too high an estimate. The figure which everyone seemed to agree on was between 4,000 and 5,000 civilian dead resulting from military actions of all sides during the siege.

Regarding the wounded, there is no doubt that the majority on all sides were civilians. If the standard military formula of four wounded to one dead is applied, then upward of 20,000 civilians were wounded in the siege. The military formula is somewhat conservative; given the distribution of the civilian population in the city and the number of wounded throughout the entire war, the figure is more likely to approach 30,000. It must be emphasized that these figures are only estimates. Yet the fact that they are accepted as reasonable by unofficial and official spokesman of most combatants, albeit off the record, suggests that some confidence can be placed in them. In any case, whether the number of dead civilians is 5,000 or 8,000, there is no doubt that the number of dead civilians in Beirut exceeded the number of military casualties by about six to one.

Property damage is easier to estimate. Anyone visiting Beirut immediately after the war was struck by the localization of the damage to the physical structure of the city. East Beirut escaped with hardly any damage at all. Much of what damage there was in East Beirut was the result of the civil war. The area north of the Corniche Mazraa, except for the port area, suffered only limited damage of moderate intensity. Most real damage in Beirut was confined to the Ouzai industrial area and the area near the airport. Heavily damaged, too, were the camps themselves—Sabra, Shatila, and Bourj el Barajneh—where the damage was severe. The present policy of the Lebanese government forbids the rebuilding of destroyed Palestinian houses anywhere in the country, which forces the Palestinians to live in tents. The Lebanese government wants to give the impression that the Palestinian presence in Lebanon as a permanent fact of life is at an end, and permitting only temporary shelters is intended to drive this point home. The Mayor of Beirut, Metreit Nammar, estimated that no more than 20 percent to 25 percent of the destruction in the entire city was the result of the recent war. Most of the damage was old damage from the 1975–76 war which the central government simply could not repair because it did not fully control the various areas of the city or because it lacked the financial resources to do so. Visiting American generals taken on a tour of the war zone noted publicly that much of the damage had been done long before this war occurred.[3]

PLO CASUALTIES AND LOSSES

The strategy adopted by the Israelis was such that its military action did not take a heavy toll of PLO fighters and their military capabilities in Beirut. Once the Israelis opted for siege warfare and decided not to go house-to-house and dig the PLO out of their strongpoints to kill or capture them, it was almost certain that not many PLO fighters would die. It is an axiom of warfare that neither aerial bombardment nor artillery kill many troops that are prepared for the bombardment; artillery tends to kill only troops (or civilians) that are in the open or taken by surprise. The PLO had had plenty of time to prepare for the bombardment and had an extensive network of tunnels and trenches from which to fight. The rubble itself was used as cover from air and artillery attack and since the PLO units were small, highly mobile, and deployed in constantly changing positions, it was difficult to hit their units from the air. Comparatively few of the PLO forces were killed or wounded by IDF ground action, and even fewer were killed by bombing and artillery.

Once again, the figures are only estimates. Nonetheless, they seem to be generally accurate. At the beginning of the war, Israeli intelligence estimated that there were some 6,000 PLO fighters in the Beirut area. As the war in the south progressed and PLO in those areas fled, at least 6,000 PLO fighters were able to reach Beirut safely to continue the war; about 2,500 or so reached the Syrian forces in the Bekaa. When the siege began, the number of PLO in the city approached 14,000. When the siege ended, the Israelis demanded a list of PLO fighters as part of the settlement, and with that list were able to confirm that 14,616 PLO of various factions left the city, including their wounded. This figure clearly indicates that not very many PLO fighters were killed in the siege. In fact, Israeli intelligence officials seem to believe that not more than a thousand or so PLO were actually killed, which, given the nature of the fighting, was not very many. Most—14,616—survived and were allowed to leave Beirut for Arab countries that had accepted them.

The PLO suffered fairly large equipment losses, as it had in the southern campaign. A list provided by the IDF showed that 960 tons of ammunition, including artillery and small-arms ammunition; 243 combat vehicles; 159 antitank weapons; 13 heavy mortars; 12 heavy field-artillery pieces; 38 antiaircraft guns; 108 pieces of communications equipment; and 643 optical instruments were captured. Taken together, this equipment is enough to equip a force of six to eight thousand fighters, except for small arms, which were in plentiful supply.

The Israeli Defense Force appears to have suffered disproportionately far more casualties in these engagements than did the PLO. In the battle for Beirut, the IDF lost 88 dead and 750 wounded, despite the fact that every precaution was taken to minimize the intensity of battle. This means that approximately 23 percent of the total war dead in all operations of Peace for Galilee and 32 percent of the total wounded were the result of the siege of Beirut—and this without house-to-house fighting and with the clear advantage of overwhelming air and firepower support.

VICTORY OR DEFEAT

The siege of Beirut was a clear-cut military victory for the Israeli forces and a major political defeat for the PLO. Although

Israel came under heavy criticism from a number of Western powers for its actions and lost some support as a consequence of the successful media campaign waged against it, Operation Peace for Galilee in the end did achieve its military objectives. The PLO in the south was driven from its major bases of operations, and its arms caches and infrastructure were systematically rooted out. In Beirut, the "expulsion" of the PLO was achieved, and for the first time since 1968 the PLO was not in a position from which to attack Israel. The siege of Beirut as well as the war in the south can generally be considered a military success.

For its part, the PLO was able to achieve only one of its goals. That was the rescue and survival of most of its fighting force. The evacuation agreement worked out by the United States allowed almost the entire PLO fighting corps and its leaders to leave intact and to take their wounded with them. Further, not a single major leader of the organization was killed, captured, or wounded. Yet, in the larger context, the PLO had suffered a major military and political defeat. The PLO no longer has a base contiguous to Israel from which to launch its military operations. From the Israeli point of view, this is a great accomplishment; for the first time, its borders are relatively secure from PLO attack. Moreover, the PLO no longer has a capital from which it can orchestrate further military or political activities or which can act as a center to sustain the image that it is a legitimate popular liberation movement. With their expulsion from the city, the PLO has been reduced to their status prior to 1968. There is simply no place to call home anymore.

The defense of Beirut actually gained the PLO little from a larger political perspective. It was unsuccessful in its attempt to secure any sort of "recognition" of the PLO as the sole representative of the Palestinian people. To be sure, this recognition had been granted by a number of Arab states several years before. But what the PLO had hoped to obtain by holding on in Beirut was recognition from the United States in exchange for withdrawal from the city. The PLO has sought recognition from the United States and other Western powers for over fifteen years, and despite the siege of Beirut, this objective has not been achieved.

The PLO forces have been scattered; most have been disarmed and are living in camps in rather remote areas of the Arab states that agreed to accept them. In some of these "friendly" countries, they are even under guard by military forces. None of these states is likely to allow the PLO forces ever to become a major movement within its borders. Most Arab governments understand the threat the PLO posed to Jordan in 1970 and its contribution to destroying the Lebanese government in 1976. No state, and especially no traditional state, is disposed to allow the PLO to become a domestic force within its borders which might one day threaten the stability and context of its own regime.

In short, the Arab governments do not trust the PLO, and it will be kept on a short leash. These governments also understand clearly that if they permit PLO activity to emanate from their areas, they themselves will become targets of Israeli retaliation. The Jordanians have a long history of suffering such retaliation, which serves as an example to most other Arab states. Finally, the PLO fighters in the camps are separated from their families—the extended family traditional to the Arab world—most of whom remain behind in the camps in Beirut and southern Lebanon. The truth is that they are ready hostages should the PLO again undertake military activities against Israel. In any case, except for small arms—most of which have been confiscated and "stored" by the host governments—the PLO has almost no equipment with which to conduct any operations.

As time passes, the PLO might easily cease to become a major factor in the Middle East as its men are allowed to rot in the camps or slowly allowed to enter the mainstream of their host societies or simply wander the Arab world in small groups in search of a cause. Their leadership is in disarray, with plenty of blame to go around for the defeat. And there is serious disagreement among the factions' leaders about how to face the future—a fact clearly demonstrated by the recent armed clashes among rival PLO factions in eastern Lebanon. As a political movement the PLO is powerless, unless some great power resurrects it by giving it status and legitimacy. This could happen if the PLO is allowed to participate in negotiations affecting the status of Lebanon or participate as an equal partner in the larger peace talks under the Camp David formula, which would inevitably focus on the West Bank. If left in their present condition, the PLO may be capable of carrying out a few attacks against targets outside Israel, as they did in the early days. But as a military threat to Israel they are finished for the foreseeable future. And as a political force they have been severely weakened.

5
Battlefield Performance

ETHICAL CONDUCT
ON THE BATTLEFIELD

Because this war was the first in which the IDF had to conduct sustained operations in major urban areas with civilian populations at risk, and because the war was not aimed at the complete destruction of the enemy, limiting military force on the battlefield became a primary concern. The IDF knew quite well that wholesale destruction of civilians and their homes would be counterproductive to any political goals. They knew that it was possible to win all the battles and lose the political war if they did not limit the damage inflicted on Lebanese towns and cities. Extensive destruction of civilians and their homes would inflame international and domestic public opinion, and bring strong pressure from the United States to stop the war. Equally important was the fact that indiscriminate destruction would reduce the military effectiveness of Israel's own soldiers. The Israelis' psychological studies have shown that military effectiveness drops when soldiers believe that what they are being asked to do is wrong. For all these reasons, the IDF took great precautions to ensure that its forces conducted themselves properly on the battlefield.

The IDF perhaps more than any other army stresses in all aspects of its training and officer selection that the use of force within the Jewish historical and moral tradition has an ethical base. This doctrine permeates all aspects of IDF military life. It is the doctrine of Tohar Haneshek, or the purity of arms. The fundamental tenet of Tohar Haneshek is that military force may be used only in self-defense; the IDF exists primarily to protect the Jewish state and the Jewish people. Moreover, there is a clear notion that there is a proper "moral conduct for war"; a state may be engaged in hostilities, but that does not lower the standards of humanity that must be applied. It is a fundamental tenet of Israeli doctrine that destruction must be limited wherever possible, and, above all, human life must be preserved. The IDF extends the doctrine of Tohar Haneshek to its enemies as well, so there are extremely rigid rules regarding the treatment of prisoners, saving lives, and giving first aid to injured civilians and enemy soldiers. The Israelis have wrapped a very effective military force within a cocoon of morality in order to assure that combat force is applied in a way consistent with Jewish historical tradition and values.

The IDF has a very long tradition of training its soldiers in the ethical dimension of war. This dimension has throughout the years led officers and men on many occasions to refuse to execute orders which they felt to be unethical. They also openly criticize their officers. Following the example of Moshe Dayan, there is a kind of folk aura which surrounds officers who for ethical reasons are slightly rebellious, even to the point where they serve time in the brig as Dayan once did. Such officers become folk heroes when they refuse to execute orders and can justify their action on ethical grounds. A true story told following the war in 1956 concerned two young battalion commanders who went over the head of their brigade commander and asked the Chief of Staff to remove and prosecute the brigade commander because he had not shown due care in the moral application of force since he did not take due care to protect his men and civilians in the battle area. While nothing much came of the case, it is worth pointing out that one of the two battalion commanders was Mordechai Gur, who later became Chief of Staff. The other was Rafael Eitan, who later also became Chief of Staff. The brigade commander against whom they brought these charges was Ariel Sharon, the Defense Minister during the Lebanese war.

The IDF links ethical action and the limits of destruction to its battlefield doctrine and links it all to the effectiveness of its military machine. It is an integral aspect of IDF training of combat soldiers that soldiers fight best when they are not asked to do things which reasonable men would judge to be immoral.

From this proceeds a concern to reduce the human and material damages of war. As one examines the conduct of the Israeli Defense Force throughout the Lebanon war, it is a simple truth that the IDF took steps that other armies would not have taken to limit damage to property and reduce the loss of human life, both civilian and military, to both friends and enemies. During the siege of Tyre and Sidon, for example, the IDF held up its attack on those cities to drop leaflets to warn the civilian population. These leaflets contained a map of the city and showed the avenues of advance that the IDF would take when it entered the city. They designated certain areas of the city which would be free of fighting and to which civilians could go and be safe. In Sidon, the safe area was the beach. Thousands of civilians went there, and the beach was not touched. In taking such steps to minimize civilian casualties, the IDF disclosed in advance what its avenue of attack would be and gave the PLO an opportunity to deploy its forces to meet the advance. The leaflet drop reduced the element of surprise. Paradoxically, while the IDF continually sought to achieve surprise in the east by moving swiftly and out-flanking PLO forces, in the west, especially in the areas with urban populations, they often gave up surprise to minimize the loss of human life. One would be hard pressed to find many examples of an army relinquishing tactical surprise in order to minimize civilian casualties.

Nowhere did the Israeli desire to minimize damage and loss of civilian lives reflect itself more than in the tactics they used in the PLO camps. This was especially so in the two major refugee camps of Rachidiya outside Tyre and in the Ein Hilwe camp outside Sidon. In both places, the PLO often used civilians as human shields and took positions in hospitals, even using the sick and wounded as shields. In most instances, the IDF stayed its firepower there. From a purely military point of view, these camps could easily have been reduced to rubble by artillery and tank fire and, of course, by air attack. Most of the houses are constructed of concrete blocks with tin roofs and are closely packed together. Moreover, the PLO forces that remained behind to fight in the camps were relatively small, certainly not exceeding 150 men in each camp. If the Israelis had wanted to reduce the PLO's military positions in the camps, they could have done so quite rapidly, easily, and virtually without any loss of their own soldiers. Instead, they moved carefully in the camps, house by house, treating civilians involved as if they were hostages. In Ein Hilwe, for example, the Israelis negotiated throughout six days and nights with the PLO, using bullhorns, with negotiators moving back and forth between opposing forces. In some instances, the IDF allowed the PLO to pull out in the darkness and escape through Israeli lines without firing on them. In the end, a great number of civilian lives were spared. Long conversations with individuals living in the camps at the time of the battles disclosed few instances where a concern was not demonstrated by Israeli soldiers.

In built-up areas, IDF soldiers were specifically forbidden to throw hand grenades or satchel charges into houses or buildings before entering them. It is a standard ground-assault technique in house-to-house fighting either to blow a hole through the wall or to throw a grenade through the door before entering. At the very least, one enters a house firing. All these tactics were denied the IDF simply to avoid killing innocent civilians. As a consequence, the PLO often ambushed Israeli soldiers from inside houses. It is a telling statistic that at least 55 percent of the total IDF casualties were inflicted by small-arms fire. The urban ambush using civilians as cover or shields became a basic PLO tactic. It was a tactic that the Israelis knew would be employed against them, and they chose nonetheless to restrain their troops rather than risk greater civilian casualties.

The ethical concern of the IDF was also demonstrated in the area of medical care. The Israeli Defense Force gave a good deal of medical care to civilians and even to wounded PLO's without question. Since most Israeli military casualties were evacuated by helicopter from the places where they were injured, the medical platoons, the roving surgical team and the battalion aid hospitals, had few patients to attend to. These medical facilities were put to treating civilians and PLO wounded. I spoke to a number of doctors who treated the wounds of young men who were suspected PLO. In a number of instances, these wounded men still had their PLO footgear on. In most cases, after they were treated, the Israelis let them return to civilian areas. Once, outside Sidon, a doctor who had been working in the Ein Hilwe PLO camp brought in an ambulance load of fourteen young PLO's who had been hit in a fire fight. Although they still had their uniforms on, Israeli doctors treated them and saved their lives.

Israeli soldiers, before they went into battle, were briefed by their officers and given pamphlets on the location of religious shrines and other important buildings and told to avoid damage to them. Soldiers were lectured almost without end about avoiding civilian casualties, and there was constant higher-staff supervision to see that these lectures were given and that proper behavior was observed on the battlefield. The Israelis had some problems with brutality and improper behavior during the 1978 Operation Litani, and it seems to have been a deliberate policy of the IDF to ensure that none of this occurred in Lebanon.

Moreover, the Israelis accorded the PLO the treatment due POW's in accordance with the Geneva Convention. International law does not consider the PLO a national fighting force and so, in a legal sense, they are not entitled to treatment due prisoners of war. During the early days of the Vietnam War, the American forces defined the guerrillas as not being entitled to Geneva Convention protections. The Israelis, although they refused to grant *official* status to the PLO as a national fighting force, nonetheless instructed their soldiers and their prison-camp personnel to extend to the PLO the rights and privileges of POW's. They did so even in the Ansar camp, and PLO captives were allowed to send letters and receive food and Red Cross visits.

It is an interesting commentary on the ethical base of the Israeli Defense Force that during the entire war, including the occupation, which has lasted more than a year, not a single Israeli soldier has been charged with a major crime. Rape, murder, and brutality—the three most common crimes of any army in war or occupation—have been *totally* absent during the involvement of the IDF in Lebanon. To be sure, minor offenses have occurred in Lebanon, and the IDF took rigid measures to stop them. Any soldier caught with any kind of souvenir— liquor, pictures, cigarettes—in any quantity, including the favorite of Israeli soldiers, the video cassette recorder, which can be purchased for one third the cost in Lebanon, is subject to immediate punishment. If the item exceeded $33 in value, the punishment is a jail term. In the early days of the occupation, the Israelis gave out scores of jail sentences. Even when the soldier had a receipt, having purchased the item, he was punished. From the early days of the war, every soldier returning from Lebanon is required to pass through Israeli customs. Officers are held responsible for ensuring that their soldiers are not smuggling. Israeli soldiers are often required to empty their pockets so their officers can be sure that they have no "souvenirs" or expropriated property from Lebanon. If contraband is found, it is destroyed in front of the soldier.

It is clear from examining the ethical conduct of the Israeli forces on the battlefield toward civilians and the PLO that the IDF has been more restrained than any modern army that comes to mind—certainly more morally restrained than the American army was in Vietnam. In Lebanon, there were no free fire zones, no torturing of civilians, no brutality, no rape, no murder, no wanton destruction of domestic farm animals, and no unnecessary destruction of houses. Israeli society has deep social values and abhors killing and hurting, perhaps as a consequence of the Jewish historical experience. These values are fostered by a military policy deliberately designed to increase the battle effectiveness of IDF soldiers by removing the temptation of being unethical.

THE COST OF WAR

The price paid by Israel for victory in Lebanon in number of dead and wounded was high. While its equipment losses were generally minor compared to other wars, its human losses were very high indeed for such a small nation. Israel lost 368 dead and 2,383 wounded in the war in the south and the siege of Beirut. During the first year of occupation, Israel suffered another 148 dead and 340 wounded, bringing the total dead to 516 and the number of wounded to nearly 2,800.[1] Relative to the population of the United States, the number of Israeli dead and wounded is the equivalent of 32,460 dead and 163,380 wounded for the United States in a period of less than six weeks of combat and one year of occupation; that is, almost three-quarters of the dead suffered by the United States during the Vietnam conflict, which lasted ten years.

From an economic perspective, the war was not terribly costly to Israel. Economists estimate that the war cost about one half billion dollars in incremental costs; that is, costs in addition to what it would have cost Israel to sustain peacetime military operations. The overall cost to the Israelis was about $1.26 billion (see Table 5 in the Appendix). The war consumed about 1.2 months of the gross national product; the 1973 war in two and a half weeks consumed a full year's GNP. The costs of occupation are minimal, since the force in Lebanon is small, under thirty thousand, and there is no need to garrison and patrol the borders. The war, then, had only limited effects on the Israeli economy. The inflationary pressures are not war-related but result from a political decision to retain indexing and a reluctance to fight inflation through unemployment for fear of increasing emigration.

The most reliable figures about equipment indicate that 140 Israeli battle tanks were knocked out of action, mostly M-60's and Centurions, with only a handful of Merkavas damaged. Of that total, a hundred were damaged but repairable; approximately forty were damaged beyond repair. All the Merkavas were back in action within forty-eight hours. In addition, the Israelis lost about 135 armored personnel carriers hit so badly that they could not be repaired. Information about other equipment lost by the IDF is unavailable for security reasons.

If one examines the distribution of casualties among various ranks, it appears that once again the number of Israeli officers dead and wounded was terribly high. Ninety-seven officers were killed, or about 26.3 percent of the total casualties. Since the officer corps comprises 6 percent to 8 percent of combat strength, its proportion of dead was about three times higher than one might expect. By comparison, during the ten years of war in Vietnam, American officers comprised about 16.9 percent of total strength and suffered 7 percent of the dead. The percentage of officers killed in Lebanon relative to their total force strength is about what it was in the 1973 and 1967 wars. In terms of leadership and courage, the figures from the Lebanese war are clear proof that the slogan of the Israeli officer corps, "*Acharei*," "Follow me," is very much practiced.

The distribution of death by rank in the Lebanon war (see Table 6 in the Appendix) is very revealing. Small-unit combat leaders bore a tremendous burden of death and sacrifice. In total, 132 sergeants died, 35.8 percent of the total dead, including some sixty senior NCO's. If the officer losses are combined with the losses suffered by sergeants, the data indicate that a total of 229 "leadership elements," small-unit enlisted and commissioned leaders, died in the war, a number of dead equal to 62.2 percent of the entire total of IDF dead.

Table 7 in the Appendix lists the number of wounded by rank. The figures, once again, reveal a high number of wounded NCO's and officers. About 14.4 percent of the total wounded were officers—almost twice their proportionate share. Leadership elements comprised 32.4 percent of the total wounded. Of this total number of wounded, 4.4 percent were "seriously wounded"; 17.8 percent "moderately wounded"; and 77.8 percent had "minor wounds requiring treatment." The percentage of wounded officers, although almost twice the average proportion, was in fact considerably below the number of wounded officers in the 1973 and 1967 wars. An investigation carried out by the medical corps revealed an interesting indication of heroism. The number of wounded officers appeared low because a significant number who suffered either moderate or minor wounds refused to disengage from their units and be treated. Many treated themselves or were treated by their unit medics and continued to fight. In addition, some officers who were taken back to be treated at aid stations demanded that the treatment of wounds not be recorded because it would have prevented them from rejoining their units.

Table 8 lists Israeli casualties suffered by the various branches of service. Of the total dead and wounded, 34.7 percent were from Israeli infantry units; that is, the elite Golani infantry, paratroop infantry, and the Nahal infantry, which was thrown into battle as the war developed. Although the Israelis are particularly loath to use the infantry for fear of heavy casualties, the ratio of dead to wounded was much higher in the armor units than in the infantry units. The ratio in the armored corps was one to five, whereas in the infantry it was one to ten, suggesting that the infantry was less vulnerable than armor personnel.

Fifty-five percent of the total casualties suffered by the Israelis were from small-arms fire.[2] Until the Lebanese war, the highest percentage of casualties from small arms (53 percent) was suffered by the American forces in Vietnam. Equally significant is the fact that most of the Israeli casualties were wounds to the head, neck, and abdomen, and 40 percent of head and neck wounds proved fatal.[3] An examination of the flak jackets after the war showed that casualties due to small-arms fire would have been 20 percent higher had the troops not used flak jackets. Only a small percentage of casualties were caused by artillery, probably less than 8 percent, and most of these occurred in the battle for the Beirut–Damascus highway and during the siege of Beirut, where Israeli units were often subject to concentrated artillery and Katyusha rocket fire.[4] Burn casualties occurred at a rate of 22 percent, about the same rate as in 1973. The Israelis found, however, that the severity of burns in this war declined greatly because of improved tank design, the fact that gasoline-powered tanks are no longer in the Israeli inventory, the existence of high-technology Spectronix fire-suppression systems, and protective clothing worn by tankers. The Israelis had twenty-six cases of severe burns as a result of M-60 and Centurion tanks being hit.[5] In addition, a significant number of burns were suffered by soldiers in armored personnel carriers, whose aluminum skins tended to ignite when they were hit by RPG's.

A particularly significant category of casualties were those of soldiers afflicted by what the Israelis call "battle reactions," what in other armies is called battle shock, or psychological casualties. In 1973, because the IDF considered the number of psychological casualties suffered in the Yom Kippur War too high, the army undertook a complete program to prevent and treat battle shock. Trained battle psychologists were with every brigade and division and made responsible for monitoring the morale and stress levels of combat units. Sophisticated methods for measuring combat morale and confidence were developed and implemented, so that it was possible to survey the entire IDF ground force through a questionnaire, transmit the results to rear headquarters for a computer analysis, and report to commanders in less than twenty-four hours.[6] The process was a continuing one and the monitoring was vigorous. The object, of course, was prevention: to find evidence of breakdowns of morale and confidence prior to battle. The IDF also developed treatment techniques for dealing with battle shock when it occurred. Usually this called for treatment by battle psychologists right at the front, often within sight and sound of the battle. The program took almost eight years to implement and was generally regarded as a success.

An examination of psychological casualties in the Lebanon

war suggests, however, that the program may not have worked as effectively as was hoped. The rate of psychiatric casualties suffered by the IDF in Lebanon was at least as high as in 1973 and probably higher. In an interview, Dr. Ron Levy, head of the IDF Mental Health Unit, noted that 10 percent of the soldiers in Lebanon suffered from some type of battle reaction, ranging from fatigue to paralysis.[7] The rate of psychiatric casualties in the Lebanon war as reported at the Third International Conference on Stress in War and Peace held in Jerusalem in January 1983 was 26 percent. The larger number includes all categories of battle reactions; the lower number, 10 percent, probably refers to the number of IDF soldiers who suffered relatively serious psychiatric reactions. Of those who suffered serious battle reactions, 40 percent were treated successfully and returned to their units. A psychiatric casualty rate of 10 percent of the total wounded would amount to 275 soldiers who had suffered some serious battle reaction. Since 60 percent of these soldiers could not be returned to their units, this meant that at least 165 soldiers were unable to fight due to psychological stress.

If the figures provided by Dr. Levy are correct, they tend to indicate that the IDF may have as serious a problem as other armies in terms of its ability to deal with battle casualties. The rate of battle-shock casualties in the Yom Kippur War was between 3.5 percent and 5 percent. The rate of battle-shock casualties suffered in Lebanon was anywhere from two to three times higher than in the 1973 war. By any comparison with the Yom Kippur War, the war in Lebanon was easy, and yet the rate of battle-shock casualties was higher. Moreover, a battle-shock rate of 10 percent is higher than that of the German army in World War II. The German army in World War II suffered a psychological casualty rate of about 2.6 percent.[8] However, the Israeli rate of 10 percent is considerably better than that of the American army in World War II, which suffered 26 percent of its total casualties due to psychological reasons.[9] It is only slightly better than the 12 percent of Americans in Vietnam who suffered some type of battle reaction.[10]

Equally significant is the number of soldiers who suffered battle reactions and were able to return to battle. The Israeli experience is much poorer than one would have expected. Return rates experienced by the IDF in Lebanon were about 40 percent, much lower than the 80 percent return rate experienced by the German army in World War II, and well below the 65 percent return rate experienced by the United States army in World War II.[11] It is likely that the extent of casualties due to psychological stress among IDF soldiers will be of great concern to the IDF as they examine the lessons to be learned from the war in Lebanon.

Conversations with battle psychologists suggest some possible explanations for the high rate of battle-shock casualties. For instance, the IDF for the first time had to fight in heavily populated areas. This raised considerable ethical problems for the soldiers and at the same time increased their physical danger. In addition, the training of Israeli soldiers on how to fight had to be modified continually as a consequence of enemy tactics and terrain. This may have led to a certain degree of confusion and uncertainty. Another contributing factor may have been the nature of the war. It was a war of ambush where the enemy often had the first shot. This is a situation for which Israeli soldiers were not trained; they are trained in rapid advance and shock action and always to take the initiative. In Lebanon, they frequently found themselves the object of ambushes.

There is also the fact that each society may have a "vulnerability constant" with reference to battle shock. As with the suicide rate, which tends to be fairly constant in certain societies, it may be that certain societies are prone to given levels of battle shock, regardless of attempts to treat or prevent it. To be sure, if no such attempts are made, the rates may increase. But even with preventive mechanisms and treatment, the rates may be relatively constant. Israeli society may be disposed to accept psychological explanations for behavior, and this may have turned into a self-fulfilling prophecy. If soldiers become convinced that battle reactions are acceptable ways of dealing with stress, they may in fact suffer battle reactions to relieve stress.

Finally, there is the possibility that for the first time the Israelis have waged war when their goals were less than clear to most of their soldiers. This may have an effect on unit cohesion, and the first line of defense against battle shock is strong unit cohesion. A high degree of battle shock may indicate lower levels of cohesion than expected. This remains an open question, however. Other indicators suggest that the level of cohesion in Israeli units is very strong.

Casualty lists released by the IDF, corollated with the days and places on which battles were fought, makes it possible to determine approximately against which enemy, the Syrians or the PLO, and where, in the south or during the siege of Beirut, IDF casualties were suffered. An analysis indicates that it was in battles with the Syrians that the IDF suffered the great majority of dead and wounded. The IDF lost 255 dead and 1,537 wounded, 69.2 percent of its total dead and 64.4 percent of its total wounded, in the "accidental war" against the Syrians. The battles against the Syrians were by far the most costly for the IDF. In fighting against the PLO in the south, the IDF had only marginal casualties: twenty-five men died fighting there, and ninety-six were wounded; these figures constitute about 6.9 percent of Israel's total dead and 4.2 percent of its total wounded.

Clearly, the most costly decision made by the Israelis was to fight the Syrians. It was the Syrians who inflicted the lion's share of casualties. The casualties suffered by the IDF in the siege of Beirut were greater in number than those incurred in the fighting against the PLO in the entire war in the south. During the siege of Beirut, the IDF lost 88 dead and 750 wounded, 23.9 percent of its total dead and 31.4 percent of its total wounded. More than twice as many Israelis, 69.2 percent, were killed by the Syrians than by the PLO, which killed 30.8 percent. The same distribution applies to the number of wounded. The Syrians inflicted 64.4 percent of the total wounded, compared to 35.6 percent inflicted by the PLO.

Casualty figures cannot be viewed in a vacuum; all wars produce casualties. The question is how serious were the Israeli casualties relative to their total strength, and how effective were Israeli battle operations against the enemy in terms of the number of dead and wounded inflicted on them. About 12 percent of the total PLO strength was killed. By historical standards, this is not very high, but it is the highest of the three major combatants. About 2.5 percent of total Syrian forces was killed, while only .5 percent of the total IDF strength committed in the war was killed. When presented in raw numbers, the kill ratio of the IDF to the PLO was about 1 to 6.5, which is to say that for every Israeli soldier, 6.5 PLO died. The ratio vis-à-vis the Syrians was not quite as good. It was 1:4, which is to say that for every Israeli soldier killed, at least four Syrian soldiers died. These kill ratios favor the Israelis, but compared to their performance in other wars, the IDF's kill ratios actually fell.

Israel paid a high toll in human lives to protect its existence. No matter how sophisticated the IDF equipment, it is men who must operate the machines. And it is manpower in both numbers and quality that remains the greatest concern to Israeli planners. Heavy losses have a particularly strong impact because Israeli society is so closely knit.

MORALE

The close identification of the IDF with society at large means that shifts in public opinion are almost immediately reflected in the opinions of its soldiers. Unlike the United States or Germany, where military service removes the citizen from the larger social arena and where dissent and open disagreement with civilian leadership decisions are not allowed, or, as in a professional army like England's, whose soldiers are not expected to dissent from public policy because the army is separate from the larger society, the IDF is a direct projection of Israel's larger social values and reacts quickly to swings in public opinion.

In the past, this connection has been a major source of strength. During the Lebanon war, however, for the first time public opinion in the larger body politic showed less than enthusiastic support for military operations. In a poll taken by the *Jerusalem Post* a week after the invasion, 78 percent of those interviewed said the invasion was "definitely justified"; 16 percent supported it with "a few reservations"; and 5 percent opposed it.[12] Basically, these numbers were consistent with past patterns of support for a war. However, a poll taken by *Yediot Aharonot* two weeks later showed that 83 percent supported the war while 14 percent opposed it. This level of opposition is particularly high by Israeli standards. Prior to the siege, 68 percent said they opposed any military action in Beirut whatsoever.[13]

This declining support for the war began to be reflected by the IDF soldiers. A poll taken by Hanoch Smith in December 1983, whose results were provided to me in a personal interview, showed that 66 percent of the Israeli populace thought the "Lebanese war was morally justified." Among serving soldiers, this percentage was lower, only 62 percent. Seventeen percent of the larger population opposed the war, saying that it was not morally justified. The percentage among serving soldiers was higher, almost 20 percent. With regard to Beirut, 38 percent of the general population said that "entrance into Beirut was unnecessary." A much larger number of serving soldiers, 48 percent, thought so too.[14] Although the lack of public support for some of the specific aspects of the war was not sufficiently deep to weaken the field performance of the Israeli forces, nonetheless it was much higher than it had been in past wars. As the war went on, soldiers came to reflect more and more the growing anti-war sentiment, and a number of incidents of overt criticism and refusal to execute orders occurred within the IDF.

The most prominent of these incidents involved Colonel Eli Geva, commander of the brigade that spearheaded the attack on the western front and struck all the way to the outskirts of Beirut. Geva had a noble and distinguished career as a tank commander. He was the son of a general and a hero of the 1973 Golan campaign, where he served as a battalion commander under Avigdor Kahalani. He was also the IDF's youngest brigade commander. As Israeli forces encircled Beirut, Geva began to have second thoughts about the wisdom of IDF forces entering the city. Accordingly, he asked to be removed from his command rather than have to lead it in an attack on the city. He was quoted in public sources as saying: "I do not have the courage to look into the eyes of the parents of the soldiers who would be killed going into West Beirut."[15] He asked for and was granted a meeting with the Chief of Staff and with Prime Minister Begin. In that meeting he stated that he would not kill children and women, which he thought would be inevitable if an attack occurred. He offered to resign his commission and fight on with his men as a common soldier, in much the same way as General MacArthur in the Battle of Bataan. The request was refused, and Eli Geva was dismissed from the IDF.

Whether or not one agrees with Geva's action, it was obviously a result of a major and open disagreement with the policies of the war. It should also be noted that the notion of moral protest is in the best tradition of Tohar Haneshek. Indeed, so personal and ethically based was his decision—and Geva said it was the only decision he could take—that he did not expect his men to follow him.[16] The Geva case became a *cause célèbre* in Israel.

Needless to say, to have a major military commander refuse to engage his forces in battle is a rare occurrence in the IDF.

However, although the Geva case was the most well-known, a number of others occurred which clearly reflected the lack of agreement within the IDF as to the course of the war. In one instance, an unidentified senior officer was dismissed after he wrote an article for a major journal, *Ha'aretz*, defending Colonel Geva's actions. It was an anonymous article, but an IDF investigation uncovered his identity and he was removed. In another incident, a number of officers, including at least one general, tendered their resignations in disagreement over the conduct of the war. One of these was General Amram Mitzna, the officer in charge of the IDF Command and Staff College, who also had a long and distinguished combat record. Still another incident involved Avraham Burg, a reserve lieutenant in the paratroops who saw action around Lake Qaraoun against the Syrians. Burg is the son of Yosef Burg, the head of the National Religious Party and the longest-serving member of the Begin cabinet. Burg also spoke out, saying: "I had to make my own personal reckoning, and in the final analysis personal experience and conviction is stronger than anything else."[17] He said that the war in Lebanon was the turning point, especially "the terrible killing on all sides, particularly of innocent civilians. I cannot get out of my mind the image of children with their hands held high in surrender because they were scared of me."[18]

Another significant incident within the IDF was the formation of an organization called Soldiers Against Silence, founded by soldiers of a paratroop antitank unit that had seen action against the Syrians. On the day of their release from duty, two thousand men from this and other elite paratroop units signed a petition expressing opposition to the war and calling for the resignation of Ariel Sharon as Defense Minister because "he is responsible for the crisis of confidence and motivation in the army that we represent."[19] The large number of soldiers signing the petition clearly indicated a disruption in the IDF over the course of the war. Two thousand men is almost the equivalent of a full Israeli brigade and, in comparative terms, would be the equivalent of almost eleven thousand soldiers openly signing a petition against the war during the Vietnam conflict. In yet another incident, Staff Sergeant Udi Shiloni, a member of Soldiers Against

Silence, said that before the battle his men came to him to say that if they were killed, he should go to their funerals and tell their families that they died in a war they did not believe in.[20] Shiloni was making the point publicly that in his view a large number of the men who fought the war did not support it.

On June 28, thirty soldiers on leave from Lebanon and in uniform openly demonstrated against the war in front of the Prime Minister's office. The group included officers and sergeants, protesting the expected invasion of West Beirut and the bombing of civilians in the PLO camps. The organizer of the protest, Sergeant Eyal Ehrlich, said his group represented the feelings of "90 percent of the soldiers in Lebanon."[21] Along with him was a captain, Ronen Ben-Shera, whose arm was still bandaged from a wound he had received. He said: "This is the most terrible war we've been in, having to confront civilians . . . You entered the camp—the people you saw in front of you were just civilians— and then someone shoots at you from some house. Well, you have to shoot back in self-defense, even when you know there are women and children inside, too."[22] This type of opposition to the war was reflected in other incidents, not least of which were reports from the front that Israeli soldiers had begun to distrust accounts of the war broadcast by the official Israeli army radio and began to listen to Radio Lebanon in English or Arabic to get a more accurate account of events.[23] And on September 26 rumors began to circulate that 260 regular army and reserve officers, some of them generals, had signed a petition calling for Sharon to quit because of his conduct of the war.

If public opinion affected the opinion of soldiers in the IDF, there is little doubt that the open demonstrations of protest and dissent by soldiers served to trigger civilian demonstrations. During the war, there were scores of anti-war demonstrations, and a smaller number in favor of the war. These demonstrations ranged in size from a few thousand to a few hundred. The largest occurred in Tel Aviv after the Sabra and Shatila massacre; the crowd was estimated as 400,000 strong, almost 10 percent of the Israeli population. By comparison, the largest anti-Vietnam rally in the United States was the Day of Protest, in which 500,000 people turned out. A comparable American protest proportionate to the 400,000 who turned out in Tel Aviv would require 20 million demonstrators!

Clearly, the need for the first time to conduct military operations against an enemy hiding in civilian areas forced soldiers and commanders to face personal crises of conscience. In order to uphold the instructions on the moral conduct of war, units were exposed to suffering casualties that might otherwise have been avoided. And Israeli soldiers for the first time saw civilians die as a result of their actions and saw the fear on the faces of civilians they encountered in the battle zone. No doubt, this made a number of officers and soldiers feel that what they were doing was not much different from what the PLO did; that is, involve civilians in war.

There is no denying that there was considerable disagreement, dissent, confusion, and questioning among the soldiery of the Israeli Defense Force in the Lebanon war. However, from the data available, it would appear that this did not have much effect on the ability of the IDF to carry out its mission in the field. Perhaps if the war had dragged on, it would have had a more significant effect, as was the case in Vietnam. But the war was short enough so that, although opinion crystalized, it did not actually disrupt operations. In any case, speaking out and dissenting openly has a long tradition in the Israeli military, and it is encouraged as a way of improving the military by bringing problems to the attention of commanders. In the officer corps, there is a strong sense of the Prussian tradition of von Scharnhorst, and officers do not fear that they will be punished merely for speaking out. Colonel Geva and other officers who dissented were all given hearings and allowed to state their case. Geva had several meetings with the Chief of Staff and was granted an opportunity to present his case to the Prime Minister. No attempt was made on the part of the IDF or the political leadership to conceal the fact that dissent was surfacing. IDF officers are trained and encouraged to speak out and to use their own judgment. Thus, the presence of dissent in and of itself does not have an effect on the IDF's ability to carry out its mission. Quite the opposite; it may be taken as a sign of health.

The health of the IDF is intimately linked with the nation's survival. While criticism and morality are stressed, there is a deep-seated belief that criticism cannot be allowed to impede the ability of the military to protect the Jewish state—a point which even the dissenters were careful to observe. Critics within the IDF justified their criticism on the grounds that the policies they objected to would hurt the IDF's ability to defend the state. This was heard at Yamit during the evacuation of Sinai, when a number of soldiers refused to participate in the evacuation precisely because it would not be in the larger interest of Jewish society. It is strongly believed, moreover, that a moral army is the best army; psychological studies by the Israeli army indicate that soldiers fight well when the morality of their actions is unquestioned in their own minds. When soldiers seriously question the morality of their actions, combat ability declines. As a consequence, the IDF feels that the ability to criticize and to question orders is a vital resource.

The individuals involved in dissent went out of their way to minimize the impact their actions would have on combat operations. Geva, for example, said that although he could not lead his men in battle, he would fight on as a common soldier; he made the point that he did not expect the men to follow his decision, leaving it instead to their own consciences. Spokesmen for Soldiers Against Silence also made the point that there was no question of their members refusing to follow orders. Their wish was to bring to the attention of military and political leaders the extent of the dissent which they felt existed within the IDF. Mordechai Bar On, former Chief Education Officer of the army and a colonel in the reserve who fought in Lebanon, continually stressed, as chief spokesman for the Peace Now movement, that the movement had no wish to impair the ability of the IDF to fight or encourage its members not to follow legitimate orders.

The major impact of the dissent in the IDF during the war would seem to have been a lower morale among the soldiers than in past wars, and perhaps a higher rate of combat-reaction cases than in the past. These seem to be the reactions of individual soldiers to their own personal experiences far more than a reaction to the protests of the larger society.

Measured by other indicators of morale, however, the Israeli Defense Force comes off rather well. Take, for example, combat refusals. During Vietnam, one of the major indicators of low morale and low discipline among the American forces was what the Defense Department called "combat refusals"; that is, incidents where units or soldiers refused to engage the enemy on order or simply refused to serve in the war zone. During the Lebanon war, not a single incidence of combat refusal to engage was reported on the part of an Israeli unit, although there were at least four such incidences on the part of individual soldiers.[24]

Another type of combat refusal, the refusal of soldiers to serve in Lebanon, was highly uncommon: four officers and nine enlisted men refused to do their military service in Lebanon. Most of these were reservists, and they were meted the standard twenty-eight days in prison. Even this small number of refusals must be seen in perspective, however. Every year the Israeli Defense Force has a number of refusals, usually soldiers who refuse to serve on the West Bank. During the evacuation of Yamit, a number of soldiers refused to serve there. On average, over the past five years, the number of soldiers each year who refused to serve was between ten and twelve.[25] The refusal of thirteen officers and enlisted men to serve in Lebanon, then, is not out of line with the yearly average; it would be difficult to make a case that their combat refusals represented a heightened opposition to the war.

Another indication of low morale or lack of cohesion would be the suicide rate. Information available on suicide is rather sketchy. Interviews with individuals who keep records on suicide indicate that the rate of suicide and suicide attempts in the Israeli Defense Force in 1982–83 was the lowest in ten years; the suicide rate of those stationed in Lebanon was, paradoxically, lower than for units stationed elsewhere; and the rate was the lowest among combat units in Lebanon as opposed to noncombat units.[26] Unlike the Soviet army, where suicide is a very common occurrence and a clear indication of low morale and low combat effectiveness,[27] the Israeli figures suggest that the suicide rate has not been affected by the Lebanon war.

In January 1983, the Department of Behavioral Science of the IDF conducted a random survey of fifteen hundred soldiers who had served in Lebanon to determine their feelings during the war. All respondents were taken from combat units. The results of the survey appear in Table 9 in the Appendix. Generally speaking, the responses of the soldiers to the questionnaires indicated that unit cohesion was very high, as was morale. For example, 60 percent of the soldiers said that their morale had been "high" or "very high" while they were in battle with their units, and

86 percent said that they had received a "high" or "very high" degree of mutual support from their peers while in their units. Eighty percent said that they had a "high" or "very high" degree of confidence in their immediate commanders; 85 percent felt that the soldiers of their own rank, their peers in combat units, had fought well and performed well under fire.[28] The data suggest that, whatever else may have gone wrong, the level of morale and cohesion was sufficiently high; no severe or even moderately severe morale problems surfaced while in battle.

CONCLUSION

The Jewish tradition demanding moral conduct in war and the expectation that Israeli officers and soldiers will use their judgment and make ethical decisions almost guaranteed that some measure of opposition to the war would emerge. Add to this the moral bias of the larger society from which the majority of IDF forces are drawn as conscripts and one could predict a much greater degree of dissent within the Israeli army than might be expected in other armies of the West. In a short war, however, a small degree of dissent presents no threat to combat ability.

It is difficult not to compare the Israeli soldiers' penchant for speaking out and bringing ethical problems to the attention of their leaders with the record of American soldiers in Vietnam, where in ten years not a single officer resigned in protest over the moral problems of that war or spoke out against them.[29] When the war was over, a number of general officers disagreed with certain policies but nonetheless carried out orders without question.[30] One might venture the opinion that if one had to choose between an army in which ethical protest is a relatively constant feature and one in which ethical protest is almost nonexistent, one would be much better off, from the perspective of the moral tenor of the military establishment as well as combat effectiveness, in selecting a military force in which moral protest is a recognized and respected mechanism for bringing protest out into the open.

6
The Lessons of War

The war in Lebanon gave the Israeli Defense Force its first opportunity to test its newly configured military machine under fire. Having introduced a number of changes in structure, tactics, weaponry, control, and equipment, the IDF that marched into Lebanon was a vastly different army from the one that took the field in 1973. The restructuring of the IDF was a direct response to its experiences in the Yom Kippur War, including a number of serious deficiencies and in one instance a near-catastrophe. Yet conditions in Lebanon bore almost no similarity to the conditions in which the Israeli army had to fight in the 1973 war. A number of shortcomings emerged in Lebanon because the IDF was not adequately prepared to fight that kind of war. An examination of the performance of the IDF under these conditions is important.

TACTICS

The tactics employed by the IDF in Lebanon were not those drawn from the lessons of the 1973 war. Here is a clear example of an army preparing for the last war it had fought, only to find itself facing battle conditions radically different from those it had prepared for. The special conditions of the Lebanese theater of battle forced the IDF to develop tactical solutions to problems that they did not adequately foresee or at least were not adequately prepared for. The degree to which Sharon orchestrated battlefield conditions by portraying Israeli advances as a reaction to enemy activity indicated that the tactical plan was less than clearly formed in the minds of the field commanders.

IDF tactics in Lebanon were affected by four major considerations: (1) its lack of experience in the particular theater of operations; (2) the configuration of its forces; (3) the nature of the terrain; (4) a great concern for human life. The IDF had almost no experience in the type of fighting they had to engage in in Lebanon—fighting characterized by combat in built-up areas and populated urban areas, and mountain warfare, with all its attendant difficulties. The only IDF experience in fighting in urban areas was in Jerusalem in 1967 and the short battle for Suez City in 1973. Neither of these battles was central to the war, and they were the only urban engagements in that war. In Lebanon, however, urban fighting and mountain warfare predominated. After the Jerusalem and Suez City battles, that limited experience in urban fighting was quickly discarded as not applicable to the kind of war Israel was most likely to fight in the future. One can find any number of commanders who fought in Lebanon who would argue that the Lebanon experience in urban warfare ought to be discarded on the same grounds—it is a type of war that Israel is not likely to fight in the future.

Equally important, Israel had no experience at all in mountain warfare. Israeli forces have almost always fought on terrain where large tank formations could maneuver and strike rapidly into the enemy's rear. As a consequence, they developed none of the tactics associated with mountain campaigns. Mountain training is rather specific and requires different types of troops, weaponry, and coordination among the combat arms. When the Israelis took the field in Lebanon, they had to develop tactics and reconfigure forces on the spot. Since none of the troops had been trained for urban warfare or mountain warfare, the tactical improvisations were often less than satisfactory; the result was a number of ambushes and significant losses as the war wore on.

Another factor which affected Israeli tactical development was the configuration of its forces. IDF forces were configured as armor-heavy, supported by mobile infantry in APC's. Since 1973, these two arms of the combined-arms teams had been augmented by highly mobile artillery capable of rapid movement and deep penetration of the mobile arms. The IDF relied heavily on rapid movement, surprise, daring, and initiative of its commanders, who were expected to strike deep in the enemy's rear to seize key defensive positions, and then have the infantry mop up. As a result, the IDF failed to develop "leg" infantry, infantry capable of sustained ground combat on its own. Instead, the Israelis stressed mobile infantry, using it as "shock" infantry in short bursts of intense combat by paratroopers or mobile forces supported by armor and artillery. Consequently, Israel lacked the capacity to conduct sustained infantry operations in which the infantry is the primary striking force supported by armor and artillery. It is precisely this type of tactical deployment that is required in mountain campaigns. Armor and mounted infantry are under severe disadvantages in terrain where they cannot move rapidly or cannot deploy off available roads, conditions which obtained commonly in Lebanon. The Israelis tended to use armor as spearheads even on the narrow roads, with armored personnel carriers transporting the infantry behind the armored spearhead. This meant that on narrow mountain roads the Israelis relinquished surprise, movement, speed, and initiative. And perhaps most important, they gave away the first shot in ambush to the enemy. It seems clear that the IDF was not able to reconfigure its forces in any significant way to deal with the mountainous terrain in eastern Lebanon where most of the war was fought.

A third consideration affecting tactics in Lebanon was the differences in terrain. There were, in effect, two wars. The war in the west was characterized by narrow roads bordered by thick citrus groves interspersed with built-up areas. It was not mountainous. However, the major urban areas of Tyre, Sidon, and Damour, and the six refugee camps on the road of advance, all provided cover and ambush points for the PLO. The war in the east was characterized by mountainous terrain, which also favored the defenders in every way. The IDF's lack of mountain infantry or any infantry capable of sustained independent operations in urban areas meant that Israeli forces came under constant ambush on both fronts. The IDF, especially in the east, came to rely on airpower to hit enemy targets. This war was one in which the Israeli ground forces found themselves at significant disadvantages most of the time as the battle developed, disadvantages created not only by Syrian determination and tactics but by the inability of the IDF to reconfigure its forces and adjust to the terrain the battlefield presented.

A fourth factor affecting Israeli tactics in Lebanon was a deep concern for human life. The Israelis seemed reluctant to use infantry in mountain terrain in the traditional manner, putting them out in front of tanks as screens for armor—a reluctance rooted in a fear of suffering too many infantry casualties. And in urban areas the IDF showed a great concern for human life, sometimes conceding surprise and initiative to the enemy as a result of the effort to reduce civilian casualties. While history never reveals its alternatives, it probably wouldn't be unfair to suggest that the caution and concern shown by the IDF to minimize civilian casualties may well have cost its troops more dead and wounded than normally would have been the case had they used the great concentrations of firepower at their disposal.

It often seemed that IDF ground operations in Lebanon were marked by tactical solutions that were sometimes inappropriate to the conditions of battle: extreme caution in built-up areas of the west; doggedly slowed rates of advance; and, of course, a clear failure to kill or capture most of the PLO. In the east, Israeli tactics often led to its forces being ambushed, to high costs in equipment, and to relatively heavy troop losses because the enemy was allowed to determine the time and place of battle. Also, in the east, the Israelis showed a tendency to substitute firepower, especially air strikes, for tactical moves. One gains the impression from detailed study that this war was not fought as efficiently as Israel's other wars. None of this suggests that any other army would necessarily have been able to do much better under these conditions. But that does not obviate the fact that the type of tactics which the Israelis used in Lebanon often seemed, if not inappropriate, then less than optimal to reach the objectives the army sought.

A number of other factors affected the conduct of the war. Three of these may influence future IDF tactical development: (1) the emergence for the first time of strongly centralized command, control, and communication links; (2) the tendency for commanders to switch commands, thus reducing unit integrity; (3) conventional thinking that tended to mark Israeli battlefield operations.

The war in Lebanon for the first time saw the development of a corps-level headquarters, seemingly in response to the force's having grown too large to be controlled directly by territorial headquarters. Along with a corps headquarters, there came the implementation of centralized C3—command, central, and communications—links from the front to corps level. "Real-time" intelligence was introduced through the use of remote-piloted vehicles (RPV's); there are real-time television monitors at division, corps, and territorial headquarters, which may indicate an inclination in the Israeli army to centralize command at higher levels. In other armies, most notably the United States army, the linking of higher headquarters to the combat units by instantaneous technological means of communication has tended, as in Vietnam, to reduce the initiative of local commanders. Commanders confronted with difficult situations are inclined to pass responsibility for these decisions up the chain of command. In addition, there is the tendency for senior commanders to seize control of local fighting units precisely because they have the technological means to do so. None of these conditions is evident in the Israeli Defense Force. At least not yet. But some Israeli commanders are concerned that centralization of command and control made possible by high technology will lead to a diminishing of the leadership, daring, and initiative that have characterized the Israeli army in battle.

The tactical deployment of the IDF in the Lebanon war was marked by much switching of units from one command to another and by the moving of field commanders in and out of their positions. Few units retained command and control integrity throughout the war; brigades that began under one commander often ended up under another commander after passing through one or two interim commands. Equally important, units often ended up fighting on entirely different battlefronts from where they had started. For example, the 36th division under Kahalani began its attack in the center. Before attacking, it lent a brigade to Sakel's forces in the east. After Kahalani had struck toward his initial objectives around Nabitiya and executed a turning movement toward Sidon, he lent a complete brigade and additional forces to Amos Yaron, who then assumed command of the operation. On the thrust to Damour and to Beirut, command of the coastal-road operation switched no fewer than four times in less than thirty kilometers: from Kahalani to Amos Yaron, back to Kahalani as far as Damour; at Damour, to Yitzhak Mordechai for the assault on Beirut, and then back again to Yaron, who commanded the forces outside Beirut.

These shifts represented a danger to the integrity of the battle units and often resulted in the presence of more than one commander of equal rank in the same operation in which the force itself was a combination of troops from both commanders. Many Israeli soldiers and officers offered the view that there were too many commanders at some battlefields, often with nothing to do or commanding piecemeal operations for short periods of time. This situation violated Israel's pattern of maintaining unit integrity, especially integrity of leadership, for the duration of a battle. In Lebanon, because of differences in terrain and rapidly changing battle conditions, the Israelis switched commanders and units throughout the war. Their success on the battlefield suggests that Israeli unit commanders have a great capability for innovation.

Lastly, the conduct of the war was influenced by the tendency of the IDF to be harnessed to conventional military thinking. Almost all Israeli battle experience has been with large-scale units in conventional wars against enemies configured in conventional ground-force patterns. Israelis had no experience fighting guerrilla forces, particularly those integrated in an urban population. Conventional battlefield maneuvers, though perfectly executed, sometimes seemed quite inappropriate. Examples are systematic air bombardment, artillery concentrations, and the rapid turning movements and deep penetration assaults that were conducted by Israeli forces throughout the war. Many of these tactics had little effect on the guerrilla enemy. The turning movement executed by Kahalani from the center to the south of Sidon would have completely trapped a conventional army and permitted it to be ground to pieces—but it had almost no effect on the PLO. In true guerrilla fashion, the PLO were quite capable of slipping through Israeli lines almost at will. In Lebanon, one often witnessed the application of tactics characterized by conventional military thinking, which, when executed against a guerrilla force, brought very few results in terms of killing or capturing the enemy.

In Lebanon, IDF commanders were forced to improvise as

battlefield conditions changed. In some instances, the improvisation was successful; in others, it proved costly in men and machines. In addition, the rapid decentralization of command required by field conditions forced the IDF to rely heavily on its excellent small-unit tactical commanders. The 1973 reconfiguration of the IDF had tended to centralize command and decision-making. In Lebanon, the IDF found many of these new organizational characteristics not very effective, or in some instances even inappropriate, and rapidly decentralized. The Israelis quite simply had tactically prepared to fight the last war, the war in 1973.

ARMOR

The war in Lebanon was the first real field test of the new Israeli Merkava tank; its performance was astonishing, yet probably no more than three hundred Merkavas were deployed of the total 1,240 tanks used.[1] The Merkava showed itself to be the safest main battle tank in the world against fire, as a consequence of a number of innovations, including seven self-sealing fuel tanks that are fully armored. In addition, the ammunition in the crew compartment is stored in fireproof containers which are so safe that, when set afire, they take a full hour to get hot enough to set the ammunition off. The number of secondary explosions that occurred in the Merkava was exactly zero—unlike other tanks, in which the ammunition is not so securely stored. Another factor which reduced casualties in the Merkava was the new Spectronix fire-suppression system, which can detect a fire in three milliseconds and suppress it in two hundred milliseconds. This fire-suppression system, coupled with the crew's asbestos protective clothing, considerably reduced the number of tank casualties due to fire. In Lebanon, not a single crewman died in a Merkava tank, and only six cases of light burns were reported. By comparison, 25 percent of all casualties suffered in the M-60's and Centurions were due to burns.[2]

The Merkava's special armor also proved itself. The Israelis have a data base of tank-armor protection against which they assess the performance of their M-60 and Centurion tanks and the enemy's T-62's. The Israeli analysis showed that, under fire, there is a 61 percent probability that a round striking a tank will penetrate. For the Merkava, the rate at which rounds striking it penetrated was 41 percent. In addition, there is a 30 percent probability that a penetrating round will also penetrate the crew compartment; in the Merkava, it was 13 percent. Its special armor and the placement of the engine in the front makes it almost invulnerable from the front. No known tank round can penetrate the front glacis to the crew's compartment. IDF data also show that in 31 percent of tank hits the tank will catch fire; by comparison, the Merkava caught fire only 15 percent of the times it was hit. The data also show that of tanks lit afire, 85 percent to 90 percent are completely destroyed. In Lebanon, no Merkava was lost as a consequence of being set aflame.[3]

The Merkava's firepower is probably the best of any tank in the world. Its 105mm gun, although small by Soviet and some Western standards, where they reach 125mm, nonetheless proved very effective. Most tank combat occurs at fairly close range, certainly under two thousand meters, where superior crewmanship is more important than gun caliber. In addition, the Israelis have developed a new round for the 105mm gun, an armor-piercing, fin-stabilized, discarding-sabot hypershot round. This Hetz, or arrow round, can reach and penetrate tank targets at a range exceeding 5,500 meters. This means that the Israeli tank's ability to engage in combat at a range of almost three miles exceeds or equals the effective range of the larger Soviet T-62 and T-72 gun.[4] The tank cannon is linked to an Israeli-made laser range finder and ballistic computer coupled with external sensors that make it very accurate. The Israelis have also developed a revolutionary new barrel shroud which operates at 90 percent efficiency, containing deviation of the gun barrel to under three mils. This compares to the M-60 tank's normal barrel-shroud operating efficiency of 60 percent. The heavy suspension of the tank and the gun-stabilizing unit also contribute to the accuracy of the gun. Accuracy is further improved by the use of a special twenty-power zoom lens in the tank sight which is slave-connected to the fire-control system, allowing automatic ranging and continuous aiming of the gun in real time. Israeli crews are well known for their ability to accurately fire a large number of rounds in a very short time. The special zoom lens slaved to the ballistic fire-control system increases that capability on the battlefield.

The Merkava has a heavy Horstmann variant external-suspension system which makes it the most mobile off-road tank in the world. The Merkava can go places that no other battle tank can go. Its wide tread allows it to gain maximum purchase on very steep slopes, and its front-loaded engine gives it a considerable degree of ground pressure so that it can climb very steep grades that other tanks cannot negotiate. In the Bekaa and the Shouf Mountains, the Merkava was able to maneuver on terrain where its rival T-62 couldn't go. In at least one place I saw, the Merkava had operated on terrain so steep that a soldier could scarcely stand erect there. Its suspension is simple and completely armored and when hit can be easily replaced. In Lebanon, it took an average of two weeks to bring back to working order any M-60, Centurion, or T-62 tanks whose suspensions were damaged. No Merkava that was hit spent more than forty-eight hours being repaired. This is highly significant because the Israelis have to fight with fewer tanks than their enemies are likely to throw into battle. Their experience in 1967 and 1973 showed very clearly that the army that could rapidly return damaged tanks to action was normally the force that successfully continued the offensive. In fact, of the 130 Israeli tanks that were hit, only forty were damaged beyond repair. No Merkavas were declared total losses.

The ability of the Merkava to carry ten infantrymen in its rear compartment was very useful in the Lebanon war. No other tank in the world can be entered from the rear. With a reconfiguration of its ammunition supply, the Merkava can carry up to ten fully equipped infantrymen or four litter cases. In addition, although its normal combat ammunition load is eighty-three rounds, extra ammunition can be stored in the troop-carrying compartment, thus extending the basic combat load to over three hundred rounds: armored units are able to advance without making frequent stops for ammunition. In Lebanon, the ability to carry infantrymen and wounded was a great advantage. The Merkava moved infantry through built-up areas and areas that had been reduced to rubble, and it served an important role in evacuating the wounded. In one instance, in the Bekaa, a Merkava tank evacuated twelve wounded men in one trip while being subjected to heavy artillery and antitank fire.

The new main battle tank performed far above expectations.

On the other hand, one published report suggested that the efficiency of Israeli tank crews had declined relative to 1973. There is no hard evidence to prove this, and none offered by the source.[5] It is clear, however, that the terrain in which Israeli tankers had to fight placed them at a great disadvantage. Narrow, steep, winding roads gave enemy tanks and infantry forces armed with RPG's great opportunity to ambush Israeli tanks.

Reliable comparative tank-crew efficiency figures are impossible to come by, as are strict comparisons of Syrian and Israeli tanks. The reason, as a spokesman for Israeli intelligence pointed out to me, is that IDF tanks that were destroyed or damaged were not hit by tank cannon from other tanks but by a range of antitank weapons, including basic antitank guns, RPG's, and Sagger missiles. The Syrians also used French Gazelle helicopters armed with HOT missiles, which took a heavy toll. There were few engagements in which tanks fought each other tube to tube. While comparisons are difficult to make, the Israelis seem to have killed about three tanks to every one that they lost. This kill ratio takes into consideration all weapons systems. Since the Syrians had absolutely no air cover and fewer tanks, the three-to-one ratio is indeed well below the 1973 figures. But there is no way, on the basis of available information, to assess the ability of rival tank crews in gun-to-gun situations to bring about tank kills. From the perspective of employing a complete range of antitank weaponry against Israeli tanks, the Syrians seem to have done quite well and taken a considerable toll of Israeli machines.

In the IDF, armor includes not only tanks and tank crews but the mobile infantry, which uses armored personnel carriers. The mobile infantry wear the armor black berets and are organically tied to armor formations and considered part of armored combat units. These units suffered heavy casualties from the range of weapons deployed by the Syrians. The M-113 Zelda armored personnel carriers in many instances became death traps; made of aluminum alloy and steel, they burned readily. At times, the troops became so frightened of burning to death that many refused to ride in the APC's and took to walking alongside them or riding on the outside. Perhaps a basic lesson of this war is simply that tanks and APC's deployed together in mountain terrain without a forward infantry screen simply do not work very well.

In addition, several tragic accidents involving armored units resulted in a number of casualties. At Ain Katina, near the town of Jezzine, two battalions of the same brigade approached the crossroads from different directions. Each thought the other was the enemy and engaged and fought a pitched battle for almost three hours. Estimates are that at least six tanks were hit and a number of tank crewmen killed and wounded.

In another incident, at Soultan Yaaquoub, the lead battalion of a brigade force ran directly into a Syrian ambush; at least seven tanks were destroyed or abandoned, and at least twenty-six crewmen were killed or severely burned. This force involved M-60's, and a number of soldiers in armored personnel carriers were also killed or wounded. A similar situation occurred near the town of Ain Zhalta in the Shouf Mountains, where lead units of an advance brigade were seriously ambushed near the great horseshoe curve as it approached the town. Heavy casualties resulted and the division spearhead was forced to stop. The ambush was finally broken when a full battalion of troops was helilifted into blocking position to break up the ambushing forces.

In yet another case, a logistics company comprised of trucks, maintenance people, logistic personnel, and armored personnel carriers somehow failed to display its orange identification bunting and was hit from the air by IDF fighter-bombers. Some estimates are that there may have been as many as one hundred casualties, with at least twenty dead; the figures remain classified.

With regard to the role of armor in Lebanon, there is little doubt that although the equipment and gunnery performed flawlessly, the terrain served to limit the Israelis' ability to bring armor to bear decisively in the type of master strokes the Israelis are famous for. Armor usually had to fight piecemeal and often was the victim of ambush. The dash and daring so common to the IDF armored corps was almost impossible to apply. One of the major critiques of the employment of Israeli armor in Lebanon is that traditional doctrines of armor turned out to be relatively useless. The terrain lent itself far more to the type of war fought by the Syrians, with infantry and commando units placed in ambush situations, and tanks used in support rather than the infantry used in support of tanks. In Lebanon, the armored corps fought far more battles against commando units armed with RPG's and missiles and against helicopters with missiles than it fought against other tanks.

It is unlikely that the experiences in Lebanon will cause the IDF to undertake any significant reconfiguration of its armored forces or, indeed, that the Israelis will rethink their armor doctrine. Conversations with a number of senior armor commanders suggest that for the most part the ground commanders in Lebanon tend to feel that the war was not typical of the wars that Israel will have to fight in the future. They may be correct. And yet any war with Syria will force the Israelis to fight in much the same kind of terrain that they encountered in Lebanon. Israeli armored commanders may be unwilling to rethink elements of their deployment doctrine and thus the IDF may make the same errors and perhaps suffer the same rate of losses as they did in the Lebanon war.

INFANTRY

Since 1948, infantry has been the bastard child of the IDF. As Israel fought its wars, it tended more and more to make the tank the king of the battlefield, without raising the infantry to the position of queen of battle, as it has been in most modern armies. Until 1973, infantry was relegated to obscurity, playing at best a marginal role in support of the tank. With the experience of the Yom Kippur War, it became apparent that many tank losses were inflicted by enemy infantry teams using missiles and that the IDF had no forces which could suppress them. To reduce the vulnerability of its tanks against infantry in 1973, the IDF chose to increase the role of mobile artillery rather than to build up its infantry. As the size of the IDF increased after 1973, available infantry forces proportionately declined. In 1973, the IDF could field fifteen infantry brigades and four paratroop-trained brigades, a total of nineteen infantry brigades. By 1982, it could field ten mechanized infantry brigades, including five paratroop brigades, and twelve territorial guard infantry brigades and Nahal infantry, a total of twenty-two brigades. Although the number of infantry brigades rose by three, the army expanded from six to eleven divisions (or fifteen divisions, if various intelligence sources can be believed). Thus, the infantry available to integrate with the other combined arms teams declined precipitously. One of the major difficulties that the IDF encountered in Lebanon was a chronic shortage of infantry to support the other combined arms.

The IDF has always had infantry forces but has refused to use them in a traditional infantry role. The Israeli forces went into Lebanon without "leg" infantry, the traditional infantry forces that can walk into battle and fight sustained infantry operations. Instead, the IDF used infantry in Lebanon as it had in 1973, either in assault operations against urban areas, where paratroopers saw most of the action, or as mobile support for the tanks. Although the Israelis have reconfigured their forces to use the combined arms team as the centerpiece of the combat units, the infantry is still relegated to the role of supporting tanks and mobile forces. The Israelis use highly mobile artillery forces to perform the traditional role of infantry in protecting tanks and other combined arms elements. In Lebanon, however, the terrain and the urban areas in which the Israeli forces had to fight did not allow for appropriate use of mobile infantry. On the other hand, the Syrians used their infantry quite properly, given the terrain in which they were fighting. They broke up their armor into one or two tanks, attached them to commando infantry, and used the infantry to good effect by deploying it in ambush and having the tanks support the infantry.

The sensitivity of the IDF to the loss of its soldiers has convinced its planners that on the modern battlefield only machines can protect soldiers. But the analysis of IDF dead and wounded in Lebanon presented earlier shows quite clearly that infantry survives far better on a modern battlefield when engaged with combined arms teams than had been thought by the Israelis. This fact notwithstanding, the IDF has made an enormous investment in its artillery arm to suppress infantry attacks, and it is unlikely that the Israelis would be willing to redirect any resources away from artillery and armor to infantry.

Since the IDF obviously cannot prepare for all contingencies, the lessons of the Lebanese war may not get a fair hearing. As Israeli planners look to the future, they may conclude that the most likely wars Israelis will fight will be wars in which combined arms forces as presently configured, although light on infantry, will be most effective. If, in fact, this is an appropriate view of the future, and many Israeli commanders believe it is, then not much is likely to change with regard to the number and type of infantry forces in the IDF. Yet it is undeniable that in Lebanon the Israelis were chronically short of adequate infantry and that their infantry was not used as effectively as it could have been had there been more of it available and had it been configured properly and employed correctly.

ARTILLERY

Artillery is the newest combat arm of the IDF, created out of whole cloth after the 1973 war. In 1973, the IDF had about 300 artillery guns, most of which were towed pieces. By 1982, the number of guns had increased to over 958, most of which were self-propelled, large-caliber artillery. Prior to 1973, artillery played essentially a support role, with limited mobility in support of the tank. Today IDF artillery is completely mobile to keep up with the rapid advance of tanks and armored personnel carriers; it has become a full partner in the combined arms team.

The IDF can field about fifteen artillery brigades. Its weaponry is comprised mostly of M-109's and M-107's, added to a number of locally produced Soltam M-71's and L-33's. In addition, it deploys a considerable number of 160mm mortars mounted on old Sherman chassis, as well as a number of M-50 105mm guns mounted on Super Sherman chassis. Mobility is further augmented by the ability of the IDF to move artillery pieces to the battlefront on transporters.

Artillery proved effective in most instances during the Lebanon war, although to some extent its effectiveness was reduced by the terrain, which prevented its playing the highly mobile, fast-moving role envisioned for it in the new combined-arms doctrine developed since 1973. Operations were often slowed to a crawl by terrain and hostile fire in urban areas. In the east, artillery proved effective in counterbattery fire against Syrian positions, a fact helped considerably by the Syrians' refusal to redeploy artillery rapidly with the changing tactical situation. The effectiveness of artillery in the eastern zone was also increased considerably by the Israelis' complete air superiority. In the west, the effectiveness of artillery was limited by self-imposed restrictions to limit property damage and civilian casualties. However, the artillery was technically very good. It made good use of new devices such as the RPV's, which were flown over the battlefield to provide real-time intelligence through TV pictures of enemy targets. It also made good use of intelligence gathered by aircraft flying over the battlefield. In addition, it used the new Rafael David fire-control computer system (made in Israel), which made it fairly effective at sheaving artillery and linking concentrated fires. It also deployed a number of new fire modes built around the new Telkoor M-131 multi-option fuse.

In Beirut, artillery played a crucial role in suppressing enemy fire and destroying PLO strongpoints within the camps and the city. Often, in responding to PLO Katyusha and mortar fire, the IDF was able to sheave its artillery rapidly and respond almost immediately by pouring scores of shells on a single area. Effectiveness of artillery is often directly related to the ability to sheave effectively, and the Israelis, with almost no experience in this tactic before 1973, seem to have learned quickly and developed the technique to a high degree. During the siege of Beirut, the IDF seems to have discovered the technique of "sniping" with large-caliber artillery pieces by firing single rounds into PLO military targets at point-blank range.

Artillery performed well in Lebanon, with no major problems. However, battle conditions presented it with considerable advantages that it may not have on a different battlefield in the future. The conditions of battle in Lebanon did not allow for a true test of the artillery and structure envisioned in 1973. Its new role was to deploy in support of rapidly moving armored infantry forces in a closely coordinated combined-arms attack. A test of that role will have to wait the future.

MEDICAL CARE

The IDF medical evacuation system is probably one of the most efficiently designed in the world—a reflection of the IDF's sensitivity to the loss of human life. The evacuation system is constructed on the Russian model more than on the American model, which is characterized by the extensive use of medical evacuation helicopters to ferry wounded from the battlefield to brigade or battalion medical stations, where they can be treated. The Israeli system positions a large number of mobile armored personnel carriers on the battlefield, each with a doctor and medical team aboard. The object is to treat the wounded as close to the battlefront as possible prior to evacuating them. Israeli experiences have shown that if a soldier can be given advanced first aid on the spot, his chances of survival are much better than if he is routinely evacuated. The Israelis have also deployed mobile surgical teams based in armored personnel carriers to perform surgery on the battlefield. Each combat unit has a medical battalion, and within it, each has a medical platoon with a doctor attached to it.

As the war developed, the Israelis made some significant changes in treating battle casualties. Anticipating that there would be a high number of casualties (because of mountainous terrain and urban fighting), the IDF assigned each medical platoon an extra doctor, so there were two doctors available instead of one. In addition, every helicopter in the combat area, whatever its role, had a doctor on board, so that it could respond to calls for help in the course of its routine missions. Helicopters, even those on purely medical missions, are not marked by the red Star of David, and the doctors aboard carry weapons. The Israeli experience has been that medical insignia on an APC or a helicopter does very little to keep it from being attacked by the enemy. The fact that there were doctors aboard helicopters and that helicopters were used in a secondary role as medical evacuation vehicles resulted in an interesting phenomenon. Fully 82 percent of the Israeli casualties were evacuated by helicopter from the medical platoon of the combat battalion where the soldier was wounded, and flown directly to rear-area hospitals. Although the Israelis had an extensive system of mobile operating teams and division medical battalions, very little use was made of them. Instead, wounded soldiers were evacuated from the point of wound to rear areas[6]—which meant that the Israeli medical evacuation system began to bear a much closer resemblance to the American model developed in Vietnam than to the Soviet model.

The types of casualties which the Israelis had to deal with

were ultimately predictable. General Eran Dolev, the Chief Medical Officer, pointed out that the Israeli experience in fighting in Jerusalem and Suez City provided the IDF with a small data base from which to predict casualty rates in Lebanon. These studies predicted very closely the number and types of casualties that occurred in Lebanon, especially in the western zone. General Dolev noted that 40 percent of the wounds suffered by Israeli soldiers were head and neck wounds, inevitably fatal. Perhaps most interesting, 55 percent of the dead and wounded were the result of small-arms fire, a rate of small-arms wounds that exceeded the 53 percent rate of the American forces in Vietnam. The casualty list would have gone much higher, however, had it not been for the flak vest which the Israelis used. The flak jacket, designed and developed in Israel and used for the first time in Operation Litani, is light, easy to keep closed, and has a higher collar than most vests. Some indication of its effectiveness can be gained from the fact that, by counting the number of hits on the jackets worn in battle, it was determined in a survey that casualties due to small arms would have been as much as 20 percent higher had the flak jackets not been used. Most small-arms wounds were inflicted at close range, a result to be expected in fighting in built-up areas.

A considerable number of APC casualties were caused by burns. Normally, when an APC was hit, the impact of the molten core of the shaped-charge round caused many deaths and burn casualties inside. The percentage of burn casualties in the armor-tank corps was about 20 percent, about the same *rate* as in the 1973 war. But in Lebanon the severity of burns was reduced greatly due to improved Merkava tank design and other factors already mentioned. However, twenty-six cases of severe burns occurred in M-60's and Centurions, the bulk of them in the ambush at Soultan Yaaquoub.

The number of casualties resulting from artillery was relatively minor for most of the war. In fact, there were no significant artillery casualties until the battle for the Beirut–Damascus highway, when both PLO and Syrian artillery was brought to bear on Israeli troops. The combat which produced the highest number of artillery casualties was in Beirut, where the PLO used its artillery effectively and also massed artillery fire from Katyusha rockets. But in comparison to other wars, the number of artillery casualties in Lebanon was quite low.

General Dolev and others in the Israeli medical service are concerned about the rate of casualties within the medical corps itself. Two doctors were killed, one in a helicopter crash and another in an APC. Sixteen other doctors were wounded; the number of supporting medical personnel who became casualties is not available.[7] There is concern expressed in the medical service that placing doctors in the medical platoons or in helicopters exposes highly trained personnel to unnecessary risk. It is felt that some way must be found to minimize the death rate of doctors without unduly jeopardizing the life of the wounded soldier. Although a number of answers have been suggested, the debate continues. One suggestion has been made that doctors might be moved out of the medical platoon and deployed farther to the rear at the medical battalion. Such a solution would represent a trade-off between the concern to keep doctors alive in the battle area and the quickest and most effective treatment of troops. The fact is that during the Lebanon campaign Israeli medical services performed very well in locating, treating, and evacuating wounded, thereby minimizing the number of soldiers who died.

ENGINEERS

Combat engineers played a crucial part in Lebanon. Their mission was to prevent the natural obstacles presented by the terrain from slowing the advance and to enhance the capacity of armor to conduct rapid maneuvers, especially enveloping or encircling movements. Engineers spearheaded the advance on seven of the ten axes and often walked alongside tanks as they performed their mission. They opened five critical routes of advance, prepared them for armor-vehicle travel, and built a considerable number of roads. They spanned a number of water obstacles, among them the Litani and the Zaharani Rivers. Engineers also saw action in Beirut, especially at the Museum Crossing, which was led by D-9 bulldozers to reduce obstacles.

Israeli engineers cleared a number of roads at great personal risk in the east. In Wadi Cheba, they made the flanking movement possible toward Rachaiya by cutting a twelve-mile road through the wadi, which allowed Israeli armor to outflank Syrian troops. At the battle of Bhamdoun on the Beirut–Damascus highway, engineers cut a five-mile detour which allowed the assault to continue, and at Souq el Gharb they cut a two-mile detour to permit Israeli forces to bypass the Syrian defenders, outflank them, and take their objective. Engineers exhibited considerable heroism under fire and suffered a significant number of casualties. They excelled at the repair of culvert bridges, which span the roads all the way to Jezzine and to the Bekaa Valley. The Syrians systematically blew up these bridges as they retreated and continued to cover them by fire from their next defensive position. Often at great risk, engineers repaired the bridges under fire, to allow the Israeli attack to continue. Israeli engineers laid or paved 400 kilometers of new roads in Lebanon. As if this were not enough, the engineers were often pressed into service as infantry. At the Museum Crossing, during the siege of Beirut, engineers were out in front of the assault, using their bulldozers to clear the road while covering their own operations against sniper fire from the PLO.

In many ways, the combat engineers are the unsung heroes of the war in Lebanon. Their actions in spanning rivers and rebuilding destroyed culvert bridges on narrow, serpentine roads made it possible in many instances for the Israeli forces to continue to advance; cutting of flanking roads often contributed greatly to tactical victory and reduced IDF casualties. Since 1973, engineer teams have been completely integrated into the combined arms teams, and in this war, given the terrain and the nature of other tactical obstacles, they came into their own. They clearly demonstrated the contribution that first-rate units of combat engineers can make to a highly mobile army fighting in hostile terrain.

LOGISTICS

Since 1973, the IDF has been configured to fight and supply an army of at least eleven divisions fighting at full strength for twenty-eight days and to do so on three separate fronts. This is a remarkable increase in a logistic capability over the 1973 war, when Israel could field and supply an army of only six divisions for some fourteen days. Much of this increase is made possible by producing more war material at home rather than relying on foreign sources. It is also a consequence of better planning, stockpiling, and distribution. For instance, the IDF estimates that in 1973 only 40 percent of its tank ammunition ever reached the front, because it got stuck in the logistics train. The IDF also ran out of tank transporters, and tanks had to move to the battle-field under their own power, with an enormous rate of equip-ment breakdown. Today the logistics train has far more vehicles to move supplies, and the handling process has been streamlined to the point where it is extremely efficient.

IDF logistics is based on the Soviet "push model" instead of the American "pull model." In the push model, supplies are ferried to the front at regular intervals to overload the fighting front with ammunition and other necessary supplies. By con-trast, the American pull model calls for supplies to be sent to the front only after a request is received from a fighting unit. The IDF experience indicates that the pull system is inadequate to sustain a rapid, long-range, armored advance, and it requires too many personnel in the fighting units to administer the distribu-tion and control of supplies.

In Lebanon, the Israeli logistical system operated flawlessly, for a number of reasons. First, its stockpiles were more than sufficient for a short war. Second, the increase in vehicles man-dated in 1973 was more than enough to move supplies into battle areas. However, the IDF quickly abandoned overland transport supply because of the lack of roads. Third, the IDF had complete control of the air over the battle area, and as a result could freely ferry supplies by helicopter, thus avoiding poor roads and rugged terrain. Finally, using the few main roads as airfields, IAF C-130's were able to play a big role in sustaining the supply effort. The IAF used the 130's to deliver supplies near the battle area, often landing on roads, and then ferried them by helicopter to the troops.

The logistic effort in Lebanon had everything going for it. It was an easy task to accomplish. It was so easy that the navy, which controlled the coastal area and a number of major ports, played almost no role in resupply.

RESERVES

The size of the reserve call-up in the Lebanon war remains a military secret. It has been revealed, however, that the call-up was much smaller than in the 1973 war. The IDF maintains a standing force of 172,000 men, of which 52,000 are regular forces and 120,000 are conscripts. Given that the initial force, including units deployed in reserve for use in Lebanon, did not in the early invasion exceed 65,000, and given that at its peak during the siege of Beirut the number did not exceed 85,000, then the regular forces augmented by their normal reserve capacity would have sufficient strength to carry off the invasion. But the Israelis are not prone to leave things to chance. Call-ups of reserve units were made to fill out the regular units and to provide reserves on the Golan and behind the border that might have been used had the war dragged on longer or had the Syrians expanded the war to the Golan Heights.

On the basis of public sources, one can determine that not more than 10 percent of the work force was disrupted by the reserve call-up. Knowing that there are 656,000 Jewish males in the work force and 362,000 females, and assuming that the need would be for fighting manpower and would exclude most females, one would estimate that some 65,000 men were probably called to active service. Using different indicators, one arrives at a figure fairly close to that one. By noting the number of people called in various economic sectors, one can also estimate the number of reservists called. Thus, 35 percent of the drivers of the Eggert Cooperative, Israel's principal public transportation company, were called. The demand for drivers was probably higher than in most other sectors, with sixty to eighty busloads of troops a day being shuttled into Lebanon. In addition, 33 percent of the Israeli Philharmonic Orchestra was called, and 20 percent of the students at Hebrew University were called. If one averages these percentages, the results suggest that 29 percent of Israel's 228,000 reservists were called to service—a figure in the vicinity of 66,000 men, or about the same as the 10 percent of the work force. On the basis of these two figures, it is probably safe to estimate that the Israelis called up between 65,000 and 70,000 reserves, which would not be more than 21 percent or 22 percent of the reserve power they could have brought to bear.

The call-up of the reserve during the Lebanon war had a much less disruptive effect on the economy than in past wars, and still adequate manpower was provided to conduct combat operations. Also, once the siege of Beirut was over, the Israelis began an immediate thinning out of their combat forces in Lebanon, demobilizing their reserve units. Within four months of the end of the war, no more than twenty to thirty thousand troops were still deployed in Lebanon.

HELICOPTERS

Among the most successful new weapons was the American-made Cobra gunship and the Hughes 500 M-D Defender helicopter gunship, also American-made. Both machines are configured to fire antitank missiles, although they can perform a variety of additional roles. The Cobra had seen action in the Iran–Iraq wars as a tank killer, but the Lebanon war was the first in which the Cobras were used by a truly sophisticated and well-trained military force in a significantly large antitank role. Military commanders reported a high degree of success, suggesting that fully 60 percent of the tanks and thin-skinned vehicles killed in the war were killed by helicopter gunships. While this seems a bit high—other sources note that they killed twenty tanks and fifty thin-skinned vehicles—there is no doubt that the Cobra and the Hughes helicopters did an excellent job.[8] Both are very fast, highly mobile machines and can fly NOE ("nap of the earth") approaches, particularly effective given the terrain in Lebanon. The deep gorges, wadis, and mountains provided good cover and allowed tank-killing helicopters to get within close range of their targets. The Syrians made use of the French-made Gazelle helicopter, armed with the new HOT antitank missile, also produced by the French. Conversations with Israeli commanders and especially tank crews suggest that the HOT missile is an extremely effective weapon which was used with devastating effect by the Syrians. While helicopter gunships were effective in Lebanon, their effective use by other military forces remains to be demonstrated. The number of ships actually employed was very small. Perhaps the most significant test of this equipment will be against concentrated antiaircraft defenses. Neither the Syrians nor the PLO were able to mount significant antiaircraft defenses against missile-firing helicopters. Should such helicopters be employed en masse against a traditional Soviet defense, for example, in which Soviet armored columns carry their own organic antiaircraft capability, the success of helicopter gunships may prove to be significantly less than it was during the Lebanese war.

7

The Light at the End of the Tunnel

More than a year after the war ended, Israeli military forces were still in Lebanon. The war that began with the limited military objectives of removing PLO forces from artillery range of Israel's northern settlements and of destroying their supporting infrastructure ended with Israel faced with the ordeal of military occupation. The military goals of the war have unquestionably been achieved; what has eluded Israel is a political settlement. In each of Israel's previous wars, military victory has failed to produce a lasting political settlement, with the exception of the 1973 war, which resulted in the Camp David agreement of 1978. Perhaps Abba Eban, the former Foreign Minister, was correct when he suggested that Israel seemed destined to fight wars in which the vanquished will forever refuse to come to the bargaining table and make peace with the victors.

Immediately following the end of the fighting, the IDF reduced its troop strength in Lebanon from 85,000 to 35,000 men. Four months later, by January 1983, that number had been reduced to 20,000. For the most part, a division force remained in the Beirut–Shouf area, while another division garrisoned the Bekaa Valley in positions which control the approaches to Damascus within reach of Israeli guns. Reserve units continued to shuttle in and out of Lebanon, staying in the country for periods of thirty-five days and returning to their bases inside Israel. As in the past, the IDF garrisoned its reserve units with active units for their annual training periods and expected them to carry out actual operational missions against a real enemy. It is this realism in their training that accounts for the excellent performance consistently turned in by reserve units in time of war. In many cases, as we have seen, they performed better under fire than regular army units.

The economic cost of sustaining a force of 20,000 soldiers in Lebanon is not significantly higher than if these units were garrisoned inside Israel. Since the Israelis are relieved of the need constantly to patrol the northern border and to mount operations against PLO forays, the economic cost may well be even less than before the war. The cost of the continuing Israeli presence in Lebanon probably does not exceed $0.2 billion in incremental costs per year.

The human costs are another matter. In the months since the siege of Beirut ended, the IDF lost an additional 148 dead, bringing the total to 516. It also lost another 519 wounded, for a total of 2,902. Many died as the result of tragic accidents within the battle area: ninety soldiers died in an explosion of a military headquarters in Tyre in November of 1982. Over forty IDF soldiers died in auto accidents or other accidents related to training. Another twenty died when Israeli forces moved into West Beirut following the assassination of Bashir Gemayel in September, and another hundred were wounded. Hardly a week goes by when some Israeli soldiers are not wounded or killed when fired on from ambush. The war zone is still hot and has a long way to go to cool down.

Israeli troops are constant targets of hit-and-run attacks, most as a result of operations undertaken by three groups of combatants: (1) PLO residues and even new recruits in West Beirut, southern Lebanon, and the Bekaa Valley; (2) other private armies remaining in the country; and (3) Christian forces. Map 16 shows the disposition of all military forces in Lebanon, along with their respective strengths, as of May 1983. There is little doubt that as many as two thousand PLO "stay-behinds" melted into the population of West Beirut and remained to play a large and active part in the hit-and-run harassment of the Israelis. Indeed, one of the bones of contention between IDF and U.S. peace-keeping forces near the airport in Beirut was that the PLO forces slipped out of the camps, passed through Marine lines, and launched attacks on Israeli vehicles moving down the Green Line road, then retreated back through Marine lines into the camps, using the Marines as a buffer to prevent IDF pursuit or counterfire. The situation was aggravated by the refusal of U.S. forces, at the direction of the State Department, to establish direct contact with IDF forces in the area. When the Marines detect PLO teams moving through their lines, they are instructed to contact the Lebanese army rather than the Israelis. The American Marines in the area became an inadvertent barrier protecting PLO ambush teams from Israeli retaliation.

IDF forces also come under attack from a number of groups of the leftist and Moslem militias remaining in Lebanon. Before the June invasion, there were anywhere from 90 to 124 private armies operating in the cities and countryside of Lebanon. A few of these armies had as many as ten thousand soldiers, and some as few as fifty. These private armies, often organized around confessional or ideological lines, are very much alive and still very well armed. None of them, except those that were openly allied with the PLO, was expelled, nor were their arms destroyed. They were able to harass the IDF almost at will—some angered by the continued detention of their coreligionists in the Ansar camp, or motivated by revenge for damage done to their families or property. No military occupation will make them disappear; they survived and thrived during the civil war and they give every evidence of continuing to do so. Some look forward to the day when the IDF leaves and they can pick up where they left off with the confessional strife which has marked Lebanon's recent history.

Strange as it may seem, there is reason to believe that Israeli occupation forces have come under fire from Christian militia as well. To be sure, the mainstream of the Christian forces are not openly hostile to the IDF, but it is to the Christians' advantage to see such attacks continue as a way of pressuring the Israelis to leave Lebanon. The Christian forces are not a unified homogeneous entity that can be controlled by a single commander, and several fringe groups have fired on IDF forces, especially in the Shouf area, where the IDF has had to position forces between Christian and Druse factions fighting over the same town or territory. Moreover, military attacks on the IDF, regardless of their origin, serve Christian interests well by keep-

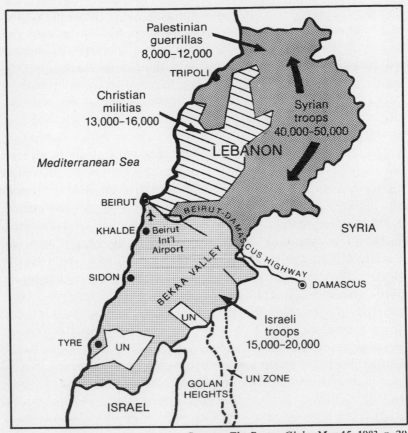

**Map 16. Major factional military dispositions in Lebanon
May 1983**

ing the pressure on the Israelis. Nor is it lost on the Israelis that every attack on an IDF soldier only fuels the fire among elements of the Israeli public that want to see an early and a quick withdrawal from Lebanon. Now that the Israelis have signed an agreement with the Lebanese to withdraw, these continued attacks on Israeli soldiers by any confessional army will undoubtedly increase the Israeli public's desire for withdrawal even more.

The IDF is having great difficulty dealing with these attacks. Without pressing the analogy too far, its position is not unlike that of a conventionally configured army which must relinquish the initiative as to time and place of attack to a guerrilla enemy. Such an enemy can hit at the time and place of its own choosing, inflict a few casualties—none of them militarily significant—and rapidly withdraw, to strike again another day. Since these attacks often occur in urban neighborhoods packed with civilians, the IDF's own moral code of war limits its ability to retaliate. Thus, the IDF has consistently refused to raze villages, burn houses, torture civilians, and otherwise take revenge on the civilian populations which shelter the terrorists who strike at the Israeli forces. This is a testament to their sense of the moral limits of war and to their military discipline. As a means of dealing with the immediate military problem, however, the Israelis' moral code is not successful.

SABRA AND SHATILA

Among the most serious problems of the war were created by the massacre of some seven hundred civilians in the PLO camps of Sabra and Shatila in West Beirut on September 16–18, 1982. No other event in the Lebanon war had such a profound impact on the Israeli public and its political leadership or did so much to undermine the rationale of the war.

The assassination of Bashir Gemayel threatened to undo the Israeli goal of establishing a friendly central Lebanese government and securing its northern border by signing a peace treaty with Beirut. Immediately after the assassination, the IDF moved into West Beirut in force to keep control of the city. At the same time, the IDF pressured the Christian Phalange finally to enter the fighting. IDF units surrounded the camps on three sides, suffering a considerable number of dead and wounded from PLO residues and Mourabitoun leftist militias in the camps. At no time did IDF soldiers enter the camps. This task was left to the Christians, who were to "cleanse" the camps of remaining pockets of resistance.

It is clear from the official report of the inquiry conducted by the Knesset that high-ranking members of the Israeli military were concerned that the Christians might use this opportunity to take revenge on their enemies; both sides had used violence and revenge on numerous occasions since the outbreak of civil war in 1975. The IDF's military intelligence branch, which did not share the high opinion of the reliability of Christian troops held by Mossad, was especially fearful. Even Chief of Staff Eitan had great misgivings, and voiced them to his superiors, that the Phalange could not be trusted to deal with their traditional enemies. However, once the political decision was made by Defense Minister Sharon to allow the Christians into the camps, the IDF provided only a limited degree of military support for the operation. The Christian forces were to enter the camps at six o'clock on Thursday evening, September 16, and IDF mortar crews were ordered to fire illumination shells over the camp to provide light for the operation. To its credit, the IDF refused to provide air strikes, tank, and artillery support, which the Phalange had also requested.

The IDF set up a joint liaison command post overlooking the camp so that IDF and Christian officers could monitor the situation as it unfolded on the ground. It is probable that Mossad advisors were also present in the camps. The fear remained that the Christians could not be trusted. And events justified that fear.

The Christian Phalange soldiers entered the camps and for three days and nights systematically terrorized, shot, and beat their civilian populations. The number of dead remains uncertain, since some were buried by their families without any official notification; some were buried under rubble as the Christians tried to conceal the extent of the slaughter; and some were trucked to Christian areas, where they were buried. Estimates of people killed vary from 350 to 750. What seems beyond question is that most of the dead were civilians, including large numbers of women and children. The men who were killed were often unarmed. The IDF played no direct role in the massacre but clearly bore at least indirect responsibility for the political decision to allow the Christians to enter the camps in the first place and for not responding fast enough to the rapidly mounting evidence that something was amiss.

The reports of the Sabra and Shatila massacres almost overnight destroyed the IDF's credibility as a humane force. They also shook to the core Israel's civilian support for the war. The Israeli government convened a tribunal to investigate and get at the truth. Behind this response was a sense of moral outrage.

In one sense, the actions of the Israeli government in rapidly condemning the men involved in the events leading to the massacre were highly courageous. Instead of covering up the incident as the United States tried to do with My Lai, the IDF and the government of Israel faced it squarely and assessed responsibility by calling for the removal of several high-ranking members of the military, including the Chief of Staff, the chief of military intelligence, the northern area commander, and the commander of Israeli forces in Beirut. The tribunal went further than any other that has dealt with such matters in the past. It raised to the status of law the doctrine of "indirect responsibility" and clarified the notion that officers, soldiers, and politicians could be held responsible not only for what they had done or knew but for what they *should* reasonably have known and what they should reasonably have done. This act alone, the establishment of a new doctrine in international law to which the Israelis were unilaterally prepared to subject themselves, redeemed the IDF and its civilian government in the eyes of many.

Yet Sabra and Shatila remained a turning point for Israel in Lebanon. The events of September derailed Ariel Sharon and the coalition of hawks within the cabinet and the military that had pushed the war to such extremes. Moreover, it gave Israel a chance to reassess its political position in Lebanon in terms of its original goals and national security. The appointment of Moshe Arens, at least as much of a hawk as Sharon, but a man of much subtler style, provided the chance to reexamine Israel's policy. Arens announced such a review in March 1983, indicating that Israel would focus on its initial war aims and on long-range security. This suggested that Arens was backing away from the political goals of war set almost unilaterally by Sharon and his supporters. Arens was not tied to "Sharon's war" and therefore had greater flexibility in conducting negotiations than Sharon had. This yielded results when on May 16, 1983, Israel and Lebanon signed an agreement calling for the withdrawal of Israeli forces. Although few if any of Israel's long-range political goals were achieved, Israel believed that its border was at least secured.

The massacres represented a turning point within the IDF as well. Although the commission's report clearly upheld the traditional notion of protection and honor for those officers and men who refused to execute orders which they believed to be unethical, the firing of so many high-level officers for what they "should have done" sent a chill through the IDF's professional officer corps. Moreover, the firings came at the very time when the IDF had to select a new Chief of Staff because of the scheduled retirement of Rafael Eitan. For months, the Israeli officer corps was frozen in its tracks.

In May 1983, as Eitan stepped down, the debate centered on who would replace him. There were two front-runners. One was Avigdor "Yanoosh" Ben Gal, who had been corps commander of the forces in the east; the other was the Deputy Chief of Staff, Moshe Levy, who had served under Eitan. Ben Gal has a reputation as a hawk and is a much decorated combat officer; many IDF officers feel a strong loyalty toward him. Among this group of officers, Ben Gal was considered the best-qualified for the job and he was expected to get it. Moshe Levy, on the other hand, has almost no combat experience but has a reputation as an excellent military planner and strategist. In April 1983, the Israeli government made its choice, and Moshe Levy was appointed Chief of Staff.

It is difficult fully to assess the impact of Levy's appointment, but it is being interpreted by many in the IDF officer corps as well as among the civilian population as an attempt by the political leadership to ensure that its top generals remain subservient to its direction. Whether true or not, there is a suspicion in Israel that Eitan strongly supported Sharon's desire to expand the war, contrary to the wish of the cabinet. Levy, who is more of a diplomat than Ben Gal, is perceived as likely to be more responsive to political direction. The appointment of Levy, who does not have a long and distinguished combat record, as did most other former chiefs, is a signal to the corps of combat officers that things may have changed: political considerations may now preempt battlefield experience as the most important requirement for promotion at the higher levels. What effect this will have on the morale of Israel's key combat leaders, the brigade and division commanders of the professional army, remains to be seen.

CONCLUSIONS

One of the basic problems faced by any army of a democratic society is how to sustain the presence of a military force in an occupied country for any period of time when the security rationale for that presence is diminished. Paradoxically, in a condition of low-intensity conflict, where the occupying force is periodically attacked by enemy forces that are insufficient to bring about a military defeat, the problem increases, since it appears to the public and to the policy-makers of the occupying country that the gains are not worth the deaths and injuries incurred in keeping the force in place. This condition is exacerbated when the military force is comprised of conscripts. Indeed, one of the major problems of modern military science is how to fight low-intensity conflict over a long period with a conscript force without risking a loss of political will in the host country.

The evidence suggests that no one has found a satisfactory answer. Consider, for instance, the French in Indochina when the French National Assembly made it illegal after 1954 to use conscript forces in military actions outside metropolitan France. The French army is really two armies: a conscript force for use in defense of the country in a European war, and the Foreign Legion, for use in military operations in other parts of the world, usually in former French colonies.

The American experience in Vietnam is a classic example of the inability of a conscript army to fight well under conditions of limited war and of a democratic society's inability to sustain a military effort for political goals in the absence of a strong argument rooted in national-security concerns. To be sure, the weakening of American will took ten years, but in the end it destroyed the army's ability to conduct battlefield operations in a foreign country.

Conscript armies are simply not very good for conducting sustained low-intensity operations. They are inherently vulnerable to the swings of public opinion within their host societies. In the case of the IDF, this is made even more acute by the traditional ethical base of the IDF and the deeply felt notion that the IDF exists to defend the State of Israel rather than to prosecute offensive wars. The IDF is not regarded in Israel as just another instrument of foreign policy, as military forces are in other nations. Rather, it is perceived as a special social instrument with fine limits of employment; namely, the defense of the Jewish state. When it is no longer possible to argue that the nation is in danger from an enemy—say, guerrilla or confessional armies in Lebanon—then support for continued military action and its attendant human cost is likely to decline rapidly.

Support for long-term low-intensity operations in Israel is limited by another consideration, the size of the country and the pain felt at the death of every IDF soldier. The country is like a large family—a *mishpocha*—and every death ramifies through the entire social structure and its web of familial and ethnic ties. It is difficult to overstate the sensitivity of Israeli society to death on the battlefield and impossible fully to realize how much outrage the death of even a single soldier can provoke if that death is seen as pointless. In larger nations, where manpower is not a problem for the military, low-intensity wars will likely take years to sap the will of a country. This is even truer if the military is an all-volunteer force, which, by the nature of the selection process and its demographics, is simply unrepresentative of mainstream society. In Israel, the loss of support for a military adventure abroad that is no longer perceived as being rooted in national-security demands can occur much more rapidly, perhaps even in a matter of months.

Such concerns affect the tactics of any army entangled in a low-intensity war. Its massive firepower and mobility are not nearly as decisive as on a conventional battlefield; indeed, they may even be a disadvantage. Often, low-intensity guerrilla wars require "special operations," perhaps involving terror, destruction of civilian homes, ruthless interrogations, and even executions. These tactics were used by the French and proved very effective in the Algerian war. But such tactics are not easily tolerated by conscript soldiers or by their families back home. To defeat guerrillas, one must operate in precisely the same manner as they do, using their tactics and techniques, and conscript armies cannot do this very well and retain a strong sense of national support. As a result, they often forego doing these things at all, which leaves them at the mercy of the enemy and prolongs the war, which in turn leads to more domestic weariness, which further restricts tactics. The circle closes, with the inevitable outcome being the wearing down of the occupying military force.

It is highly unlikely that the IDF will be asked to sustain a long-term presence in Lebanon. Moreover, if it does remain, military lines will be redrawn so that casualties and actual incidents of combat are reduced to a minimum. But it will probably begin to reflect all the problems outlined above. More likely, however, the IDF may face these problems in other areas, most specifically on the West Bank.

If, as seems probable, Israel functionally if not formally annexes the West Bank, and if, as seems probable, a large population of Arabs and Palestinians is allowed to remain in the West Bank, the IDF must learn to deal with various levels of low-intensity conflict. These may range, over a long period of time, from demonstrations to rock throwing to bombings and sniping. Yet to be considered by the IDF is the type of force to develop for such a purpose. An ancillary problem is to determine what tactics are acceptable and, probably more important, what limits are to be placed on military activities.

If history is any guide to the success or failure of such operations, it seems that whatever IDF forces are developed for low-intensity operations, they cannot be conscript-based. They may even have to be separate from the larger IDF establishment, perhaps in the same way that the Foreign Legion is separate from the larger French military conscript force. It may even be necessary to set them apart from the values of the larger democratic society, perhaps after the fashion of intelligence units, to permit a wider range of tactical actions against guerrilla operations, actions which the Israeli people are not likely to condone if they come to their attention. Whether Israeli society and the IDF can tolerate such a force or are even capable of generating one is open to question.

If the IDF wants to remain in Lebanon or on the West Bank, it must alter its basic assumptions about its role in defense of national policy. This may require redefinition of its nature and its basic ethical thrust, a factor which distinguishes it from other armies. The war in Lebanon has challenged for the first time since independence the relation of the IDF to the political structure and to the society it serves. The question is fundamental: shall the IDF be used in its traditional ethical and historical context as a defensive force, or has Israel become like other nations whose armed forces are used to achieve political goals that have little to do with defense of the homeland? The war in Lebanon has forced many Israelis to ask these questions. The answers remain uncertain.

Notes

1: THE ISRAELI DEFENSE FORCE

1. For a brief but good history of the origins of the IDF, see *Israel: A Country Study* (Washington, D.C.: Department of the Army, 1979), pp. 231–42.
2. Reuven Gal and Richard A. Gabriel, "Battlefield Heroism in the Israeli Defense Force," *International Social Science Review*, Autumn 1982, pp. 232–35.
3. Much of the material in this section is taken from Irving Cohen, "Israeli Defense Capability," *National Defense*, January 1976, pp. 271–73.
4. An excellent article dealing with the basic strategic assumptions of Israeli defense policy is Israel Tal's "Israel's Doctrine of National Security: Background and Dynamics," *The Jerusalem Quarterly*, Summer 1977, pp. 51–55. Much of the information contained in this section is also drawn from extensive conversations with General Tal in Tel Aviv in March 1983.
5. Ibid.
6. Ibid.
7. The data presented here are extracted from *The Military Balance* (London: International Institute for Strategic Studies), volumes for 1973 and 1982.
8. Many of the problems highlighted in this section are drawn from the comments of a number of high-ranking IDF combat officers in personal interviews. Some of these problems are also discussed in a somewhat strident article by Martin van Creveld, "Not

Exactly a Triumph," *Jerusalem Post Magazine*, December 10, 1982, pp. 5–10.
9. Meir Pa'il, "The Israeli Defense Forces: A Social Aspect," *New Outlook: Middle East Monthly*, January 1975, pp. 40–44.

2: THE PLO IN LEBANON

1. These figures are based on estimates obtained in interviews with various journalists and political and police sources who lived through the Lebanese civil war. Exact figures are unavailable, since no official records were kept. However, the figures given here are generally considered accurate by the people interviewed, including sources in Israeli intelligence.
2. Ibid.

3: WAR IN LEBANON

1. *Newsview*, July 20, 1983, p. 18.
2. Ibid.
3. *Newsview*, July 20, 1983, p. 19.
4. Ibid.
5. Ibid.
6. Interview with Brigadier General Amos Gilboa, Deputy Director of Military Intelligence, as quoted in *Military Science and Technology*, January 1983, p. 116.
7. The account of the Bekaa raid given here was put together from a number of interviews with knowledgeable Israelis. There are two public accounts which strongly support this version of the facts. See Paul S. Cutter, "EW Won the Bekaa Valley Air Battle," *Military Science and Technology*, January 1983, p. 106; also see, in the same issue, an article by Paul Cutter, "Elta Plays a Decisive Role in the EOB Scenario," on pp. 136–38.
8. Ibid.
9. Estimates provided by Israeli intelligence sources.
10. Not to be confused with the IDF Chief of Staff, Rafael Eitan, who has the same name. The Chief of Staff is known as "Raful"; the advisor on terrorism is called "Rafe."
11. Gilboa, op. cit., p. 116.
12. *Time*, July 5, 1982, p. 36.
13. Ibid. An excellent account of damage done to Lebanon during the war can also be found in the *Boston Sunday Globe*, December 26, 1982, pp. A13–A14.
14. *IDF Spokesman* briefing in Tel Aviv, March 1983.

15. Ibid.

16. T. N. Depuy, "The Big Lebanese Lie," *Jerusalem Post International Edition*, October 31–November 6, 1982, pp. 4–5.

17. Drawn from an interview in Beirut with Arab press sources; I do not speak Arabic and was unable to verify the original article.

4: THE SIEGE OF BEIRUT

1. Estimates of artillery casualties were provided by Brigadier General Eran Dolev, Chief Medical Officer of the IDF, in a personal interview in March 1983.

2. *An Nahar*, September 1, 1982, p. 1.

3. *Jerusalem Post*, October 22, 1982, p. 3.

5: BATTLEFIELD PERFORMANCE

1. Notes accurate as of September 1, 1983. Total casualties include those killed in accidents.

2. These are estimates provided in interviews with General Eran Dolev, Chief Medical Officer of the Israeli army.

3. Ibid.

4. Ibid.

5. Ibid.

6. The system is explained in detail in Richard A. Gabriel's "Stress in Battle: Coping on the Spot," *Army Magazine*, December 1982, pp. 36–42.

7. *Jerusalem Post International Edition*, July 25–July 31, 1982, p. 13.

8. These figures are taken from Martin van Creveld's *Fighting Power: German and U.S. Army Performance, 1939–1945* (Westport: Greenwood Press, 1982), pp. 91–97.

9. Ibid.

10. Ibid.

11. Ibid.

12. The poll is cited in *Newsview*, July 20, 1982, p. 9.

13. Ibid.

14. My sincere thanks to Hanoch Smith for sharing these data with me in a personal interview at his home.

15. Interview with Eli Geva, March 1983.

16. Ibid.

17. *Jerusalem Post*, November 12, 1982, p. 15.

18. Ibid.

19. *Jerusalem Post*, June 2, 1983, p. 11.
20. Ibid.
21. *Jerusalem Post*, June 29, 1982, p. 2.
22. Ibid.
23. Ibid.
24. My thanks to Hersh Goodman, military correspondent for the *Jerusalem Post* and an expert on the Israeli military, for sharing this information with me from his own sources.
25. Ibid.
26. Ibid.
27. For an examination of suicide rates in the Soviet army and their impact on combat effectiveness, see Richard A. Gabriel, *The New Red Legions: An Attitudinal Portrait of the Soviet Soldier* (Westport: Greenwood Press, 1980), pp. 176–81.
28. Unclassified portions of the report appeared in the Israeli military magazine, *In the Camp*, February 25, 1983, p. 7.
29. See Richard A. Gabriel and Paul L. Savage, *Crisis in Command* (New York: Hill and Wang, 1978), pp. 8–99.
30. One of these silly apologies for useless lives is found in Douglas Kinnard, *The War Managers* (Hanover: University Press of New England, 1977).

6: THE LESSONS OF WAR

1. This estimate of deployed Merkavas is taken from *Defense Attaché*, no. 4, 1982, p. 31.
2. Interview with General Eran Dolev, Chief Medical Officer of the IDF.
3. These data, as well as most of the data on armor, are gathered from interviews with individuals involved in the design, production, and evaluation of the Merkava tank. For security reasons, specific individuals will not be identified as to what information they provided.
4. Interviews with individuals in the tank-gunnery division of the production facility that makes the Merkava.
5. The charge appears in Martin van Creveld's "Not Exactly a Triumph," *Jerusalem Post Magazine*, December 10, 1982, pp. 6–7. Interviews with the author to discover the source of the report were unsuccessful; I was told that the original data supposedly were based on "a classified Pentagon Report."
6. Interview with General Dolev.
7. Ibid.
8. Ibid.

Tables

Table 1. Manpower and Equipment of IDF Ground Forces

Regular (standing) force strength: 135,000
Total strength with mobilized reserves: 450,000

Organization: 11 armored divisions
  33 armored brigades
  10 mechanized infantry brigades (5 paratroop-trained)
  12 territorial infantry brigades
  15 artillery brigades (each with 5 battalions)

Tanks: 3,600 main battle tanks
  1,100 Centurions
    650 M-48
  1,010 M-60
    250 T-54/55
    150 T-62
    250 Merkava I/II

4,000 armored fighting vehicles
  Ramta
  BRDM 1/2
  Shoet Mk. 2/3

4,000 armored personnel carriers
  M-113
  OT-62
  BTR-60

Artillery: 2,000 or more
   60 M-107   120 M-109
   30 M-101   48 M-110
   30 122mm M-68 900 mortars (81mm, 120mm, 160mm)
  500 L-33   Lance surface-to-surface missiles

Antitank weapons
  Ze'ev rockets
  106mm
  TOW, Cobra, Dragon, Picket, Milan, antitank missiles

Antiaircraft weapons
  2 batteries of 24 Vulcan/Chaparral 20mm guns and missiles; 900 AA
  guns 20, 30, 40mm

Source: *The Military Balance: 1982–83* (London: Institute for Strategic Studies, 1983), pp. 56–57

Table 2. Combat Formation of IDF Ground Division— Tank and Mechanized Infantry

Tank division: 12,000 men, compared to about 10,000 in 1973

- 3 tank brigades, each with 111 tanks
  Three battalions per brigade, each with 36 tanks; additional tanks are commanders' vehicles; thus, 333 tanks per division
- 1 artillery brigade mounting three battalions of artillery, almost all self-propelled; three batteries to each battalion
- 1 logistics brigade comprised of
  - 1 intelligence recon battalion
  - 1 engineer battalion
  - 1 division hq—one jeep company
  - 1 transport battalion
  - 1 medical battalion
  - 1 maintenance battalion

Mechanized infantry division: 9,000 to 10,000 men (Has two configurations)

- 2 infantry brigades mounted on APC's
  10 men per APC, 36 APC's in a battalion and 360 men per battalion
  110 APC's and 1,080 men per brigade × 2
- 1 support brigade equal to the logistics brigade of the tank division
- 1 tank brigade with 111 tanks, or sometimes two tank brigades

Note: When deployed with one tank brigade, the mechanized infantry division has a tank battalion of 50 tanks attached to it.

Source: *IDF Spokesman,* March 1983

Table 3. Syrian Order of Battle in Lebanon

A Syrian division deploys about 12,000 men. It fields 40 tanks to the battalion and 4 battalions to the brigade, or about 160 tanks to a tank brigade. A mechanized infantry brigade will mount about 40 tanks for support, while a normal infantry brigade will mount about 32. Commando battalions comprise about 250 men each. (Source: Colonel Benjamin Fitzgerald, "Syria," in Richard A. Gabriel, ed., *Fighting Armies: The Antagonists of the Middle East* [Westport: Greenwood Press, 1983], pp. 24–35.)

In the Bekaa

1st armored division

91	tank brigade	160 tanks
76	tank brigade	160 tanks
58	mechanized brigade	40 tanks
62	independent brigade	32 tanks
10	commando battalions	2,500 men

Total: 392 tanks

In Beirut–Damascus highway area

85th infantry brigade

2,500 men and 32 tanks
unknown infantry brigade: 32 tanks
unknown tank brigade: 160 tanks (perhaps the 68th brigade)
20 commando battalions: 5,000 men

Total deployed force
30,000 men
612 tanks
30 commando battalions (with Sagger, Milan, RPG, antitank guns)
150 armored personnel carriers
300 artillery pieces and antitank guns
30 SAM batteries (SA-3, -2, -6)

Table 4. *Table of Ground Distances between Major Lebanese Cities and Towns*

Western Zone of Operations

Israeli border to Beirut	106 km
Israeli border to Tyre	24 km
Tyre to Sidon	32 km
Sidon to Damour	20 km
Damour to Khalde	5 km
Khalde to airport	4 km
Airport to Baabda	3 km

Center Zone of Operations

Metulla to Hasbaiya	15 km
Metulla to Nabitiya	16 km
Israeli border to Jouaiya	21 km
Nabitiya to coastal road (Sidon)	27 km
Nabitiya to Jezzine	21 km

Eastern Zone of Operations

Hasbaiya to Lake Qaraoun	18 km
Hasbaiya to Rachaiya	23 km
Marjayoun to Masghara	20 km
Nabitiya to Jezzine	21 km
Jezzine to Beit ed Dein	23 km
Jezzine to Barouk	21 km
Barouk to Ain Zhalta	5 km
Ain Zhalta to Ain Dara	6 km
Jezzine to coastal road	20 km
Beit ed Dein to coastal road	12 km
Beit ed Dein to Deir el Qamar	6 km

Beirut–Damascus highway operations

Damour to Ain Aanoub	5 km
Ain Aanoub to Souq el Gharb	2 km
Souq el Gharb to Aley	3 km
Mansourieye to Bhamdoun	2 km
Ain Dara to the highway	3 km

Note: Despite short distances between most points, Lebanese roads are extremely narrow, steep, and often serpentine. Thus, in actual field operations the "Lebanese kilometer" is often considerably greater than the air distances would indicate.

Table 5. Economic Costs of the Lebanon War

Total Cost	$1.26 billion
Ammunition	32 million
Man-hours	62 million
Construction/transport	8.9 million
Fuel (land vehicles)	3.9 million
Food	3.2 million
Miscellaneous	16.5 million
Total damage in Lebanon	1.9 billion

Source: *IDF Spokesman*, March 1983. All figures in 1983 U.S. dollars converted at the official Israeli shekel exchange rate.

Table 6. Israeli Soldiers Killed in Action, by Rank

Privates	49	13.3%
Corporals	90	24.4%
Sergeants	132	35.8%
Lieutenants	46	12.5%
Captains	28	7.6%
Majors	19	5.1%
Lt. colonels	2	.5%
Colonels	1	.2%
Generals	1	.2%
Total dead:	368	

Source: *IDF Spokesman*, October 1982

Table 7. Israeli Soldiers Wounded in Action, by Rank

Privates	566	19.5%
Corporals	1,385	47.7%
Sergeants	530	18.2%
Lieutenants/Cpts.	348	11.9%
Majors/Lt. colonels	67	2.3%
Colonels/Generals	6	.2%

Source: *IDF Spokesman*, January 1983

Table 8. Israeli Casualties by Service Branch

Branch	Dead	Wounded	% of Total Dead and Wounded
Armor*	154	642	28.9
Infantry	86	870	34.7
Training units†	40	180	7.9
Artillery	4	176	6.5
Engineers	7	107	4.1
Communications	6	122	4.6
Medical Corps	4	124	4.6
Other branches (maintenance, supply, transportation, etc.)	40	91	4.7
Air force	18	58	2.7
Navy	9	13	.9
	368	2,383	100

* Armor casualties include more than tank crews; they include armored infantry (APC), which wear the black armor beret and are organically attached to armor brigades.
† Training units are school units, from, say, the officers course, the platoon-commanders course, etc. When mobilized, such units deploy and fight as units rather than having the members return to their parent outfits.

Table 9. Survey of IDF Morale, January 1983

85% felt that the soldiers at their own level (their peers within their combat units) had fought and performed well under fire.

60% said that their morale had been "high" or "very high" while they were in battle with their units.

86% said that they received a "high" or "very high" degree of mutual support from their peers in their units while in battle.

80% said they had a "high" or "very high" degree of confidence in their immediate superior commanders.

76% said they had a "high" or "very high" degree of confidence in their equipment and the way it performed in battle.

40% were "not satisfied" with their own level of physical fitness during the war.

Source: Extracted from an official IDF report as it appeared in the IDF military journal *In the Camp*, February 25, 1983, p. 7

Index